INEQU

AND STRATIFICATION

THIRD EDITION

INEQUALITY AND STRATIFICATION

Race, Class, and Gender

ROBERT A. ROTHMAN

University of Delaware

PRENTICE HALL, Upper Saddle River, New Jersey 07458

Library of Congress Cataloging-in-Publication Data

ROTHMAN, ROBERT A.
  Inequality & stratification: race, class, and gender/Robert A.
Rothman.—3rd ed.
    p. cm.
  Includes bibliographical references and indexes.
  ISBN 0-13-269531-6 (alk. paper)
    1. United States—Social conditions. 2. Equality—United States.
3. Social structure—United States. 4. Social classes—United
States. 5. Social status—United States. 6. Minorities—United
States. I. Title.
  HN57.R577 1999
  305′.0973—dc21
                                                98-22521
                                                CIP

Editorial director: Charlyce Jones Owen
Editor-in-chief: Nancy Roberts
Acquisitions editor: John Chillingworth
Managing editor: Sharon Chambliss
Editorial/production supervision and interior design: Rob DeGeorge
Copy editor: Margaret Pinette
Buyer: Mary Ann Gloriande
Electronic art creation: Publishers' Design and Production Services, Inc.
Marketing manager: Christopher DeJohn
Cover art director: Jayne Conte

This book was set in 10/12 Times Roman by Publishers' Design
and Production Services, Inc., and was printed and bound
by Courier Companies, Inc. The cover was printed by Phoenix Color Corp.

Printed in the United States of America

10 9 8 7 6 5 4 3 2

ISBN 0-13-269531-6

PRENTICE-HALL INTERNATIONAL (UK) LIMITED, *London*
PRENTICE-HALL OF AUSTRALIA PTY. LIMITED, *Sydney*
PRENTICE-HALL CANADA INC., *Toronto*
PRENTICE-HALL HISPANOAMERICANA, S.A., *Mexico*
PRENTICE-HALL OF INDIA PRIVATE LIMITED, *New Delhi*
PRENTICE-HALL OF JAPAN, INC., *Tokyo*
PEARSON EDUCATION ASIA PTE. LTD., *Singapore*
EDITORA PRENTICE-HALL DO BRASIL, LTDA., *Rio de Janeiro*

**To Nancy
For Everything**

Contents

Preface

When the first edition of this book appeared late in the 1970s, reviewers noted that it was unusual to devote systematic attention to minorities and gender in analyzing the structure and dynamics of class systems. This more inclusive approach has come to dominate the social sciences in the intervening years and has stimulated a reconsideration of the nature of social inequality and generated a large body of new scrutiny of the interaction among class, race, ethnicity, and gender. Moreover, dramatic social and economic change is reshaping contemporary industrial stratification systems. These developments mandate a third edition that incorporates the most recent work in the field. Therefore, theory and research of the 1990s prevails over older material outdated by events.

There are also several organizational changes designed to improve the flow and coverage of the subject. Part One provides a broad overview and introduction to the field. Part Two is an expanded discussion of the evolution and institutionalization of industrial class systems. The three chapters that focus on the basic elements of inequality—economics, prestige, politics—define Part Three. Part Four includes separate chapters on life chances and lifestyles as well as class consciousness. Social mobility is the subject of Part Five. Although the American experience remains the central emphasis of the book, the scope has been broadened to include more attention to other industrial systems of social stratification.

One thing that has not changed is the central pedagogical thrust. This edition, like earlier ones, is written with the undergraduate student in mind. It is intended to provide the fundamentals of social stratification for undergraduates in a concise and readable format. One new feature is that *Key Concepts* are highlighted with boldface in the text and listed at the end of chapters to facilitate review. Consequently, this book may be used in different ways: as a basic text for stratification courses; or in newer sociology courses that focus on the intersection of class, race, and gender; courses in stratification; or as one component of courses such as introduction to sociology, social problems, race and minorities, or gender studies. The concise format makes it convenient to combine it with any of several useful anthologies.

Any book that attempts to lay out the fundamentals of an area as complex and broad as stratification cannot elaborate all the areas of debate and controversy. Therefore, more advanced students are directed to the material contained in footnotes and annotated Suggested Reading sections for the resources needed to explore these issues in more depth and detail.

This project has benefited from the ideas and comments of numerous friends and colleagues, but especially Nancy Horak Randall, Wingate University, and Michelle A. Smith, Kent State University. Stacy Osnick helped with the research, and Sharon Chambliss and Rob DeGeorge at Prentice Hall guided the manuscript through the production process. The entire effort was sustained by the unflagging support of my wife, Nancy.

INEQUALITY
AND STRATIFICATION

PART ONE

The Nature
of Inequality
and Stratification

Industrial societies are divided into social classes based on position in an economic system of production and distribution, and occupation is the best single measure of social class position. Some of the most significant rewards and opportunities for people are shaped by social class position. The implications of class are most pronounced in the distribution of earnings and wealth, social judgments and evaluations, and access to political power but extend to most facets of modern life, including matters of life and death. The system of classes and the distribution of inequalities are supported and maintained by the culture and social structure of the society. Chapter 1 develops the basic ideas and concepts that are central to the sociological analysis of inequality and stratification. Chapter 2 reviews three major theoretical conceptualizations and interpretations of the origins of class systems that inform current theory and research.

CHAPTER ONE

Structural Inequality and Social Stratification

THE STRUCTURE OF INEQUALITY

Inequality is readily evident in the contemporary world. Discrepancies—sometimes vast discrepancies—in wealth, material possessions, power and authority, prestige, access to simple creature comforts, and the way people are perceived and treated dominate the social life of contemporary societies. There are many forms of inequality, but sociologists tend to focus on three major forms—economic, social status, and power and authority—following the lead of the German sociologist Max Weber. At the extremes are the homeless and the super-rich, the esteemed and the degraded, the powerful and the powerless, and there are many levels between them.

Economic Inequalities

Disparities in wealth and material resources are usually the most visible form of inequality. Industrial societies contain millions of people whose daily lives are a struggle against economic hardship. Hundreds of thousands of the destitute are homeless, compelled to wander the streets and fill the shelters in Los Angeles, London, and Moscow. One child in ten lives in poverty in the major industrial nations—Australia, Britain, Canada, Ireland, Israel, and Italy (Pear, 1996). In America, it is one child in five. An even greater proportion lack health insurance. According to one study, about one child in three in the United States during 1995–96 was without insurance for at least one month, and 3.5 million (five percent) were without protection for the entire period (Bacon, 1997).

While many struggle for survival, others in the same society enjoy great wealth. Professional athletes, entertainers, and corporate executives earn incomes of millions of dollars. Others, fortunate enough to have been born into prosperous families with names such as duPont or Rockefeller or Walton (Wal-Mart), never need to worry about the source of their next meal or confront the fear of being unable to pay the rent. On the contrary, some indulge in ostentatious and extravagant lifestyles. Wealthy tobacco heiress Doris Duke, for example, always felt it necessary to fly her two pet camels with her on her trips to Hawaii (Clancy, 1988). Ranged between such extremes are smaller gradations of monetary inequality, often measured by the size of homes in which people live, the kind of cars they drive, or the quality of the schools their children can afford to attend.

Social Status

A second important form of inequality is social status. **Social status** is the social standing, esteem, respect, or prestige that positions command from other members of society. It is a judgment of the relative ranking of individuals and groups on scales of social superiority and inferiority. Social status is relevant because people are sensitive to the evaluations of others, valuing the admiration and approval of their peers, as is readily evident when people attempt to enhance their social standing through the public display of clothing, jewelry, cars, and homes, or by their choice of careers and lifestyles.

Individuals may earn social status on the basis of their own efforts (athletic ability) or personal attributes (physical attractiveness, intelligence), but there is also a powerful structural dimension to social status—occupations, social classes, racial and ethnic groups, and the sexes are ranked relative to one another. For example, at various times and in various places, women and men have formed clearly demarcated status groups. In the United States, as recently as the 1950s, it was common for males to be openly rated as superior to females by both men and women (McKee & Sherriffs, 1957). Occupational prestige rankings are probably the status hierarchies with which most people are familiar. Occupations around the world are typically arranged on a strict hierarchy of prestige, with physicians and lawyers and scientists usually found at the top and garbage collectors and janitors near the bottom. This ranking holds true for societies as diverse as China (Fredrickson, Lin & Xing, 1992), Czechoslovakia (Penn, 1975) and the United States (Bose & Rossi, 1983).

The significance of social ranking extends beyond questions of social approval and ego gratification. Status considerations can dictate the form of social interaction between people at different levels. People are likely to show deference to those ranked above them and tend to expect deference from those below them. Social ranking can also lead to practices designed to limit social contacts and social interaction that show up in residential segregation and other forms of exclusionary behavior.

Power and Authority

There is a third salient, more complex form of inequality, dealing with the unequal distribution of power and authority in society. Although there is a lack of consensus on precise definitions of such terms, there is agreement that the essence of **power** is the ability to control events or determine the behavior of others in the face of resistance and to resist attempts at control by others. **Authority** refers to a specific form of control where the right to command is considered as appropriate and legitimate. Authority may be based on tradition or may reside in organizational position (as generals' right to direct the behavior of lieutenants, or supervisors' ability to sanction workers) or in expert knowledge (physicians' right to prescribe the actions of patients) (Weber, 1947).

Discrepancies in power are difficult to document, but it is clear that enormous power is concentrated in the hands of the people who direct the large organizations that dominate the political, military, corporate, and social landscape. Sociologist C. Wright Mills (1956) was among the first to point out that the growth of massive organizations, during the twentieth century, consolidated unusual amounts of power in governmental offices such as the President of the United States and cabinet officers, military leaders such as the Joint Chiefs of Staff, corporate CEOs, church leaders, and university presidents. In contrast, a majority of Americans feel quite powerless politically, feeling they have little or no influence over the activities of the government, and four out of five believe the government is run by special interests (Apple, 1995).

SOCIAL STRATIFICATION

The terms **social stratification** and **stratification system** focus on the societal context of inequality. Social stratification envisions societies as divided into a hierarchy of levels or layers of individuals and families in which the distribution of rewards is linked to hierarchical position, *and* the values, beliefs, laws, and ideologies that serve to support and maintain the distribution of inequality. Attention to the idea of a system is an important component of social stratification because the various dimensions are interrelated and mutually supportive. Social and cultural ideas explain and legitimize the division of society into levels and the distribution of rewards, and the patterns of inequality confirm the legitimacy of the values. Powerful nations have, for example, enslaved other groups as a source of cheap labor and rationalized their actions on the grounds that the victims were somehow inferior populations.

Social stratification has taken many forms in different places and at different points in history, but the three most familiar forms are slave, caste, and class systems. Slave systems divide people into two fundamental groups, the free and the unfree. Despite a great deal of progress in the area of human rights, some forms of slavery survive in a number of places around the globe such as Mauritania (Masland et al., 1992). Caste systems organize people into fixed hereditary groups in which there is little or no chance for children to escape the caste of their parents. Caste systems have existed at various times in Rwanda (East Africa), Swat (Pakistan), Japan, Tibet, Korea, and India (Berriman, 1973). The Hindu caste system was in place as early as the ninth century and prevailed until the nineteenth century. The British began to formally dismantle the system at that point, but vestiges remain in many rural areas (Beteille, 1992). Class systems are the product of industrialization, where major social and economic rewards are determined by position in the economic system of production, distribution, and consumption. Each type arises under different historical conditions, identifies distinctive social categories of people, generates alternative kinds of hierarchies, and differs in the scope and magnitude of inequalities.

CLASS, RACE AND ETHNICITY, AND GENDER

Class, race and ethnicity, and gender are sometimes approached as distinct and separate social categories and sources of inequality in contemporary society. However, they are best understood as overlapping or intersecting bases of inequality and stratification in what has been called a **matrix of domination** (Andersen & Collins, 1992). None can be fully understood or explained without analyzing the interrelationships among them. For example, the experiences of middle-class African-American women must be approached as the convergence of class, race, and gender. Therefore, each of the concepts requires clarification.

Social Class

A **social class** (or simply **class**) is a group of individuals or families who occupy a similar position in the economic system of production, distribution, and consumption of goods and services in industrial societies.[1] For the overwhelming majority of people social class position is defined by occupation. Social class position is much more complex than jobs, but work is the most useful starting point. People's work sets effective limits on financial rewards and social status, influences the stability of employment and the chances for social mobility, locates them in systems of workplace authority and power that have consequences that extend beyond the workplace, defines some features of social relations on and off the job, contributes to the way people think about themselves and others, and has enduring implications for their children.

Many of the problems of the poorest members of society can be traced to their tenuous link to the economic system. The unemployed and the working poor form a large pool of people lacking a secure position in the workplace. They are handicapped

---

[1]Sociologists are unable to agree upon a single definition of the term *social class,* in large part because meanings vary with ideology and methodology. Classes are often defined as "groups with roughly similar earnings." However, this measure is inconsistent with the usage here, because earnings are determined by class position. Alternatively, educational levels are sometimes used to identify classes, but educational credentials are better understood as one of the key factors in opening or limiting access to structural position. In some places in the text, income or education is used to identify classes, because that was the approach used by the authors of the study being cited.

by a lack of experience, weak educational credentials, a lack of job opportunities, discrimination, or personal habits. Whatever the combination of reasons that explains the plight of specific individuals, their collective impoverishment has its origins in an economic system that is unable to provide jobs at decent wages for all who want them.

One of the issues that divide sociologists is the problem of distinguishing the number and form of classes in contemporary industrial societies.[2] Despite some areas of ambiguity and the lack of clear boundaries between class levels, American society can conveniently be divided into five broad social classes.[3] At the top of the stratification system is a small "elite class" that wields unusual economic, political, and social power. The elite is actually composed of two analytically separate groups, an "institutional elite" that directs the dominant national organizations and institutions (government, business and industry, the media, education, and religion), and a "capitalist elite" made up of individuals and families whose power derives from wealth and property. In some instances the wealth of the capitalist class has been passed down through several generations in families such as the Mars candy family and the Heinz food family, while others have amassed fortunes in their own lives, as is the case of Bill Gates of Microsoft. Specific individuals may, obviously, simultaneously be members of both groups as is illustrated by the members of the Kennedy and Bush families whose careers in politics were built upon inherited wealth.

The next level, the "upper middle class," combines occupations based on expert knowledge (professional people such as physicians and scientific personnel) and administrators and managers below the executive level. The "lower middle class" includes technicians, lower-level administrators, and most clerical and sales personnel. In the United States the term "working class" means manual work, also called blue-collar work, and describes those who do the physical labor in the factories, mills, and mines. Some are engaged in highly skilled work (auto mechanics) while others do more routine work on assembly lines, and skill differentials are an important consideration in understanding how manual workers perceive themselves. At the bottom of the hierarchy are "the poor," who live on the very margins of the productive system. Numbered in this class are both the "working poor," who fill the least skilled jobs in the economy, and those caught up in unstable and poorly paid jobs (the unemployed, under-employed, and discouraged because they believe they cannot find work).

Developing an accurate picture of the class structure of American society is a complex and controversial task, but one model is suggested by Exhibit 1.1. The elite is small, comprising no more than one or two percent of the population. About one-quarter of the society can be defined as upper middle class on the basis of administrative, managerial, and professional occupations. One-third of the population hold lower-middle-class jobs in clerical, sales, and administrative support positions, and another one-quarter fill the manual occupations of the working class. Perhaps one in

---

[2]There is one school of thought that argues that discrete classes have been eroded by the social and economic forces of post-modern society (Block 1992). The case for the persistence of classes is given by Hout, Brooks, & Manza (1993).

[3]The composition of classes is discussed in more detail in Chapter 3.

EXHIBIT 1.1 A Simplified Model of Social Classes

SOCIAL CLASS	PERCENT OF THE POPULATION	NUMBER EMPLOYED
Elite	*1–2%*	
Upper middle class	*25–30%*	
Professionals		18,752,000
Managerial		17,746,000
Lower middle class	*25–30%*	
Sales workers		15,404,000
Technicians		3,926,000
Clerical		18,353,000
Working class	*20–25%*	
Craft workers		13,587,000
Operatives		7,874,000
Transportation workers		5,302,000
Protective services		2,187,000
The poor	*20–25%*	
Service workers		14,186,000
Domestic workers		804,000
Unskilled workers		5,021,000
Farm workers		1,889,000
Unemployed		7,000,000

Note: Class designations are based on standard occupational categories employed by the Bureau of the Census. The unemployed are estimated at five percent of the workforce.

Source: Employment and Earnings. 1997 "Employed Civilians by Detailed Occupation, Employment and Earnings," 61 (January, 1997), Table 12, page 177.

four Americans may be counted among the poor, holding marginal jobs or facing unemployment.

Race and Ethnicity

Members of racial and ethnic groups are, to quote a widely used phrase, clusters of people who, "because of physical or cultural characteristics, are singled out from others in the society in which they live for differential and unequal treatment" (Wirth, 1945: 347). Several different collective terms are used to describe these groups in a society. Sociologists originally introduced the phrase **minority group** to emphasize power differentials that maintain their subordination by the majority. Some contemporary analysts prefer terms such as "dominant" and "subordinate groups" because they more clearly emphasize power differentials. Other analysts favor the phrase "people of color." **Race** is a social construction typically based on visible physical characteristics such as skin color, stature, and facial features. **Ethnic groups** are identified by cultural (or national) origins, which may be manifested in language, religion, values, beliefs, or customs and practices.

The bringing together of peoples of diverse cultural or racial origins does not necessarily produce social, economic, or political subordination. A case in point is the Cossacks and Tungas of Manchuria, who coexisted for centuries within a context of political independence and mutual respect (Lindgren, 1938). Switzerland has since 1815 been a nation with three official names and languages, Schweiz (German), Suisse (French), and Svizzera (Italian), where members of these three groups peacefully coexist. Unfortunately, conflict or some form of economic or social exploitation is a more common outcome of the meeting of groups than is peaceful coexistence. The former Yugoslavia is, for example, wracked with ethnic hostility.

New groups enter societies by different paths, and each route has important implications for subsequent intergroup relations. Immigration is the flow of peoples in search of religious or political freedom or economic opportunities. The immigration of non-English ethnic groups, to the United States, began on a large scale in the 1840s and continues today, as waves of newcomers pour into America. In Europe, the 1990s witnessed a massive movement of people in response to the dissolution of the communist block and civil wars, producing some unrest and the tightening of immigration policies in some western European nations. Groups are sometimes explicitly recruited to provide specific kinds of labor (contract labor). Chinese laborers, for example, were recruited to help build the U.S. railroad system during the 1850s.

Immigration and contract labor tends to be a more or less voluntary process, but there are also involuntary contracts. Peoples are sometimes forcibly incorporated into a new nation as a result of territorial expansion. More powerful groups pursuing military, economic, or political goals encroach on previously independent populations, as was the experience with Europeans encountering Native Americans, and relegate them to the lower levels of the stratification system. In the most extreme cases subjugated groups are enslaved to fill the need for cheap labor. Slaves may also be imported for the express purpose of providing cheap labor or other duties.

Racial and Ethnic Groups in the United States

American society is a mosaic of peoples of diverse racial and ethnic origins. Natives (or their descendants) of at least 150 different countries and 557 Native American tribes live in the United States. Typically, the government gathers data for five major racial and ethnic groups, African American, Asian American, Hispanic, Native American, and white. The combined population of the four nonwhite groups was 64 million in 1992 (O'Hare, 1992). Each of these groups has an extended history in America, and the language used to identify each group hints at the social and political realities of their histories. In each case, there is some disagreement over self-identification among members of these groups(Exhibit 1.2).[4]

---

[4]Census Bureau enumeration of membership in racial and ethnic categories is based on self-identification by respondents, and thus is subject to variation over time. Moreover, people of multiracial background must often choose a single designation. Residents will, in the 2000 census, for the first time have the opportunity to elect more than one category. The issue of multiracial identification is discussed in more detail in Chapter 6.

EXHIBIT 1.2 How People Prefer to be Identified

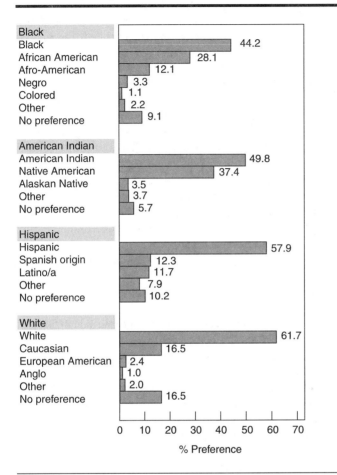

Source: Clyde Tucker and Brian Kojetin, "Testing racial and ethnic origin questions in the CPS supplement," *Monthly Labor Review* 119 (September, 1996): 3–7.

African American, Black.   Blacks or African Americans are the largest single minority group in the United States, comprising approximately twelve percent of the population. Most are descendants of families that have lived in the United States for generations. More recent immigrants have their origins in Ghana, Ethiopia, and Nigeria. The institution of slavery was firmly established by the end of the seventeenth century. Some slaves apparently favored the term "African" over the more insulting and derogatory terms used by others, at least until white supremacist groups mounted a campaign to deport freed slaves. "Negro" dominated social discourse until the 1960s when the former racial slur "black" was adopted as a statement of group solidarity and identity. Late in the 1980s some leaders began to champion "African American" to encourage people to identify themselves by their history and culture rather than their skin color. Recent surveys show that "black" is the most favored form of self-identification, but "African American" tends to be favored by the younger and better-educated.

Asian American.   The number of people whose origins are in Asia or the Pacific is expected to reach about 11 million by the year 2000. They come from China, Japan, Korea, Vietnam, the Philippines, Cambodia, and India, making them the fastest-growing minority group of the 1990s (Goldberg, 1996). Asian Americans were not included in this survey, but other research suggests that most people in this category prefer to identify with their native land rather than a collective category.

Hispanic, Latino/a.   Over 20 million Americans have Spanish-language roots. This too is a diverse population. The largest group within this category is Mexican, including about 13 million persons, and they are geographically concentrated in the Southwest. Puerto Ricans, about 3 million, have tended to settle in the Northeast, and Cubans (1 million) in Florida. The remainder are from Central and South America, the Caribbean, or Spain.

The Census Bureau originally referred to members of this group of people as Spanish-speaking, but adopted "Hispanic" in the 1970s in response to political pressure and in recognition of the fact that many Spanish-surnamed people did not use the language (Gonzalez, 1992). "Hispanic" has Latin roots, referring to the Iberian peninsula. Some Americans feel that "Hispanic" is like the word "Negro," imposed on diverse individuals by an English-speaking government, and favor "Latino" (male construction) or "Latina" (female). Some Mexican Americans describe themselves as "Chicano," and most others prefer to identify themselves as members of their native lands. When asked to choose one collective term, "Hispanic" is the most favored choice, but it is clearly a secondary form of self-identification (Garcia, 1997).

Native American, American Indian.   The original inhabitants of the North American continent were a dissimilar group of cultures including the Eskimos of what is now Alaska, the Pueblos of the Southwest, the Iroquois of the Northeast, and the hunters of the Great Plains. There are currently over 2 million Native Americans and four out of ten are members of four tribes, Cherokee, Navajo, Chippewa, and Sioux. As is well known, these people were erroneously named "Indians" on the assumption that Europeans had reached Asian India. About one-half choose American Indian, but Native American is the favored form of identification for a sizable proportion of residents, and natives of Alaska and the Aleutian Islands (Aleuts) typically choose that designation.

White.   The white segment of the American population is also a heterogeneous category, composed of people who trace their origins to countries such as England, Ireland, Italy, Germany, Sweden, Russia, Poland, and scores of others. People have been making distinctions among human beings based on skin color and physical appearance for centuries. Terms such as "Caucasian" emerged later as scientists unsuccessfully attempted to classify people on physiological or biological criteria. The phrase "white race" seems to have gained popularity at the beginning of the nineteenth century as a way of maintaining social distance from Native Americans and African Americans (Allen, 1994). Most white Americans prefer that term today.

Gender

Gender refers to the social characteristics that distinguish between the sexes.[5] The social construction of gender is a subtle and complex process that includes tangible presentations of people (clothing and grooming), a sexual division of labor between women's and men's work, and subtle behavioral and attitudinal expectations. Gender is embedded in the social and cultural heritage of a group, and individuals are introduced to it as they encounter differential expectations and are exposed to dissimilar treatment that emphasizes differences at the expense of similarities.

One of the most significant obstacles that women everywhere confront is the failure to place economic value on their productive efforts. Women worldwide work more hours than men and perform more than one-half of all the economic activities in societies, both industrial and developing, but their work is divided differently (UNDP, 1995: 87–91). Only about one-third of women's work is in a paid labor market, compared to about three-fourths of men's work (Exhibit 1.3). The bulk of time devoted to unpaid work in industrial countries involves housework and child care. Social class has an effect on hours worked in the home because members of more affluent families can afford to purchase some of the services that others must perform themselves—laundry, cleaning, prepared meals, lawn and yard care. Women in developing nations typically bear an even heavier burden for they must also do things such as collect water and firewood and are involved in planting and harvesting. Unpaid work is essential to the survival of families, but labor market work is valued in the sense that it is recognized as "productive work," pays tangible monetary rewards, and earns social status in the society. Thus, men derive greater benefits from their labor than women.

THE INSTITUTIONALIZATION OF INEQUALITY

Inequalities are embedded in the very fabric of society. The phrase, the **institutionalization of inequality,** is used to summarize the configuration of social arrangements that combine to generate, support, and perpetuate social inequalities. Included among the most salient features of the institutionalization of inequality are social val-

---

[5]Social scientists typically reserve the term *sex* for the physiological and biological differences that distinguish males and females, while *gender* refers to socially defined and acquired behaviors and expectations for males and females in a particular culture at a historical point in time.

EXHIBIT 1.3 Time Devoted to Paid and Unpaid Work in Industrial Nations

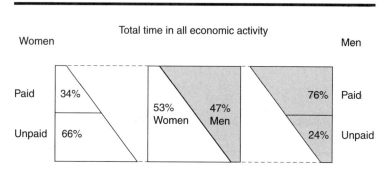

Source: United Nations Development Program, *Human Development Report,* New York: Oxford University Press, 1995, Figure 4.2, page 89.

ues, beliefs such as stereotypes that confirm the unequal distribution of rewards, laws and prevailing patterns of power that limit people's ability to redistribute rewards, and patterns of social organization that constantly reinforce and legitimize prevailing differences. Each of these is important in its own right, but they also combine into broad configurations called ideologies.

Values. **Values** are standards of desirability. They are collective expressions of what is precious or worthless, respected or disdained, commendable or deplorable. Values are intangible but are powerful motivators, encouraging certain courses of action and discouraging others, rewarding some accomplishments and penalizing others. Values may place a premium on things such as material objects (possessions), ideals (democracy and opportunity), behaviors (courage or bravery), or symbols (grades) and serve as a guide and a justification for the conduct of individual affairs.

At the most basic level it is important to remember that the very desirability of wealth and status that is so prevalent in the United States is a cultural value. The American value system emphasizes displays of wealth, consumption, and invidious distinctions based on personal possessions. The pursuit of such goals does not extend to all segments of American society. Displays of wealth through clothing, jewelry, homes, or possessions are actively discouraged by the Old Order Amish because its members are devoted to a lifestyle that deliberately rejects the materialism of modern industrial systems in favor of a stable, homogeneous, and devout religious value system (Kephart, 1994).

Widely shared values often underlie the distribution of status. The dignity and worth of human life is a powerful dimension of the social and religious heritage of Western civilization, with the result that occupations that contribute to the preservation of life (physician) tend to enjoy higher social status than work that makes no apparent and direct contribution to the quality of life. A conspicuous example of the cultural value–social status linkage was embodied in the Hindu concept of an "untouchable" caste. Hindus considered it wrong to harm any form of life, and that meant that butchers, hunters, fishers, and even shepherds raising animals for human consumption were in occupations that "defiled" or "polluted" them. They were united in a caste and excluded from common forms of social discourse.

Beliefs.   **Beliefs** are ideas or assumptions about the nature of social and physical reality. Beliefs define the way people and events are perceived and experienced and shape responses to them. Beliefs need not be supported by objective evidence. Early twentieth century sociologist W. I. Thomas nicely summarized the implications of beliefs by noting that, "If men define situations as real, they are real in their consequences" (Thomas, 1928). It is a reminder that beliefs have repercussions because people act on them, regardless of their validity. Knowledge based on scientific research is a belief in this context, but so too are stereotypes, urban legends, and religious revelations. They all qualify because they serve to explain the social and physical world and interpret the causes of events even if they cannot be validated by modern science.

Beliefs about the nature of individuals and groups are interwoven with the distribution of rewards. It is, for example, common to discover beliefs that suggest members of racial or ethnic minorities have social, cultural, or biological deficiencies that explain and justify discriminatory treatment toward them. The waves of Polish and Italian immigrants to the United States in the nineteenth century, were often relegated to dead-end, unskilled jobs on the grounds that they were lazy or morally dishonest.

Laws.   Inequality is frequently formalized in the legal system of a society. The legitimacy of excluding women from high-status occupations such as law was actually upheld by the U.S. Supreme Court in the nineteenth century (Bradwell *v.* Illinois, 1873). Moreover, the Court subsequently upheld so-called **"protective legislation"** that excluded women from a whole range of jobs then defined as too strenuous or dangerous for them (Muller *v.* Oregon, 1908). Protective legislation was legitimized on the grounds that women needed protection because they were not as strong as men, were dependent upon men, and were the mothers of future generations (Hill, 1979). It is no coincidence that such jobs were often better-paying positions with greater chances for promotion.

Social Institutions.   Social institutions such as religion, education, and the family also play a role in the perpetuation of inequalities. For example, the church has sometimes provided overt sacred support for secular inequality. Medieval feudal estates were imbued with a religious-moral purpose by Christian philosophers who maintained that the feudal system was the only possible way of defending the Church against its pagan enemies (Nottingham, 1954). A more subtle link between religion and inequality was proposed by Karl Marx in his criticism of organized religion. He claimed the attraction of other-worldly salvation distracted the attention of the poor away from their present suffering and contributed to their acceptance of the existing system.

Formal educational systems may perpetuate existing patterns of inequality and help to guarantee that each generation will inherit the same social position as that of their parents. A network of elite preparatory schools and colleges trains upper-class children in America to assume the reins of power held by their parents (Kingston & Lewis, 1990). Tracking systems in secondary education tend to benefit the children of upper-middle-class parents, while the children of the poor and the working class are more likely to be channeled into unrewarding, dead-end careers in blue-collar or service work (Oakes, 1985).

Ideologies.   The ideas and values that explain and justify prevailing patterns of inequality tend to be joined in loose systems or **ideologies** in which the component elements support and reinforce each other. Many different ideologies flourish to bolster inequality. Some ideologies have entered the language and are widely discussed— "sexism," "racism," "patriarchy," "meritocracy" and "white supremacy"—although there is usually a discrepancy between conventional usage, which is notably vague, and the precise meanings employed in the social science literature. Economic inequalities in the United States are, for example, grounded in a competitive, individualistic ideology that teaches rewards are earned on the basis of talent and hard work (Kluegel & Smith, 1986). This labels the less fortunate as not enterprising or industrious or prudent enough to succeed. The ideology thus simultaneously justifies the affluence of the wealthy and the impoverishment of the poor and homeless.

Ideologies may be elaborate and coherent systems of ideas deliberately promulgated by a dominant group, or they may be loose collections of ideas that emerge in the process of everyday social relations among groups. In the first category are explicit ideologies developed and advanced by dominant groups to justify their advantaged position. For example, medieval European aristocrats espoused the position that they were the descendants of the Teutons (later called Aryans), who had defeated the Romans, while commoners were descendants of the Romans and other inferior cultures (Shibutani & Kwan, 1965). Members of the aristocratic class were thus members of the line responsible for the flowering of Western civilization and hence destined to rule. Not all ideologies are deliberately created. Rather, they may be understood as emerging in a more unsystematic way when isolated ideas are selected out and embraced simply because they can be interpreted to justify inequality.

Social Relations

Broad patterns of inequality are deeply set in the structure of society, but they are also constantly enacted and reinforced on a daily basis in social relations. At the most obvious level, class, race and ethnicity, and gender incidents show up in countless small, but maddening, instances of condensation, hostility, and discrimination. More consequential episodes appear in settings such as job interviews, loan applications (Loeb, Cohen, & Johnson, 1995), and the quality of legal defense (Coyle, Strasser, & Lavelle, 1990).

EXHIBIT 1.4 Criminal Victimization and Income

FAMILY INCOME	VICTIMS PER 1000 PERSONS
$ 7500 or less	49
$ 7500 to $14,999	34
$15,000 to $29,999	26
$30,000 or more	20

Source: U.S. Department of Justice, *Sourcebook of Criminal Justice Statistics,* Washington, DC: Government Printing Office, 1990, page 239.

CLASS AND LIFE CHANCES

Class, race and ethnicity, and gender have direct and readily observable consequences, but they also combine to touch many other aspects of people's lives in subtle and indirect ways. Max Weber used the concept of life chances to describe the unobtrusive implications of class. His phrasing remains descriptive, "the typical chances for a supply of goods, external living conditions, and personal life experiences" (Weber, 1946: 180). Thus, **life chances** refers to the role of class in increasing or decreasing the probability of enjoying experiences and opportunities that enhance the quality of life or facing problems that diminish it. Infant mortality, the chances of going to college, the risk of suffering mental illness, loneliness, obesity, and countless other incidents are encompassed by this phrase (Gilbert & Kahl, 1993: 3). The concept of life chances is highlighted by examining the probability of being a victim of violent crime (robbery, assault, rape). The poorest in American society are more than twice as likely to be victimized as are the most wealthy (U.S. Department of Justice, 1988: 26). Such examples can only hint at the broad implications of social stratification.

CONCLUSION: THE INTERSECTION OF CLASS, RACE, AND GENDER

It is possible to identify class, ethnicity, and gender as separate social constructions because they are based on different criteria and institutionalized differently, but they are impossible to separate in practice or in the understanding of patterns of inequality.[6] At the personal and individual level they are lived simultaneously (Andersen & Collins, 1992: xxi). Class, race and ethnicity, and gender are never irrelevant in everyday social interaction and social experience. In the realm of inequality these three fundamental dimensions of social structure converge to produce stratification

---

[6]The conceptual problems of simultaneously dealing with class, race and ethnicity, and gender and the ineffectiveness of available terminology to convey the complexity of the issues are explored in West & Fenstermaker, 1995a and 1995b.

EXHIBIT 1.5 Class, Minority Status, Gender, and Income in the United States

Social Class	MEN			WOMEN		
	White	Black	Hispanic	White	Black	Hispanic
Upper middle class						
Professions	$36,975	$28,775	$32,846	$19,324	$21,122	$21,302
Managers	39,273	29,712	32,264	20,800	20,281	19,819
Lower middle class						
Technicians	27,238	19,404	20,402	17,250	16,227	n/a
Sales	28,242	16,358	20,494	10,752	7,937	9,336
Clerical	20,018	17,590	16,417	12,712	14,068	12,498
Working class						
Craft workers	22,068	18,066	17,246	14,040	13,378	12,994
Semiskilled	19,249	15,501	15,214	10,684	11,167	8,560
The Poor						
Service Work	10,510	8,595	10,282	6756	7855	7022
Unskilled	12,110	11,041	11,930	8615	8113	7865

Source: U.S. Bureau of the Census, *Money Income of Households, Families and Persons in the United States, 1989,* Washington, DC: U.S. Government Printing Office, Table 40.

systems. Class, race and ethnicity, and gender combine and interact to facilitate or frustrate access to rewards, amplifying the impact of any one individually.

The broad implications of the relationship between class, race and ethnicity, and gender are suggested by exploring the distribution of income in the United States as shown in Exhibit 1.5. There are pronounced differences in earnings, as illustrated by a gap of more than $10,000 between the upper middle class and the lower middle class. The income of the clerical sector of the lower middle class, dominated by women (80 percent), is actually much closer to the earnings of the working class. A similar $10,000 gap separates the poor from those higher in the stratification system.

However, the overall pattern is modified by minority status and gender. Minorities and women consistently command lower average wages than men, but it is a pattern that also varies by class level. Several items illustrate the situation. The earnings of African-American men in lower-middle-class clerical work are 87 percent of those of white males, but only about 58 percent in sales occupations. Women's income is consistently lower than men's, but the discrepancy widens at higher class levels. Interestingly, the income of African-American women approaches that of white women and is actually higher in a number of occupations, notably the professions, clerical work, and operatives. It is a complex situation, but it often reflects the fact that minority women have historically been forced into the paid labor force to aid in family expenses and have therefore accumulated long seniority.

KEY CONCEPTS

authority	life chances	power
beliefs	matrix of domination	protective legislation
ethnic group	minority group	race
gender	social class (class)	values
ideology	social status	

institutionalization of
    inequality
	social stratification
	    (stratification system)	

SUGGESTED READING

MARGARET L. ANDERSEN, *Thinking about Women: Sociological Perspectives on Sex and Gender.* (4th ed.) Needham Heights, MA: Allyn & Bacon, 1997. A thorough and comprehensive overview of feminist social science scholarship.

MARIO BARRERA, *Race and Class in the Southwest.* Notre Dame, IN: University of Notre Dame Press, 1979. An examination of the exploitation of men and women Mexican immigrants as urban and agricultural laborers.

ROGER DANIELS, *Coming to America.* New York: HarperCollins, 1990. A comprehensive history of immigration to America.

JOE R. FEAGIN AND CLAIRECE BOOHER FEAGIN, *Racial and Ethnic Relations.* Upper Saddle River, NJ: Prentice Hall, 1996. This text, now in its 5th edition, provides a comprehensive overview of the history and contemporary status of racial and ethnic minorities in the United States.

DAVID B. GRUSKY, ed., *Social Stratification: Class, Race & Gender.* Boulder, CO: Westview Press, 1994. A useful collection of articles suitable for advanced students.

JUDITH LORBER, *Paradoxes of Gender.* New Haven, CT: Yale University Press, 1994. The author reveals the social construction of gender and the implications for women in contemporary society.

KEVIN PHILLIPS, *The Politics of Rich and Poor: Wealth and the American Electorate in the Reagan Aftermath.* New York: Random House, 1990. An overview of the sources of the widening gap between rich and poor in the United States.

H. EDWARD RANSFORD, *Race and Class in American Society: Black, Latino, Anglo.* Rochester, VT: Schenkman, 1994. A broad review of the intersection of class, race, and gender inequalities.

RICHARD SENNETT AND JONATHAN COBB, *The Hidden Injuries of Class.* New York: Vintage, 1973. An older but still relevant analysis of the subtle and invidious consequences of social class.

ERIK OLIN WRIGHT, *Class Counts.* London: New Left Books, 1997. An articulate Marxist approach to the implications of class.

CHAPTER TWO
Theoretical Approaches to Social Stratification

THREE THEORETICAL TRADITIONS

Inequality and stratification have captured the attention of social philosophers, moralists, intellectuals, and social theorists since the origins of recorded history. Plato may have been the first Western theorist to attempt a systematic examination of the nature and consequences of inequality. One of the central goals of his utopian *Republic* was to construct a society in which inequalities corresponded to the inherent differences among people. But, because of his belief that extremes of wealth and poverty generated undesirable behavior, he also proposed placing limits on the economic assets people could accumulate. The theorists with most relevance to contemporary analysis date from the mid-nineteenth century when industrialization began to reshape the structure of Western societies. Three major theoretic traditions tend to dominate in American sociology.

The works of Karl Marx and Friederich Engels are the starting point in any consideration of stratification theory for they were among the first to perceive the internal dynamics of the emerging industrial order. They asserted primacy to control of the physical means of industrial production and emphasized the social relations inherent in different forms of production and the role of this factor in shaping society and in the dynamics of social change. After the death of Marx, Engels developed a systematic analysis of gender stratification.

Max Weber was one of a number of people who carried on a dialogue with the "ghost of Marx." On several occasions he is quoted as defining part of his work as "positive criticism of materialistic conceptions of history" (Bendix, 1962: 591). This should not imply a single-minded attempt to discredit Marx and Engels; rather Weber challenged some interpretations, admitted some insights, and attempted to elaborate on still others. It is more accurate to recognize that Weber objected to the idea that any single factor such as class relationships could provide a universal explanation of social phenomena; hence, he developed a multidimensional model of stratification based on economics, status and lifestyles, and power.

American interest in social stratification intensified during the 1930s and 1940s and tended to emphasize social status and patterns of social interaction. W. Lloyd Warner and his associates studied small communities with quaint names such as "Yankee City" and "Jonesville" to disguise their location. Their original formulation emphasized economic considerations, but they eventually came to argue that subjective measures of "status" and reputation superseded economic considerations (Warner, 1941). It was Warner who popularized stratification terms such as "upper upper class" and "lower middle class" that have become a permanent part of the American vocabulary.

Harvard sociologist Talcott Parsons' theoretical formulations, and those of some of his students, were particularly influential during this period. Probably the most controversial single contribution was a brief paper by Kingsley Davis and Wilbert Moore (1945) that purported to explain why stratification was universal and necessary. These developments contributed to the emergence of "functional" theories focusing on prestige and an accompanying decline in interest in conflict and political and economic inequalities. Functionalism eventually dominated American sociology for several decades.

The 1990s are a period of multiple models and multiple perspectives on inequality and stratification. Theory and research in the classic traditions initiated by Marx and Weber continue by attempting to reconcile twentieth-century developments with models formulated in earlier stages of industrialization. Two major challenges face contemporary theorists. One is the need to come to grips with changes in the nature of capitalism in advanced societies that include the globalization of the world economy, developments in the electronic manipulation and transfer of information, and the growth of the service sector of the economy. This era is variously referred to as "post-industrialism" or the "information age." The other major development is recognition of the interrelationship among class, race and ethnicity, and gender as intersecting and interrelated sources of inequality and the need to systematically explore these links.

THE MARXIAN TRADITION

Karl Marx (1818–1883) and Friedrich Engels (1820–1895) lived and wrote during a period of rapid and disruptive social change stimulated by the upheavals produced by industrialization, urbanization, and democratization. In light of their environment, it is not surprising that they were forcefully concerned with the consequences of fledgling capitalist production. Perhaps their most fundamental insight was that capitalism is not simply a way of producing goods and services but an economic, social, and political system. Marx was dismayed by the abuses, misery, and oppression of the urban industrial factory but could not help being impressed by the more positive aspects of the emerging economic system. In the *Communist Manifesto* there is praise for the capitalist class, which, "during its rule of scarce one hundred years, has created more massive and colossal productive forces than have all preceding generations together" (Marx & Engels, 1959: 8). The development of science, the command over nature, the rise of cities, and the breakdown of rule by the feudal nobility could all be attributed to this group. However, in the future he anticipated the revolutionary overthrow of capitalism.

Social Stratification

Marx's collaborator, Friedrich Engels, has provided a frequently quoted passage that provides a succinct summary of their conception of history and social stratification:

> The materialist conception of history starts with the proposition that the production of the means to support human life—and next to production, the exchange of things produced—is the basis of all social structure; that in every society that has appeared in history, the manner in which wealth is distributed and the society is divided into classes or orders is dependent on what is produced, and how it is exchanged. From this point of view the final causes of all social changes and political revolutions are to be sought . . . in changes in the modes of production and exchange (Marx & Engels, 1959: 90).

Thus, the key to understanding the flow of human history, as well as the distribution of inequality and stratification, is the organization of the productive forces of the society.

They viewed the whole of human history as divided into a number of major phases that they called primitive communism, slavery, feudalism, and capitalism. Each period was dominated by a pair of social classes defined by their relationship to the means of production and to each other—masters and slaves or landowners and serfs. Central to Marxian analysis of capitalism was the belief that the idea of private property created a basic cleavage between those who owned economic resources and those who did not, or to use their terms, the **bourgeois** (who owned capital) and the **proletariat** (nonowners who had only their own labor to sell). Inequalities of wealth in capitalist societies were directly based on ownership of land, buildings, machinery, factories—the means of production. Propertyless workers had nothing but their labor to sell, and owners exploited workers by paying them wages that were less than the market value of the products they created. Thus, capitalists' wealth was accumulated by taking control of their resources and expropriating the surplus wealth created by workers. Moreover, as a result of loss of control of the things they built and the loss of most of the wealth that they created, workers became alienated from their work. Work lost its joy, its meaning, and its rewards.

Interestingly enough, despite the central importance of classes in his vision of society, Marx did not define class in any systematic way. However, it is clear that he visualized class in two separate ways (Wright, 1985: 26–38). First, class could be structurally defined by ownership (or lack of it) of productive capacity—capital and land. And, second, it could be defined relationally; that is, classes exist in relation to one another. Moreover, they are antagonistic in the sense of having opposing interests and exploitative in that the advantages of one class are gained at the expense of the other. Capitalist wealth was also translated into power in the political sector by control of the apparatus of government and use of government to maintain wealth and advantaged position. Marx and Engels argued that the potential for domination of society was not simply economic and political but is also social and cultural in that a "ruling class" will be able to shape the laws, values, art, beliefs, and institutions of society—the **ideological superstructure**—to their advantage. The ideas of the ruling class are in every epoch the ruling ideas; *i.e.,* the class that is ruling the material force of society is at the same time the ruling intellectual force. The class that has the means of material production at its disposal has control at the same time over the means of mental production (Marx & Engels, 1959: 78). Their ideas are disseminated through the press, the church, the schools, and the various political institutions and are calculated to legitimize their advantaged position.

Class Consciousness and Class Conflict

Marx believed that capitalism was destined to be supplanted by socialism and eventually communism. The concepts of class and social change intersect with the idea of class conflict, for the disadvantaged classes spawned by the economic system are to be the instruments of social change. Therefore:

> The history of all hitherto existing society is the history of class struggles. Free man and slave, patrician and plebeian, lord and serf, guild-master and journeyman, in a word, oppressor and oppressed, stood in constant opposition to one another, carried on an uninterrupted, now hidden, now open fight, a fight that each time ended, either in a revolutionary reconstitution of society at large, or in the common ruin of the contending classes (Marx & Engels, 1964: 78).

Since ruling classes never voluntarily relinquish their position, conflict is inevitable. In this context, Marx introduced and explored the critical link between economic position and subjective class awareness. Both bourgeois and proletariat form nominal groups as a result of their relative location in the economic system. He called such groups *klasse an sich* (class of itself), with class position defined by structural position. Members of the opposing classes have shared interests by virtue of their position. These common interests are most clearly perceived by the bourgeois, for it is more readily evident that their advantaged position is based on private property. Yet, members of disadvantaged classes need not be aware of their common interests. Their interests may be fragmented by differing religious beliefs, ethnic loyalties, and prestige distinctions or obscured by rhetoric. Therefore, Marx raised the question of conditions that could transform a heterogeneous aggregate into a cohesive, organized group, a *klasse fur sich* (a class for itself) aware of its interests and acting to realize its own interests.

Marx anticipated that a combination of several social and economic forces would combine to stimulate self-conscious action on the part of workers. A major factor would be economic deprivation. He expected that the discrepancy between wealth of the bourgeois and proletariat would widen for two reasons. Increases in productivity would produce ever-greater profits, and ever-more wealth would be concentrated in the hands of an ever-smaller number of capitalists as they competed among themselves for a larger share of the wealth. Another factor in awakening class consciousness would be the homogenization of the proletariat. Divergent interests would become less meaningful as members of the working class became more similar. For example, mechanization would reduce all workers to unskilled laborers, thus reducing rivalries among different crafts. Finally, continued confrontation with owners (*e.g.,* boycotts and strikes) would expose and solidify their common interests.

The sources of revolution were not explained in any detail, nor did they spell out the nature of the societies that would follow the downfall of capitalism (Grabb, 1997). It appears that capitalism would first be replaced by a temporary period of socialism. Marx sometimes referred to this period as the "dictatorship of the proletariat," in which control of the economic system would be centralized in the hands of a government that would represent the interests of all segments of society, not just the special interests of the bourgeois. The state would make the changes necessary to alleviate the worst abuses of capitalism, such as abolishing child labor, taking ownership of some industries, and instituting a graduated income tax, all of which were radical ideas at the time. Taxes were to be used for education, health care, and social service. Workers would be rewarded fairly but not equally, on the basis of effort. Each "receives back from society . . . exactly what he gives to it."

Socialism was seen as a transitional historical phase in the progression toward communism. The centralized state would be replaced by a system of decentralized administration, and the distribution of goods would be guided by Marx's famous declaration, "From each according to his ability, to each according to his needs." Communist society is only vaguely defined and is obviously utopian. This is because Marx had profound faith in the innate decency of people and believed that the greed and self-interest spawned by capitalism would disappear once it was abolished. It must be noted that the sociological work of Marx and Engels is often embroiled in controversy because the words "socialism" and "communism" became entangled with a variety of totalitarian political regimes around the world, and critics were quick to seek to discredit all of their ideas. Therefore, it is important to focus on their ideas rather than the ways they have been utilized in the pursuit of political objectives.

Engels and Gender Stratification

Engels is often credited with the first sociological theory of gender stratification (Collins & Makowsky, 1984: 49–54). His approach is a continuation and extension of the basic Marxian perspective. In fact, he links the origins of gender stratification to the first decisive step in the process that eventually produced capitalism—the transition from communal to private property. "The first class opposition that appears in history coincides with the development of antagonism between man and woman in monogamous marriage, and the first class oppression coincides with that of the female sex by the male" (Engels, 1972: 129).

Based on the anthropological research of his time, Engels concluded that both hunting and agricultural societies were characterized by matrilineal descent and gender equality. (More recent anthropological research does not support the thesis that all hunting societies are or were equalitarian.) Because they fully participated in the production of food, women enjoyed equal social status. However, as advanced agricultural methods created the potential for an agricultural surplus, males wanted to be able to pass their accumulated property on to their children. Patrilineal descent and monogamous marriages were created to foster this, and women became excluded from economic production and relegated to household tasks. As a consequence of not producing for the market, women became economically subordinate to their spouses.

Thus, Engels effectively links gender subordination to the dynamics of industrial production systems. More recent thinking in the Marxian tradition has elaborated on that perspective, suggesting that women have been forced into playing a vital but largely invisible role in perpetuating the economic system. They reproduce the working class by bearing and socializing children to become the next generation of workers.

The Legacy of Marxism

In retrospect it is easy to emphasize that Marx and Engels were so wedded to the idea of dichotomous classes that they failed to fully anticipate the future of capitalism in the West, especially the implications of an emerging middle class. Perhaps they were too much products of their time, led to overgeneralize from what was occurring in nineteenth-century England. From that historical vantage point, it was tempting to visualize industrialization and urbanization producing a small class of industrial capitalists ranged against an expanding mass of propertyless and impoverished urban laborers. It was a period of some of the worst industrial abuses—crowded tenements, hazardous factories, subsistence wages, child labor, and minimal standards of public health. It was also the era of unrest and ferment in the fledgling labor movement; trade unions and socialist political parties were active and industrial conflict common. However, it must be remembered that both were political reformers as well as social analysts, and it has been argued that "prophets have always been dualists," seeing history as a conflict between the forces of good and evil, lightness and darkness (Feuer, 1959: xviii). The fact remains that Marx and Engels' writings have stimulated extensive analysis of industrial society and isolated some of the key issues that continue to form the basis of current thinking about inequality and stratification.

Classes.   The concept of classes based on position in a specific productive system, in which some groups are in a position to exploit others, remains a powerful tool for understanding the distribution of wealth, power, and privilege in industrial societies.

The Middle Class.   The tendency of Marx and Engels to view the world in dichotomous categories led them to minimize the role of the emerging middle class of office workers, professionals, and managers who occupy an intermediate position between proletariat and bourgeois. Marx clearly recognized a growing middle class "who stand between the workman on the one hand and the capitalist and landlord on the other" but did not work out the long-term implications of this development (Burris, 1986). For example, at one point he merely suggested that intermediate groups such as small businesspersons, farmers, shopkeepers, and craftsworkers would "sink down into the proletariat," although he was not clear about precisely how that might happen.

The proliferation of a broad middle class creates a dilemma for that part of Marxian theory that emphasizes the polarization of society into two opposing groups. Some feel that the evolution of capitalism has created a new middle class that falls outside the traditional bourgeois–proletariat division. One way of handling this issue has been to expand the basis of exploitation by showing that the evolution of industrialization has created additional forms of exploitation (see the accompanying Case Study)(Wright, 1997). Others insist that the basic owner versus nonowner dichotomy

---

CASE STUDY:
A Contemporary Marxist Approach to Social Class

University of Wisconsin sociologist Erik Olin Wright is among the most prominent contemporary social scientists pursuing a Marxist model of class in modern capitalist societies. He notes that there are quantitative divisions within the class of owners of capital assets. This category encompasses independent self-employed persons (petty bourgeois) and includes a range of employers from those employing but one or two people (small employers) to the managers of giant industrial corporations (capitalists) employing hundreds of thousands. This is the basic Marxian idea of control of productive resources or "assets" (Exhibit 2.1).

All others are employees, but there are new kinds of resources or assets that shape the social relations of work. There are what are called "organizational assets," the authority to make policy decisions (managers) or direct the work of others (supervisors), and "skill assets," employees whose job requires unusual educational credentials (experts). The class location of managers, supervisors, and experts remains a quandary because they are simultaneously proletariat in the sense that they work for others *and* bourgeois in the sense that they control productive resources or supervise the working of others. Hence, they occupy a contradictory class position. By far the largest category of employees (workers) possess no productive assets. They do not exert control over the production process, other workers, or even their own effort. The working class in the United States defined by this criteria would include approximately one-half of all employed persons (Wright & Martin, 1987).

EXHIBIT 2.1 A Contemporary Marxian Model of Class Structure in Capitalist Societies

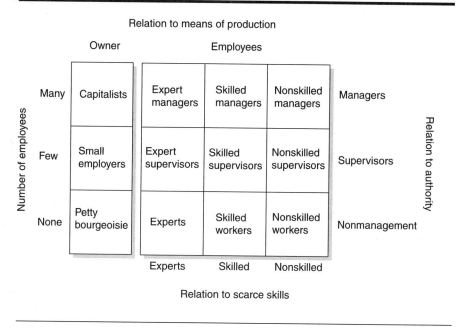

Relation to means of production

	Owner	Employees		
Many	Capitalists	Expert managers	Skilled managers	Nonskilled managers	Managers
Few	Small employers	Expert supervisors	Skilled supervisors	Nonskilled supervisors	Supervisors
None	Petty bourgeoisie	Experts	Skilled workers	Nonskilled workers	Nonmanagement

Number of employees (vertical axis label)

Relation to authority (right vertical axis label)

Experts   Skilled   Nonskilled

Relation to scarce skills

Source: Eric Olin Wright, *Class Counts,* Cambridge, England: Cambridge University Press, 1997, page 25.

continues to be the most fundamental cleavage in society, because it focuses on the fact that a tiny minority are in a position to control the work of the vast majority.

Class Consciousness.   The question of defining the conditions that facilitate or hinder the emergence of class consciousness and collective action is the subject of continuing interest and research. It is clear that most Americans are aware of class divisions in society and willing to identify with a particular class (Jackman & Jackman, 1983). Consciousness of class is important because it contributes to understanding lifestyles and helps to explain voting patterns.

Power Structures.   The idea that a small elite may form a dominant class in industrial society has stimulated a great deal of analysis. Contemporary sociologists have explored the interrelationship between the industrial and political sectors, with some suggesting that business and other special interest groups exert unusual influence on the conduct of the state. Other social scientists are pursuing the concept of ideological domination by exploring the ways that cultural ideas and beliefs support systems of inequality.

Class, Race, and Gender.   Marx and Engels were clearly aware of the disadvantaged position of women and minorities within the stratification system, and contemporary analysis increasingly focuses on the intersection of class, race, and gender in understanding the dynamics of inequality.

THE WEBERIAN TRADITION

Max Weber's (1864–1920) approach to analysis of social stratification is a more multidimensional approach to stratification than that of Marx. Weber recognizes the central importance of position in the social organization of industrial production, but he emphasizes the existence of three forms of inequality in society—economic, status, and power. His words are direct:

> Whereas the genuine place of "classes" is within the economic order, the place of "status groups" is within the social order, that is, within the distribution of "honor," . . . (and) "parties" live in the house of "power." Their action is oriented toward the acquisition of social "power," that is to say, toward influencing communal action no matter what the content may be (Weber, 1946: 194).

In short, capitalism generates three kinds of groups.

Class

The first groups are economic, based on "market situation," which does not differ in principle from the Marxian division of propertied and propertyless. However, Weber distinguished three different types of market situation. There is the labor market, which divides society into employers and employees; the money market, which separates creditors from debtors; and the commodity market, which differentiates between buyers and sellers (landlords and tenants). Accordingly, those who participate in all three markets could be members of three distinct economic classes. In addition, Weber noted that the propertyless have different levels of skill (ranging from the unskilled to the professional worker), a point that Wright uses to refine Marxist conceptions of class. Weber's observations about skill differentials among those who are without significant capital resources marks his attempt to deal with the question of the emerging middle class.

Weber noted that classes are groups of people who share a common market situation, and, in turn, class position strongly influences their rewards and their opportunities. (This is where he introduced the concept of "life chances.") Common economic position does not imply or even guarantee a sense of common identity. An awareness of common interests and collective action might emerge under the right conditions. For example, class action by workers is fostered by a presence of a clear and unambiguous opponent; physical concentration of workers in a single place, which facilitates interaction and communication; and, finally, clear goals articulated by political leaders (Weber, 1946: 180–184). Thus, he does not differ substantially from Marx on the question of class consciousness.

On the matter of gender stratification, he displayed a strong interest in Engels' analysis of the family and feminist theory of his day (Collins, 1986: 269–271). He challenged Engels' notion of the evolution of sexual domination but accepted his perspective as making a valuable contribution to understanding the situation. His own ideas on the family define it as a set of sexual and economic relationships regulated by political power (Collins, 1986: 277).

Status and Status Groups

Weber termed his second form of inequality "status honor" (or what is today referred to as social status or prestige), grounded in the prevailing values, beliefs, and ideals of the society. Economic resources and status form separate hierarchies, but Weber admitted that those with the most economic resources also tend to have the highest status. Taking this a step further led him to visualize society as a hierarchy of "status groups" having unequal prestige. Status groups are, in Weber's thinking, communities of people having some degree of awareness of commonality. These communities may be based on property, income, ethnicity, ancestry, education, or occupation, but consumption patterns and styles of life are primary.

The way in which status groups develop is one of Weber's most influential and enduring contributions. Because members of prominent status groups are aware of their shared interests, they are likely to attempt to develop mechanisms for maintaining and protecting their position and that of their children. A set of formal and informal exclusionary rules will be established, and members of higher status groups will selectively interact only with others whom they consider to be their social equals— socialize with them, join the same organizations, and send their children to the same schools. Outsiders viewed as social inferiors will simultaneously be deliberately excluded from such contacts. It follows that marriage partners will also be among social equals, for restricted patterns of interaction will limit the pool of potential partners to members of the same status group. It is in this way that privilege is maintained through generations.

Weber believed that in the most extreme cases, status groups evolve into what he called "castes," where distinctions of social status are maintained by rigid social conventions or even laws that prohibit marriage outside the group. Moreover, even physical contacts with lower caste members can be considered degrading, as though physically encountering lower caste members might contaminate them. He felt that exclusionary practices were usually associated with class position, but other bases of exclusion were race, language, and religion, and he cited the Jews as the most persistent historical example, along with other cases that can be assumed to include the "untouchables" of Hindu India.

Parties

Finally, Weber focused on the question of power and identified **parties,** groups or associations deliberately organized for the pursuit of power. His term "parties" would encompass the contemporary idea of political parties but is broader, more inclusive, including any group whose "action is oriented toward a goal which is striven for in a planned manner" (Weber, 1946: 180–184). Thus, parties encompass professional associations such as the American Medical Association and special interest groups such as a Chamber of Commerce or the National Organization of Women. Although vague on the nature of parties and how they coalesce, he did point out that economic or status interests are very important. However, other motives besides class interests and status may be operative. He would thus include environmental groups, such as the Sierra Club, or consumer groups as parties. The ways in which they may gain power can range from naked violence to persuasion, subterfuge, or hoax.

The Weberian Legacy

Max Weber actually devoted but one relatively short essay directly to the topic of social stratification, yet he is widely quoted. His importance derives from his multidimensional model of social phenomena, which is more consistent with social science reasoning that emphasizes the complexity of society and social behavior. Consequently, Weber's legacy has often been more generalized than specific.

Multiple Forms of Inequality.   Many theorists feel that Weber's most enduring contribution to the study of social stratification is his recognition of the many forms of social inequality. Thus, while not disputing the Marxian concept of economic classes, Weber did postulate a more complex picture of inequality and stratification. His scheme encompasses a broader view of economic classes and also includes status groups and parties, thus allowing individuals and families to be located on at least three hierarchies of inequality. He asserts that inequalities of lifestyles, prestige, and power can be independent of one another but concedes the primacy of the economic factor in most situations. "Property as such," he notes, "is not always recognized as a (prestige) qualification, but in the long run it is, with extraordinary regularity" (Weber, 1946: 185).

Bureaucracy.   Although not explicitly linked to his work on stratification, Weber did extensively explore the implications of the role of emerging bureaucratic structures and correctly predicted that they were destined to be the dominant form of social organization in industrial society. Most individuals are subject to some form of bureaucratic control, whether industrial, political, educational, or religious. Thus, while Marx and Engels emphasized the alienation of people from their work, Weber worried about the implications of bureaucracy that threatened to rob individuals of their individuality and their initiative. Obviously, there is also the question of the concentration of power, because leadership in these bureaucracies is the source of unusual power and influence over individuals and society, a point developed later by other theorists.

Religion and Capitalism.   One of Weber's best-known works, *The Protestant Ethic and the Spirit of Capitalism* (1958), develops the thesis that Protestant beliefs set the stage for the emergence of capitalism in the West. His theory earned quick fame because it challenged the Marxian premise that gives primacy to economic relations in shaping social institutions and offered a new connection between religion and economic development. As Weber saw it, the unique combination of religious ideas developed by Luther and Calvin fostered certain kinds of secular behavior—disciplined effort, self-denial, devotion to work, emphasis on material success, and individual responsibility—values that encouraged and fostered the emergence of capitalist economic organization. His theory has generated considerable controversy but commands attention to an alternative interpretation of interrelationship between social institutions and the stratification system.

Patriarchy. Weber explored gender inequality as a form of male domination that had its origins in the sheer physical strength of men (Collins, 1986; Grabb, 1997). Eventually actual physical domination was replaced by "patriarchy," a system of social values and beliefs that legitimize the subordination of women in the family and other institutions and the economic system. One consequence is that gender can become the basis of the formation of status groups that results in the exclusion of women from male-dominated groups.

THE STRUCTURAL FUNCTIONAL TRADITION

The tradition of **structural functionalism** has diverse theoretical and empirical roots, traceable to the work of Emile Durkheim and British social anthropologists A. R. Radcliffe-Brown and Bonislaw Malinowski. The most influential work in this tradition in the United States was produced in the 1940s and 1950s by Talcott Parsons (1940; 1953) and two of his students, Kingsley Davis and Wilbert Moore (1945). Structural functionalists approach society as an organic system of interrelated elements or structures and attempt to explain the function of these structures for the workings of society (Grabb, 1997). Some functionalists argue that societies have "needs" that must be fulfilled if society is to survive, while others define functions more broadly as simply the results or consequences of structures for the operation of the whole system.

Occupational Status

Parsons focused on the social status (prestige) dimension of inequality, not ignoring differences in wealth and power, but assigning them secondary importance. His emphasis on prestige follows logically from his broader perspective on society, which was aimed at the analysis of some fundamental questions, "How is social order possible? What integrates and holds society together?" His perspective emphasizes that one of the most important integrative structures of a society is a common value and belief system that serves to weld members of society together. That value system is also the basis of inequality because rewards are distributed on the basis of importance of people's roles in society.

In his first article on the subject of stratification, the focus is clear, "the differential evaluation (of members of society) in the moral sense" (Parsons, 1940). Within any society, Parsons argues, its members are evaluated and ranked by other members of the society on the basis of conformity to a shared value system. The link between societal values and social prestige was made earlier by Weber. Parsons further suggests that some institutions are more important than others, and that, consequently, higher value will be attributed to those who make the most important contribution to society. In industrial societies that will be the economic system; in other societies at other times, religious or cultural institutions might have higher priority. This leads him in the direction of assuming that prestige will be allocated primarily on the basis of the type of work that people perform.

Is Stratification Universal and Necessary?

Parsons suggests that a hierarchy of prestige will emerge in every society, and his students Davis and Moore address the question of why it is apparently universal. They take the position that the universality of inequality means that it must serve some vital social function, because they claim that the social institutions and social patterns that survive in a society must play some fundamental role in the continuation of that society. Their view is that every society is confronted with the need to motivate people to fill the most essential positions and perform them effectively and diligently. Phrased differently, it is the question of how society can assure that enough people will want to become physicians (or judges or computer scientists). It is a crucial issue because such jobs require lengthy and costly training, depend on finding people with scarce talents, and are more crucial to the survival of society than other occupations such as janitors.

Their answer is direct: Those positions must be handsomely rewarded materially and symbolically in the form of things that contribute to sustenance and comfort, humor and diversion, and self-respect and ego expansion. "Social inequality is thus an unconsciously evolved device by which societies ensure that the most important positions are conscientiously filled by the most qualified persons" (Davis & Moore, 1945: 249). Medicine is an apt example; training is costly, arduous, and long, and people would not be inclined to become physicians without the lure of societal rewards. The Davis-Moore functional theory of stratification can thus be reduced to a series of propositions (see the accompanying Case Study).

Inequality thus has its origins in consensus and ensures that the most competent and well-trained persons will conscientiously fill the most important positions in a society. The rewards are both economic and the subjective approval of others. Since structural functionalism is a general framework, it does not claim to explain either the relative degree of inequality or the form of stratification in a particular society, because that will depend upon social values, external conditions, level of development, and historical circumstances.

Functional theory is the subject of wide-ranging debate (Tumin, 1953). One group of critics points out that the theory has a strong ideological bias, asserting that

---

CASE STUDY:
A Functional Theory of Social Stratification

Some positions in society are functionally more important than others for the survival of the society. The continuation of society requires that these positions be filled by qualified people.

The number of people with the talent to fill these roles is limited.

Translating this natural talent into useful skills requires a period of prolonged training.

People must be induced to make the sacrifices of time, effort, and cost to undertake the training.

Therefore, society allocates proportionately greater rewards to those positions that are more important and require unusual or scarce talents.

Inequality is thus a socially evolved mechanism for enhancing the potential survival of society.

Inequality and stratification are both indispensable and positively functional for society.

Sources: Adapted from Kingsley Davis and Wilbert E. Moore, "Some principles of stratification," *American Sociological Review* 10:(1945) 242–249, and Kingsley Davis, "Reply to Tumin," *American Sociological Review* 18 (1953), 394–397.

---

it serves as a rationalization for the existing unequal distribution of rewards as both just and moral. Moreover, it fails to take account of constraints on individuals' opportunities (poverty, discrimination, unequal education). A second problem is conceptual and methodological. The idea of "functional importance" is, at best, a vague idea, meaning that there are no objective criteria for establishing the relative importance of social institutions or positions. There have been a number of attempts to test this theory, but they fail to provide consistent support for the theory (*e.g.*, Cullen & Novick, 1979). Moreover, it is often asserted that functional theory depends upon some obscure anthropomorphic reference to the role of "society" in allocating rewards that ignores the dynamics of power.

The Legacy of Functionalism

Despite its narrow focus, it must be noted that functional theory did have a powerful influence on theory and research in sociology during its ascendance.

Occupational Prestige.   Probably the most important single consequence of functionalism was to direct attention to the distribution of occupational prestige. It is clear that there is broad consensus within societies on the ranking of occupational prestige. Sociologists continue to debate the sources of social prestige and have accumulated a large body of research on prestige rankings in societies across the world (*e.g.,* Treiman, 1977).

A Classless Hierarchy.   A focus on occupational prestige suggests a continuous distribution of social status rather than classes as distinct social groups with common interests as suggested by other theorists. Classes are thus translated into groups of people with similar occupational prestige. This is more consistent with the ideas of individualism, open opportunity, and democracy that typify American society. Therefore, this theory provides legitimization for the existing distribution of inequality.

Pluralism.   The structural functional view that society is composed of a system of different institutions that contribute to the overall working of society is consistent with the pluralism of Weber and other theorists. Each institution, religious, governmental, educational, is a separate source of rewards (Parsons, 1953; Alexander, 1990). This increases the number of opportunities for mobility and access to rewards.

Structural Constraints.   It is also possible to suggest that functional theory has stimulated theory and research that is a reaction to it, rather than an elaboration of it. For example, one weakness of the theory, recognized by the authors themselves, is that there is no guarantee that the most qualified persons will actually be able to gain access to the highly rewarded positions. At a minimum, wealthy and advantaged parents will be able to provide their children with access to the education and other advantages that are prerequisites to more desirable rungs on the ladder of prestige. These are advantages not available to the poor. And obviously, race and gender matter. Moreover, as Weber pointed out, members of groups that enjoy privileged positions can actively close off access to others. Consequently, there is the need to analyze the ways in which social classes act self-consciously to protect their position.

CONCLUSION: OCCUPATION AND CLASS

These disparate theoretical traditions continue to offer valuable insights into the dynamics of inequality and stratification, and contemporary sociologists continue to pursue answers to the issues raised by earlier theorists, although there are currently many different strands of thought within each. If there is any single area of agreement it is that occupation is a central variable in understanding the distribution of rewards in industrial societies. However, there is deep disagreement over the meaning and implications of work.

The central feature of Marxist analysis is the exploitation of workers by owners who do not return full value to the workers for the products they create. More current analysis also considers the exploitation of workers by experts and organizational superiors. Thus, the Marxist tradition focuses on social relationships that are grounded in work relationships. Weber's concept of market situation reemphasizes location in the labor market, although he explores other forms of economic advantage and considers questions of power and status. The structural functional tradition emphasizes the differential value of jobs and focuses on occupational prestige as a measure of value to society.

At a practical level, sociologists often depend upon occupation because there is such a high correlation between jobs, educational attainments, prestige, and earnings. Occupation is also linked to distinctive lifestyles and influences the way in which people experience their lives and world. Thus, there can be no question that occupation is a central consideration in understanding the dynamics of inequality.

KEY CONCEPTS

bourgeois	*klasse an sich*	proletariat
ideological superstructure	*klasse fur sich*	structural functionalism
	parties	

SUGGESTED READING

JEFFREY C. ALEXANDER, *Structure and Meaning: Rethinking Classical Sociology.* New York: Columbia University Press, 1990. Contemporary structural functional thinking by a leading proponent of the approach.

RINEHARD BENDIX, *Max Weber: An Intellectual Portrait.* Garden City, NY: Doubleday, 1962. The standard intellectual biography of Weber and his contribution to sociological theory.

RANDALL COLLINS. *Weberian Sociological Theory.* New York: Cambridge University Press, 1986. A comprehensive review of the work of Weber and his successors.

RANDALL COLLINS, *Four Sociological Traditions.* New York: Oxford University Press, 1994. A useful history of sociological theory including stratification theory.

RALF DAHRENDORF, *Class and Class Conflict in Industrial Society.* Stanford, CA: Stanford University Press, 1959. A pioneering attempt to elaborate Marx's incomplete theory of classes and class consciousness.

EDWARD G. GRABB. 1997. *Theories of Social Inequality: Classical and Contemporary Perspectives,* 3rd ed. New York: Harcourt Brace. This readable volume provides a comprehensive overview of stratification theory, historical and contemporary.

JOHN F. SITTON, *Recent Marxian Theory.* Albany, NY: SUNY Press, 1996. A discussion of the many different strands of contemporary Marxian theory for advanced students.

ERIK OLIN WRIGHT. *Class Counts.* Cambridge, England: Cambridge University Press, 1997. A current Marxian analysis of the implications of social class by a leading scholar in the field.

PART TWO

Stratification in Industrial Societies

Social classes are the product of the industrial transformation that began in the eighteenth century and supplanted stratification systems based on agriculture and land ownership. The industrial transformation involved a combination of technological and organizational changes that reorganized societies into five basic class levels. Economic and technological changes were accompanied by social and cultural trends that provided a rationale for the existing distribution of rewards. Chapter 3 focuses on the industrial transformation and outlines a basic five-class model of industrial nations. Chapter 4 traces the evolution of the ideology of individualism that supports the distribution of inequality and related values and beliefs that define the place of minorities and women in the stratification system.

CHAPTER THREE
Industrial Class Systems

THE INDUSTRIAL TRANSFORMATION

Prior to the eighteenth century, societies were largely rural and agricultural, with most people devoting their lives to some form of farming. Cities were small by today's standards, and most products were handcrafted. Most wealth was based on trade or land ownership. A process of revolutionary change called the industrial transformation (or the industrial revolution) began to reshape Europe at that point and displaced social stratification systems based on land and agriculture with those based on class. The industrial transformation took shape in Europe and North America over the course of the nineteenth and first half of the twentieth centuries. Other nations experienced the process at different times and at different rates, and much of the world is still in the early stages of the process. Advanced industrial nations are now in the midst of a second industrial transformation driven by computers and telecommunications.

There is a tendency to measure the **industrial transformation** solely on the basis of inventions that facilitate the mechanization of the productive process—the cotton gin or the steam engine—but it is more appropriately understood as a complex and interrelated set of social, economic, demographic, and organizational changes that transform work and have an impact on the entire structure of societies. The list of major developments includes: technological innovations, the evolution of the factory system, slavery, and immigration (in North America), the consolidation of businesses, and the expansion of government. The internal politics of industrializing nations took them in different directions with respect to the role of government in the production and distribution of resources. The industrial transformation in the West was typically driven by **capitalism,** private ownership of productive property and the distribution of goods and services through a market system. Dramatic differences in politics must not obscure the fact that industrialization also produces some common structural arrangements and major similarities in class structures.

Technological Innovation

The industrial transformation was stimulated by a series of technological innovations that increased productivity by the introduction of power-driven machinery and inventions that magnified the productive capacity of workers. The earliest innovations occurred in the British textile industry, where the cotton gin mechanized the separation of cotton fiber, and steam power (later replaced by electricity and the internal combustion engine) made it possible for machines to take over the spinning and weaving of cloth. These developments spelled the demise of a cottage industry system of production where people performed those tasks by hand in their homes. New machinery was not always welcomed by workers, and there were many instances of workers sabotaging equipment. In 1769, the British Parliament actually made the destruction of some kinds of machinery a crime punishable by death. The cost of the new machinery and the demands of production stimulated the need for workers and led to the centralization of manufacturing in factories and mills.

The Factory System and an Urban Working Class

Some workers were displaced by machines, but the new system also created a demand for more factory workers as well as iron and coal miners to provide the raw materials of industry, many of whom migrated from rural areas. Industrial production thus accelerated the process of urbanization. For example, nearly 75 percent of all Americans lived on farms in 1820, compared to less than 3 percent today, and many present-day farmers supplement their incomes with paid jobs in the urban work force. The industrial transformation also accelerated the decline of individual autonomous workers and increased the proportion of people who are employees working for someone else in return for wages. In the United States, blue-collar jobs were filled by waves of immigrants, first from Western Europe and later from Eastern Europe. There was also a flow of internal migration of African Americans from rural to urban areas and from the South to the North after the Civil War.

The situation of the emerging urban working class was bleak in the early stages of industrialization. It was the desperate condition of the urban working class that caught the attention of Karl Marx and Frederick Engels. Wages were low, hours were long, working conditions dangerous, urban life squalid. Women, men, and children as young as ten sometimes worked ten to fourteen hours a day. This situation prevails even today on a large scale in countries in the early stages of industrialization and in sweatshops scattered around the United States and other advanced societies. The working hours in factories were not necessarily much longer than those in farming or domestic production, but the pace of the machines was unremitting and working conditions hazardous. In many places workers rioted to protest low wages and intolerable working conditions.

Slowly, over the course of the nineteenth century and into the early decades of the twentieth century, blue-collar workers were able to improve their situation. Labor unions played a large role in the process. As a result, wages and working conditions improved, and manufacturing jobs came to offer stable and secure employment for almost one in five American workers.

Slavery

Many nations relied on **slavery** to handle the arduous work in the early stages of industrialization. The use of slaves is an ancient system of forced labor, existing in Mesopotamia, Egypt, Greece, and Rome. The final formal worldwide abolition of slavery did not occur until a United Nations Convention in 1956 subsequently ratified by virtually all nations. Yet, many groups claim that it still exists in several places scattered around the globe. The nation most frequently accused of allowing chattel slavery to flourish is Mauritania in Western Africa, where antislavery organizations assert that 100,000 men, women, and children are subject to being bought and sold (Montefiore, 1996). Slave auctions were held there publicly until 1994 but are now conducted in secret. Slave owners are likely to be Moors and slaves the descendants of the original black inhabitants—the Bafours, or conquered peoples. The slaves haul water, tend the herds, and pick dates, and the women bear the next generation of human property (Burkett, 1997).

The key feature of all slave systems is the division of society into two basic categories—free and unfree. Slaves are typically denied political and civil rights granted to other segments of the society. For example, slavery in both ancient Rome and the nineteenth-century United States included stipulations that slaves could not own property, enter into contracts of any kind (including marriage), or make a will (or inherit anything), and were excluded from participation in most legal proceedings (Sio, 1965). Thus, those relegated to slavery can be denied their freedom, endure personal indignities, be deprived of the rights and privileges of others, and suffer severe economic and social deprivation. Perhaps the most important consequence of slavery is that it strips people of their basic humanity, relegating them to the status of property.

Although involuntary servitude is a common feature of all slave systems, it is important to note that colonial American slavery included a racial dimension not found everywhere. Slaves and masters came from different racial and cultural backgrounds—African and European. In addition, Europeans who had immigrated voluntarily tended to think of America as their home and see displaced Africans as outsiders, meaning that even second- and third-generation slaves, although born in America, were still considered aliens. Consequently, slavery was intermingled with claims of racial inferiority. The result was that involuntary servitude, race, and social definitions of inferiority became inextricably linked; race meant inferiority, and race was the basis for slave status (Sio, 1965; Davis, 1966; Kolchin, 1988; Russell, 1994). This is not always the case in compulsory labor systems. Slavery in Greece, Rome, and Russian serfdom made no such link; slaves were not inferior persons, merely legally *unfree* persons. Once an ideology of innate differences among the races becomes institutionalized, there are enduring consequences. Among the most important is that although the formal abolition of slavery can grant legal rights to former slaves, it cannot not guarantee them social rights. Emancipation does not necessarily bring about the demise of the ideological underpinnings that exist to legitimize and justify enslavement.

Immigration

The United States is often described as a "nation of immigrants." The first large group of immigrants was English, and their language, institutions, and culture dominated the nation during the colonial period and contributed more to the shaping of American culture than any other single group. All groups that followed contributed to the evolution of that culture, but individuals needed to assimilate that culture. The indigenous Native American population was decimated during the process. It is estimated that there was a pre-Columbian North American population of 2 to 5 million (Snipp, 1989). A combination of disease, famine, and military casualties reduced that number to merely 250,000 by the end of the nineteenth century. The Native American population expanded to approximately 2 million during the course of the twentieth century.

Several major waves of immigration to America occurred during the nineteenth century, some groups fleeing desperate economic or political conditions in their native lands or openly recruited for agricultural or industrial labor. Famine and political conflicts with the English between the 1830s and 1860s attracted over a million Irish Catholics, and many found urban jobs in the mining industry. About the same time 4 million Germans fled poor economic conditions. A large number of Scandinavians moved to America in search of farm land, and many settled in the Midwest. Between the 1850s and 1870s Chinese workers were recruited to build the railroads and fill service jobs. Italians came in the 1880s, and most found work in construction or in the factories. Japanese were recruited in the 1880s as agricultural workers on Hawaiian fruit plantations and later moved to California as unskilled and domestic workers. Eastern European Jews—many from Russia—sought to escape religious persecution.

Immigration patterns for most of the twentieth century were dominated by movement within the hemisphere. Poverty and the Revolution of 1910–11 prompted a major immigration of Mexicans that has continued until the present. Many aspects of the American economy employ Mexican immigrants, both legal and undocumented. There is, for example, a continuing demand for seasonal agricultural workers. Between 1942 and 1964 over 4 million workers were granted permits for temporary employment in the United States, largely in seasonal agricultural labor, under the *bracero* program. At the peak of the program, *braceros* harvested 75 percent of sugar beets and 90 percent of cucumbers (Valdes, 1991). More recently, poverty and political unrest brought large numbers of immigrants from the Caribbean (Dominicans, Haitians, Puerto Ricans, Cubans, and Jamaicans).

Since the 1960s there has been a large influx of Asians. This represents the reversal of a major trend, since most Asian nationals were excluded by immigration acts initially passed during the 1920s. Those laws set immigration limits on people from certain areas based on the share of the current population having similar origins. It thus favored Western Europeans and discriminated against Asians and Eastern Europeans. The four largest Asian-American groups are Chinese, Filipino, Japanese, and Korean.

In the 1990s, approximately 1.2 million immigrants have arrived each year. About 900,000 enter legally and another 275,000 illegally. The shape of contemporary movement is illustrated by the country of origin of immigrants to the United States in 1995 (Exhibit 3.1).

Scientific Management and the Organization of Work

Factory owners and managers were confronted with complex organizational problems as they sought to coordinate the labor of the emerging urban working class. Their goal was to maximize productivity and profits, but many workers were foreign immigrants or rural migrants lacking the skills and attitudes necessary to function effectively in the new factories. In other cases, skilled craftsworkers such as printers and steel makers were reluctant to surrender control of the work process to factory owners. The making of steel was, for example, in the hands of skilled steel makers—not factory owners—well into the 1920s (Braverman, 1974).

The social organization of industrial firms became dominated by the thinking of Frederick W. Taylor and a management philosophy called **scientific management.**

EXHIBIT 3.1 Immigration to the United States, 1995

NATION OF ORIGIN	NUMBER	NATION OF ORIGIN	NUMBER
Mexico	86,960	Russia	14,560
Philippines	50,962	Haiti	13,892
Vietnam	41,752	Poland	13,804
Dominican Republic	38,392	Canada	12,913
China	35,459	Britain	12,311
India	34,717	El Salvador	11,563
Cuba	17,932	Colombia	10,780
Ukraine	17,432	Pakistan	9,743
Jamaica	16,335	Taiwan	9,374
Korea	16,034		

Source: U.S. Immigration and Naturalization Service, *Statistical Yearbook, 1997.* Washington, DC: U.S. Government Printing Office.

The basic principle of scientific management is specialization. Complex jobs are minutely subdivided into numerous separate operations that can be assigned to unskilled or semiskilled workers. Using this approach, the meat packing industry replaced the need for skilled butchers with a series of simple operations that semiskilled workers performed on animal carcasses that moved past them on conveyor belts. The work involved continuous repetition of one task that could be closely monitored. The result was that countless blue-collar jobs became narrow, routine, repetitive tasks. Narrow specialization of work tasks reduced many jobs to unskilled labor, thus reducing workers' bargaining power because they could easily be replaced by other workers.

The Growth and Concentration of Industry

In the first stages of industrial capitalism relatively large numbers of small companies compete with one another, but over time there is a tendency for larger firms to eclipse smaller ones. The auto industry is a good example. In 1904 thirty-five separate firms were manufacturing cars in the United States, but the Chrysler Corporation's purchase of American Motors in 1988 left only three major American manufacturers. Large firms are also in a position to expand beyond national boundaries, as when Ford Motor Company acquired British Jaguar in 1990. In 1996, just ten auto makers accounted for 80 percent of the 35 million vehicles produced worldwide (*The Economist,* 1997a). Thus, industrialization has the potential to concentrate great wealth in the hands of businesses and business owners.

American history has witnessed several different phases of industrial growth, each fueled by different kinds of enterprises. Early in the nineteenth century industrial expansion was centered in the iron industry, railroads, and textiles, and owners amassed vast fortunes that are the basis of the contemporary wealth of families such as the Stanfords and Vanderbilts. The second half of the nineteenth century saw expansion in oil, steel, banking, and meat packing, creating fortunes for families such as the Rockefellers, Mellons, Morgans, and Swifts. These nineteenth-century capitalists, along with wealthy southern land owners and northern merchants, formed a national upper class. The descendants of these nineteenth-century capitalists form a contemporary elite class with tremendous economic power and influence. Over the course of the twentieth century, other areas flourished: cars (Ford), newspapers (Hearst), entertainment (Disney), telecommunications, and computers.

Dual Labor Markets.   In the 1960s the term "dual economy" was coined to emphasize the emergence of a broad structural division of employers and employment. The result is that some workers enjoy meaningful opportunities for advancement while others have limited chances for individual progress. This approach emphasizes that one aspect of the industrial transformation involves the creation of businesses that are large, stable, efficient, highly profitable, and oligopolies (where a few companies dominate an industry). Firms in the auto, steel, and oil industries illustrate this idea. These firms offer secure employment and have a hierarchical system of jobs that grants workers chances for promotions into positions of greater responsibility and higher pay within that company. Remaining firms tend to be small, unstable, marginal, and competitive. The clothing industry is a good example, where many relatively small manufacturers compete among themselves resulting in low profit margins and, in turn, lower wages, poorer working conditions, less reliable employment, and fewer opportunities for advancement.

Governmental Expansion

Industrialization and urbanization, population growth, and shifting attitudes about the role of government stimulated tremendous growth in the size and influence of governments. Governments almost always assume responsibility for basic public services (education, law and order), national defense, and infrastructure expenditures (roads and sewers). Nations vary significantly in the range of activities undertaken by government beyond these fundamental functions. For example, the communist socialist governments of Eastern Europe owned virtually all of the productive capacity of the society until the 1990s. The United States is at the other end of the continuum with government ownership generally limited to railroads and some major utilities. Democratic-socialist nations of Western Europe have often controlled a broad range of basic industries including airlines, banks, telecommunications, and health care, although there is a current movement toward privatization. The size of government can be measured by state spending as a proportion of total domestic spending (Exhibit 3.2).

The governments of major industrial nations account for nearly one-half of the domestic national product of these societies. The United States is at the low end at about 33 percent, and Sweden is highest at 64 percent. By this criterion it can be seen that governments in all industrialized nations have expanded all during the twentieth century, with a notable acceleration occurring after World War I and a more dramatic expansion occurring since the 1960s. The role of governments in industrial nations began to increase in the 1920s and 1930s as the scope of state activity increased. For example, public services such as education were expanded to ever-broader segments of the population. The worldwide depression of the 1930s stimulated governmental intervention in the economy, public works, and the expansion of the sheer number of public employees. Military budgets became a major factor from the 1940s onward. Since the 1960s, social welfare payments in the form of health care, pensions, and income support to the unemployed and poor have consumed a major share of total government spending (Crook, 1997).

Governments are thus both major employers and major consumers. In addition, governments influence the distribution and redistribution of wealth through social welfare programs and tax policy. Moreover, regardless of the political system, all industrial governments centralize unusual political, economic and social power in the hands of top governmental officials in legislatures, courts, and executives. This raises the question of the ability of citizens to influence government actions in democratic societies.

EXHIBIT 3.2 Government Spending in Industrial Nations, 1870 to 1996

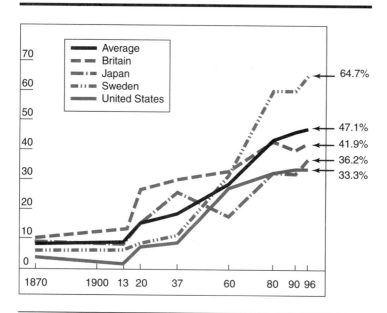

Note: The graph shows government spending as a proportion of gross domestic product. The average base includes seventeen industrial nations in Europe and North America as well as Japan.

Source: Clive Crook, "The future of the state." *The Economist* 344 (September 20, 1997), Chart 1, page 7S. © 1997 The Economist Newspaper Group, Inc. Reprinted with permission. Further reproduction prohibited.

The Knowledge Explosion

The first scientific journal appeared in the middle of the seventeenth century as new knowledge began to accumulate so rapidly that scientists needed some mechanism for sharing their discoveries with each other. The expansion of knowledge prompted the emergence of the modern professions that form the bulk of the upper middle class. They are occupations devoted to the creation of knowledge (biologists, chemists), its application (engineers, physicians, nurses, computer programmers), and dissemination (accountants, lawyers, educators). Their expertise places them at an advantage over other white-collar workers in the competition for wages and helps to elevate their position in the class system.

Overall Occupational Trends

The impact of the industrial transformation is evident in the changing occupational structure of the United States during the twentieth century (Exhibit 3.3). The professions based on expert knowledge grew dramatically, as did technicians, and are expected to continue to expand into the next century. The expansion of business,

EXHIBIT 3.3 The Changing Shape of the Workforce, United States, 1900–2005

OCCUPATION	PERCENTAGE OF PAID WORKERS					
	1900	1920	1940	1960	1980	2005
Professional	4.3%	5.4%	7.5%	11.4%	16.0%	15.5%
Managerial	5.8	6.6	7.3	10.7	11.2	10.4
Technicians	—	—	—	—	—	3.7
Clerical	3.0	8.0	9.6	14.8	18.6	16.7
Sales	4.5	4.9	6.7	6.4	6.3	11.4
Crafts	10.5	13.0	12.0	13.0	12.9	10.3
Operatives	12.8	15.6	18.4	18.2	14.2	8.7
Service	3.6	4.5	7.1	8.9	12.6	16.7
Laborers	12.5	11.6	9.4	5.4	4.6	3.6
Private household	5.4	3.3	4.7	2.7	1.2	.5
Farmworkers	37.5	27.0	17.4	7.9	2.8	2.5
Labor Force (millions)	29.0	42.2	51.7	65.7	99.3	144.7

Note: Labor force data is not strictly comparable over time due to changes in methods of enumeration.

Sources: U.S. Bureau of the Census. *Historical Statistics of the United States,* 1975. Washington, DC: U. S. Government Printing Office, 1975; U.S. Department of Labor. *Handbook of Labor Statistics.* Washington, DC: Government Printing Office, 1985; George T. Silvestri, "Occupational employment to 2005," *Monthly Labor Review* 118 (November, 1995), Table 1, page 61.

industrial, and government organizations is apparent in the growth of managerial, clerical, and sales occupations. Blue-collar jobs employed over one-third of the work force at the turn of the century, but the demand for operatives and unskilled laborers is in the midst of a long-term contraction. The fastest-growing sector of the economy by most estimates is the service sector that includes food preparation, cleaning services, health care, and personal service work. Perhaps the most obvious pattern is the intensification of industrialization and urbanization to the point where less than 3 percent of the population earn their living in agriculture.

A FIVE-CLASS MODEL

These are the major factors that have shaped the class structure of advanced industrial societies. It is possible to identify five basic classes in contemporary America. The distinctions among classes are not always clearly defined, and not every occupation can be neatly classified in a particular class. For example, schoolteachers occupy an ambivalent position in the stratification system, certainly professionals but lacking the financial rewards of other professions and not enjoying the same degree of control over their work. Moreover, there is a often a great deal of variation within a single occupation. Law illustrates this situation, with some attorneys filling low-paying government positions while others advise members of the elite.

Elite Class

The apex of the American stratification system is occupied by a small group of individuals and families who enjoy unusual wealth and power. Membership in this class is based on inherited wealth, institutional position, or some combination of the two. Members of the two segments of the elite often do travel in the same social circles.

Capitalist Elite. One segment of the elite is comprised of individuals and families who possess vast economic resources in the form of land, businesses, property, and stocks and bonds. In short, they own wealth derived from ownership of productive resources and are, therefore, referred to as the **capitalist elite.** There are some families where wealth has passed through many generations. They often have familiar names—Ford, Mars (the candy people), Rockefeller (oil), Heinz (foods), and duPont (chemicals)—and are called "old money" to underscore their tradition of wealth. Others, typically referred to as the "new rich," have amassed their fortunes more recently, people such as Sam Moore Walton who founded the Wal-Mart retail store chain, Bill Gates of Microsoft, and Wayne Huizenga of Blockbuster movie rentals.

Institutional Elite. The other segment of the elite is positional, based on leadership of the major institutions of society. In the early stages of industrialization entrepreneurs owned and ran their own firms, but most have been supplanted by a cadre of professional managers. The sheer size of governments, massive global businesses, and other institutions concentrates unusual power in the hands of the people who direct these enterprises. This group was originally identified as the "power elite" (Mills, 1956), but the term **institutional elite** (Dye, 1986) is more appropriate because it focuses attention on structural position.

There is no standard way to define membership in this group, but a widely used approach focuses on a specific number of leadership positions (Dye, 1986). The value of this approach lies not in the specific numbers but rather the identification of the most powerful institutional spheres in industrial societies. In the corporate sector, it is the top executives of the 215 largest industrial corporations, banks, insurance companies, and investment firms. Combined, these organizations control over one-half of the nation's total corporate assets. In the governmental sector there are the President, Vice-President, cabinet officers, the chairs of major Congressional Committees such as Finance and Armed Services, Supreme Court justices, and staff-rank officers in the military. In the public sector are executives of the major media (the ten major newspaper chains that reach one-third of total circulation, the news magazines, and television networks), the twenty-five largest private colleges and universities, the fifty largest foundations that control about half of all endowments, the senior partners in the twenty-five largest law firms, and various civic and cultural organizations (Red Cross, Kennedy Center for Performing Arts). It is clear that this relatively tiny group has tremendous potential to shape society.

There are, of course, more than a few cases of a convergence of economic and institutional elites in specific individuals or families. The Ford family is a prime example within the corporate world, both owning and controlling the auto company that bears its name. Moreover, the current practice of supplementing executive pay with substantial stock options means that some executives acquire great independent wealth.

Upper Middle Class

Expertise and organizational position define the **upper middle class.** The expansion of knowledge that accompanied the industrial transformation created a group of knowledge-based occupations such as science, law, and medicine. In addition, the proliferation of public and private organizations stimulated the need for managers to coordinate and direct the operations of these organizations and manage their employees. Thus, the upper middle class is made up of managers, administrators, and professionals with college educations, and increasing numbers hold advanced degrees. Most are salaried employees, but some members of professions such as law, dentistry, and medicine remain self-employed. The bulk of this class occupy midlevel positions in large public and private organizations. They are stockbrokers, accountants, biochemists, systems analysts, university faculty, engineers, and the plethora of organizational middle managers with ambiguous titles such as "associate director." At the upper levels are plant managers, directors of human resources, deans, research scientists, chiefs of surgery, and undersecretaries of cabinet departments in the federal government. At the lower levels of this class are clergy, teachers, and social workers.

Lower Middle Class

The **lower middle class** occupies the lower levels of organizational hierarchies in clerical and administrative positions that involve internal communications and the flow of information among organizations. Members of this class collect, code, transcribe, file, record, and transmit data. Among the specific jobs are bank tellers, postal clerks, receptionists, and secretaries. There are, in addition, a large number of sales workers who act as representatives of the company to customers, telemarketers, and retail sales personnel. There is also a large group of workers—approximately 4 million men and women—holding first-line supervisory jobs at the lowest levels of organizational authority with job titles such as foreperson or team leader. Members of the lower middle class generally work directly for members of the upper middle class. The scope of their authority is typically narrowly circumscribed, seldom extending to decisions about job structures or rates of production—decisions made at higher levels.

Working Class

The **working class** labors in the factories and fields, garages and repair shops, mills and mines, largely isolated from the white-collar world of offices, laboratories, law courts, and classrooms. The world of the blue-collar worker is manual work organized around the production, distribution, and repair of products (Hall, 1994). Blue-collar workers build houses and skyscrapers, assemble cars, pack boxes, construct furniture, operate sewing machines, repair telephones and Xerox machines, drive trucks, and harvest crops. There is great diversity within this group, with some workers earning high wages and enjoying stable well-paying employment while others face harsh working conditions and an uncertain future. Skill differentials within the working class are an important consideration, producing an internal division between the more skilled crafts and the less skilled work of machine operators, assembly line workers, and truck drivers.

Craft Workers.   All craft occupations involve a combination of manual dexterity; mastery of a broad knowledge of tools, materials, and processes; and expertise gained from long experience. Included in this segment of the working class are people in the construction trades (electricians, carpenters, plumbers), automotive technicians, metal workers, and printers. Preparation for craft work combines both formal and experiential knowledge. Formal knowledge is taught in apprenticeship programs that emphasize classwork and experiential knowledge that is acquired, refined, and sharpened by prolonged on-the-job training. Their high level of skill results in their sometimes being labeled the "aristocracy of labor" (MacKenzie, 1973).

Working the Machines.   The second major block of blue-collar workers have traditionally been called operatives to emphasize their connection to the machinery of modern manufacturing. Much of their work involves operating, adjusting, feeding, tending, or maintaining machines of one sort or another. This occupational category only makes sense if we recognize that it includes the whole range of tools and equipment from the simplest to the largest and most complex, hand-operated power tools, trucks and planes, textile machines, and steel furnaces. Moreover, it also includes tasks in which the worker does not really control the machinery, such as assembly line work, but rather attends a mechanized, machine-paced process. Scientific management defined operatives' jobs in many American plants as narrowly specialized and repetitive, with workers denied much discretion in the control of the work. This was the dominant pattern until the 1980s when worker dissatisfaction, rapid turnover, absenteeism, and declining quality made it clear that high wages and job security were not, in and of themselves, sufficient to overcome boring, repetitive, unchallenging work. At one GM plant, for example, turnover was 8 percent per month, and an average of 10 percent of the assemblers failed to show up on any given Friday or Monday (Braverman, 1974). Such problems, combined with an impressive record of product quality and foreign competition, are encouraging many firms to reorganize work to empower blue-collar workers.

The Poor[1]

Economic systems are not always able to create jobs that provide stable employment at reasonable wages. **The poor** as a social class includes both those working on a reg-

---

[1]This class was sometimes called the "lower class" in earlier sociological analysis, but that term has been abandoned because it carries pejorative connotations and has been replaced by "the poor." However, this term is not without problems. One is that it tends to emphasize financial circumstances rather than structural location. Another problem is that it can lead to confusion with "poverty," which is a measure of economic condition used by the government and discussed in detail in Chapter 5.

ular basis—the working poor—as well as those not currently in the labor force, some for extended periods of time.

Working Poor.   The **working poor** fill the most marginal jobs in the economic system, those who do routine physical and mental labor, usually in unpleasant conditions with rigid and often harsh supervision and facing the threat of periodic unemployment. The defining feature of the work is low pay, pay that is sometimes insufficient to raise workers above the poverty level even if they work year-round on a full-time basis. Approximately one-half of Americans living below the official poverty threshold worked for at least some part of the previous year (U.S. Bureau of the Census, 1995). This would include urban occupations such as stock handlers, machine feeders, parking lot valets, construction laborers, gas station attendants, dishwashers, cleaning workers in offices and hotels, and some food service people. And, to this must be added paid agricultural workers who do routine physical farm labor—cleaning, clearing, and harvesting fruits and vegetables. It is difficult to enumerate this group because many are paid in cash and some are undocumented workers, but one estimate put the number of seasonal farm families at over 4 million (DeParle, 1991).

Unemployed.   Virtually all workers face the threat of unemployment at some point in their careers, but the risk of unemployment is greatest among those in the marginal jobs at the bottom of the stratification system. Over the course of any decade approximately one person in four is at risk, with people in unskilled and service jobs the most vulnerable (Duncan, 1984). Thus, the poor also includes people who face recurring bouts of unemployment. There are also hundreds of thousands of discouraged workers who want jobs but are not actively seeking work because they feel unqualified or believe there are no jobs.

For most people spells of joblessness are relatively brief. The average duration of unemployment in 1996 was 16.6 weeks (and a median of 8.3 weeks). Job loss and change in family status are the major reasons that people fall into poverty. Most people are covered by unemployment insurance that buffers the early stages of unemployment, but those who face prolonged failure in job seeking exhaust their benefits. The result is that only one unemployed worker in three is currently receiving benefits (McCurrer & Chasanov, 1995). Social welfare programs also protect the most vulnerable.

The Poorest of the Poor: An Enduring Underclass?   Some poor people face prolonged periods of unemployment and persistent poverty, a group currently referred to as the **underclass.**[2] Although there is no consensus on the definition or

---

[2]The term *underclass* was apparently first used by Swedish sociologist Gunnar Myrdal (Gans, 1995). The concept of an underclass is sometimes linked to Karl Marx's idea of a "lumpen proletariat," but the idea of a permanent group of impoverished people different from mainstream Americans can more accurately be traced to Oscar Lewis' "culture of poverty" (1966) and Edward Banfield's "lower class" (1970). Subsequently, the work of William J. Wilson (1987) launched a structural analysis.

measurement of this segment of the poor, William J. Wilson's (1987: 8) definition is a useful introduction:

> that heterogeneous grouping of families and individuals that are outside the mainstream of the American occupational system. Included in this group are individuals who lack training and skills and either experience long-term unemployment or are not members of the labor force, individuals who are engaged in street crime and other forms of aberrant behavior, and families that experience long-term spells of poverty and/or welfare dependency.

The underclass is, in short, a group of people at risk of being trapped in a cycle of persistent poverty and lacking the resources to break free, a bleak prospect for both the society and the individuals involved.

There is deep disagreement between behaviorists and structuralists over the origins and future of the underclass (Prosser, 1991; Jencks & Peterson, 1991). The behavioral interpretation focuses on individual pathology as the root cause, manifest in a lack of commitment to jobs or the future causing people to behave in ways that facilitate a descent into the cycle of poverty (*e.g.,* dropping out of school, substance abuse). The structural interpretation traces the creation of an underclass to the convergence of broad economic, political, and demographic sources (Wilson, 1987). Among them are: racial discrimination, a decline in the demand for low-skill entry-level jobs, unresponsive and under-funded schools, the flight of jobs and the middle classes from center sites, and the lure of a lucrative underground economy. Depressed levels of effort are thus borne of frustration and disappointment but could be revived by redress of the causes of disillusionment.

Analysis of the underclass is also hampered by a lack of consensus about the definition and measurement of the term *underclass.* Many social scientists feel that it has been used indiscriminately, especially in the media, rendering it devoid of any analytic meaning. Systematic attempts to identify this group have used such criteria as poverty, geographic location, educational level, and dysfunctional behavior. Some research does confirm the existence of urban and rural concentrations of people with low educational attainments, persistent unemployment, high rates of crime, and welfare recipients. The underclass is, by any criteria, a small segment of the total poverty population. Underclass neighborhoods by these estimates contain somewhere between 1 and 2 million people. In addition, although it is mainly a minority population, the underclass includes less than one in five of the African Americans living in poverty (Mincey, Sawhill & Wolf, 1990).

Unfortunately, there is a tendency to stigmatize the very poor as "morally inferior" because of their situation (Gans, 1995). For example, in Britain, media coverage of a highly publicized 1992 murder clearly created the impression that sexual violence was a crime almost exclusively of the unemployed and other economically marginalized men (Grover & Soothill, 1996). There is also a tendency to equate race and persistent poverty. The major media (news magazines and television) consistently exaggerate the number of African Americans among the underclass, and underreport their number among the working poor. One study revealed that between 53 and

66 percent of the poor are portrayed as African Americans, more than twice their actual representation among the poor (Fitzgerald, 1997). This is not necessarily an intentional bias, but it does perpetuate a myth. The consequence of this is to set this group apart, to suggest some form of moral inferiority that would render useless any attempt to rehabilitate the long-term poor.

CONCLUSION: RESHAPING THE CLASS STRUCTURE

The industrial transformation is an ongoing process that continues to reshape economies and societies and, as a result, the class system. This newest phase in the evolution of industrial societies has been called the "post-industrial age," the "information age," and the "service era." Among the most salient forces having an impact on the class system are deindustrialization, the creation of the world economy, the escalation of skill and educational requirements, and the expansion of contingent employment. Many observers worry that the result will be an increase in the gap between the top and the bottom of the class structure.

Deindustrialization

The early phases of industrialization generate the need for a large force of blue-collar workers; unskilled laborers to dig canals, lay railroad tracks, load and unload trains, pack boxes, and move and haul materials; and factory workers to operate the sewing machines and steel furnaces. At the dawn of the twentieth century one worker in four in the urban labor force in America was an unskilled worker or machine operator. As economies mature the proportion of jobs in manufacturing begin to decline, a process that has been noted in advanced industrial nations since the 1960s. The loss of manufacturing jobs is referred to as **deindustrialization.** To illustrate, the share of manufacturing in total employment in industrial nations slipped from 28 percent in 1970 to 18 percent in 1994 (*The Economist*, 1997b).

Deindustrialization is prompted by improvements in productivity and by technological changes that mechanize or automate less skilled work, as when earth-moving machines eliminate the need for construction laborers. The loss of low-skill work has important implications for those with limited educational credentials or lacking work experience. At minimum, it was paid work, and it provided a point of entry into the labor force where individuals could acquire job skills and demonstrate ability, and some could subsequently hope to move on to better jobs. Deindustrialization represents the disappearance of the more stable sector of the working class that provided jobs for successive waves of immigrants to America.

Global Capitalism

Nations have always engaged in trade, but improvements in telecommunications, transportation, and the ability to move people and goods around the globe are creating a world economy. On the one hand, **global capitalism** opens markets and offers opportunities for exports that create jobs in advanced economies such as the United States and Canada (Ross & Trachte, 1990). On the other hand, it simultaneously becomes easier to move plants and less skilled jobs to nations with lower labor costs, thus threatening the loss of jobs in those same advanced industrial nations.

Education Credentials

The rate of growth of knowledge obviously continues to accelerate at an unprecedented rate, and it has several important implications. One is the proliferation of new occupations organized around specialized areas of expertise. Consider the field of computers, which did not even exist fifty years ago, or medicine, where literally scores of specialized new occupations have emerged over the course of the twentieth-century—physicians' assistants, neonatal surgeons, surgical technicians, physical therapists, dietitians, nuclear medicine technologists, occupational therapists, clinical pharmacists, and geneticists among them. The second implication is the increasing segregation of the labor force into high- and low-skill occupations. At one extreme are low-skill occupations with low pay and limited chances of advancement, notably in the lower middle class, the working class, and the poor, and at the other are high-paying upper-middle-class jobs that demand advanced education. Projections of job growth into the twenty-first century plainly show this (Exhibit 3.4). The occupations with the largest anticipated growth are clearly divided between low-skill, low-paying jobs (cashiers, janitors and cleaners, retail salespersons, waiters) and jobs requiring a minimum of a college education and paying above average wages (nurses, systems analysts, and teachers). The earnings gap between university-educated and the less educated rose sharply in the United States and Britain during the 1990s. This development will contribute to a growing disparity between the top and bottom of the stratification system.

EXHIBIT 3.4 Occupations with the Greatest Projected Growth, United States, 1995–2005

OCCUPATION	PROJECTED EMPLOYMENT	NUMERICAL CHANGE	PERCENTAGE CHANGE
Cashiers	3,567,000	562,000	19
Janitors, cleaners	3,602,000	559,000	18
Retail salespersons	4,374,000	532,000	14
Wait staff	2,326,000	479,000	26
Registered nurses	2,379,000	473,000	25
Executives	3,512,000	466,000	15
Systems analysts	928,000	445,000	92
Home health aides	848,000	428,000	102
Guards	1,282,000	415,000	48
Nursing aides	1,652,000	387,000	31
Teachers	1,726,000	386,000	29

Source: George T. Silvestri, "Occupational employment to 2005," *Monthly Labor Review* 118 (November, 1995), Table 4, page 81.

Contingent Employment

The phrase **contingent employment** was coined in 1985 by Audrey Freedman to call attention to the increasing number of people who have a transitory and temporary relationship with their employer (Polivka & Nardone, 1989). The key feature of contingent work is the lack of a long-term (explicit or implicit) bond between employer and employee. Examples of contingent workers are temporary workers, consultants, leased workers, independent contractors, and some part-time workers.

Temporary employment has long been a part of industrial economies, agricultural day laborers migrating to harvest crops, sales workers employed to cope with the holiday crush of shoppers, bookkeepers added as tax deadlines approach, and seasonal help in beach towns. What is different about the current situation is the increasing proportion of the workforce that fits into this category. Temporary employment, once generally limited to female clerical help filling in during vacations and peak business periods, has spread to virtually every kind of work imaginable. It is possible to hire not only a secretary, security guard, janitor, factory worker, or telemarketer, but also a temporary executive or professional—a lawyer, registered nurse, or physician. Temporary help agencies employed a million people *per day* in 1989 and 1.9 million in 1994, and the number is expected to be 3.5 million at the start of the twenty-first century (Rose, 1994). Several different factors have combined to produce the expansion of contingent work. Cost-containment and flexibility seem to be the major advantages for employers. The flexibility of being able to bring together workers as needed is obvious, but many contingent workers are less costly in a number of ways; training costs and record keeping are reduced, and workers are not paid during slack periods.

The penalties of contingent work include lower pay and fewer benefits such as health care and pension benefits. Part-time workers, for example, earn 38 percent less than full-time workers when controlling for age, gender, and education (U.S. General Accounting Office, 1991:5). Moreover, about one-half are not covered by health insurance. The uncertainty and financial disadvantages of contingent work mean that a proportion of contingent workers accept this arrangement only because of other obligations such as child-care responsibilities. About 30 percent of part-time workers actually want full-time employment (Collins, 1994: 53). Contingent employment thus creates a cadre of workers to whom employers have no long-term commitment and who are at a significant financial disadvantage.

KEY CONCEPTS

capitalism	industrial transformation	slavery
capitalist elite	institutional elite	underclass
contingent employment	lower middle class	upper middle class
deindustrialization	poor, the	working class
global capitalism	scientific management	working poor

SUGGESTED READING

Tom Bottomore and Robert J. Brym, eds., *The Capitalist Class.* New York: New York University Press, 1989. A collection of essays on the capitalist class in industrial nations, debating their power and influence.

Harry Braverman, *Labor and Monopoly Capitalism.* New York: Monthly Review Press, 1974. An original analysis of the emergence of monopoly capitalism.

Eliot Friedson, *Professional Powers: A Study of the Institutionalization of Formal Knowledge.* Chicago, IL: University of Chicago Press, 1986. A lucid sociological analysis of the evolution of the professions in industrial society.

Kevin Henson, *The Temp.* Philadelphia, PA: Temple University Press, 1996. An exploration of the implications of a contingent labor force.

Stephen P. Waring, *Taylorism Transformed: Scientific Management Since 1945.* Chapel Hill, NC: University of North Carolina Press, 1991. A critical examination of scientific management that suggests its goal is worker control rather than industrial efficiency.

Erik Olin Wright, *The Debate on Classes.* London: Verso, 1989. A discussion of the class structure in industrial societies using a Marxist perspective.

CHAPTER FOUR

Institutionalizing and Legitimizing Stratification

THE ORIGINS AND MAINTENANCE OF STRATIFICATION SYSTEMS

Social classes are the product of the industrial transformation that began late in the 1700s. The application of power-driven machinery and the development of factory-based manufacturing transformed rural and agricultural societies into urban, industrial systems. The explosion in productivity that accompanied industrialization created great wealth for merchants and factory owners and fostered the emergence of a comfortable urban middle class of business and professional families. Most factory workers did not prosper at first, but eventually they won better wages and working conditions, eventually raising the standard of living of broad segments of the population. Industrialization generated stratification systems with the potential for both great wealth and deplorable poverty.

Two analytically separate sociological processes are involved in the origin and maintenance of stratification systems. The first, the institutionalization of stratification, refers to the social mechanisms that enhance or inhibit access to the social class positions; the systematic exclusion of categories of people from formal education that opens opportunities for well-paying jobs is one dimension of the process. In contrast, the rationale or justification that sustains the distribution of rewards is a different process, a process that sociologists call legitimation. The idea that certain people are incapable of benefiting from formal education is an example of this process. The two processes overlap and interact and cannot be understood independent of one another.

The Institutionalization of Inequality

The **institutionalization of inequality** refers to the collection of customs, laws, and social practices that combine to create and sustain the unequal distribution of rewards based on class, minority status, and gender. Openly discriminatory laws and codes have often played a role in this process. Early in the twentieth century contractors openly advertised to pay "whites" $1.50 per day but only $1.15 to "Italians" (Feagin, 1984: 123). In addition, women and racial and ethnic minorities were long formally excluded from professional schools, apprenticeships, crafts unions, and other opportunities that could lead to well-paying jobs. Such practices often survived informally long after they were prohibited by law.

The institutionalization of inequality often operates in more subtle and invidious ways. Schools and school systems, for example, sometimes offer unequal educational opportunities for students. Money is an obvious factor, because richer school districts are able to devote more resources to education than poorer districts. Moreover, even in integrated schools, upper-middle-class students are more likely to be found on college preparatory tracks that feed to higher education, while minority students and poor and working-class children are more likely to be on tracks that lead to more modest educational and occupational attainments (Oakes, 1985).

The institutionalization of inequality is, in extreme cases, maintained by physical force, intimidation, or even terrorism. The period between the Civil War and World War II in the South witnessed the exercise of both private (the Klan) and public (law enforcement) violence and intimidation. As late as the 1940s, city police departments were implicated in forcibly providing workers for the cotton plantations (James, 1988). However, discrimination and exclusionary practices are seldom maintained exclusively by naked force and are usually sustained by social ideas that make such actions legitimate.

The Legitimation of Inequality

Legitimation refers to the social definitions, beliefs, and values that serve to support, rationalize, and justify patterns of inequality by making them seem valid or right or moral. For example, the doctrine that slaves are members of an inherently inferior group is a perfect justification for enslaving them. When ideas are organized into a more or less consistent system of elements they are said to form an **ideology,** a system of beliefs and ideas that support discrimination against socially defined groups. In the pre-British Hindu caste system, members of lower-level castes were seen as ritually impure and limited to the most odious occupations such as cleaners and shepherds. Nineteenth-century racism was an ideology that combined "science" and biology to guarantee the relegation of African Americans to the lower ends of the stratification system. It is important to emphasize that ideologies need not be logically consistent or based on an accurate picture of the situation.

Several points about ideology must be understood at the outset. First, the elements of an ideology may be consciously recognized and accepted by dominant members of society or may operate below the conscious level. Long-standing ideologies often enjoy the force of tradition. Patterns are learned and passed on to subsequent generations through the socialization process and seem to have no other justification than their antiquity. This kind of ideology is often evident in social stereotypes that are grounded in unrecognized beliefs and assumptions about categories of people.

Second, ideologies may be elaborate and coherent systems of ideas, deliberately promulgated by a dominant group, or they may be loose collections of ideas that emerge in the process of everyday social relations among groups. In the former category are explicit ideologies developed and advanced by advantaged groups to justify their privileges (Barrera, 1979: 198). Groups in power have, throughout history, defended their privileges on the grounds that the survival of civilization depended upon their continued rule. For example, medieval European aristocrats espoused the position that they were the descendants of the Teutons (later called Aryans) who had subdued the Romans, and commoners were descendants of the defeated Romans and other inferior cultures. Members of the aristocratic class were thus members of the biological line responsible for the flowering of Western civilization and hence destined to rule. Later versions of this civilization ideology showed up in the United States in this century among those who sought to erect barriers to the influx of immigrants from Eastern and Southern Europe. Not all ideologies are deliberately created (Shibutani & Kwan, 1965). Rather, they may be understood as emerging in a more unsystematic way as certain ideas are selected out and embraced simply because they can be interpreted to justify inequality.

Institutionalization and legitimation are thus interlocking features of the dynamics of stratification. The analytic distinction between two processes is important in understanding the persistence of inequality through time. Institutionalized discrimination may be discredited and outlawed, but underlying ideologies (attitudes, beliefs, and stereotypes) can persist long after formal barriers to opportunity have crumbled. There are any number of contemporary examples that can be understood in this way. To illustrate, white-collar workers continue to enjoy higher social status than blue-collar workers, despite the fact that the original basis of the distinction has been eroded by economic and technological change. Racial stereotypes still plague African-American workers in job applications, although formal occupational barriers are illegal.

THE AMERICAN DREAM AND THE IDEOLOGY OF INDIVIDUALISM

Contemporary American perceptions of the legitimacy of the distribution of wealth, social status, and political power continue to be influenced by a complex ideology that most people think of as the "American Dream." It emphasizes a link between individual effort and success in an open, merit-based system. The American Dream lured countless immigrants to America and rural migrants to the cities. Social scientists are more apt to refer to it as the **ideology of individualism,** and it may formally be phrased as follows (Huber & Form, 1973; Feagin, 1972; Klugel & Smith, 1986; Lipset, 1990; J. Hochschild, 1995):

> *There are abundant economic opportunities.*
>
> *Individuals must be industrious and competitive.*
>
> *Rewards in the form of education, jobs, income, and status are, and should be, the result of individual talent and effort.*
>
> *Therefore, the distribution of rewards is generally fair and equitable.*

Although there may be a weakening of the power of this ideology, especially since World War II, it continues to have relevance for significant segments of the population and provides legitimation for stratification in America.

The Puritan Ethic

The origins of the ideology of individualism can be traced to the Protestant Reformation of the sixteenth century. A key element in this religious philosophy was an emphasis on individual responsibility for one's own fate (both religious and secular). Puritans brought this individualistic spirit to America with them, and it came to form the centerpiece of the colonial cultural value system. The importance of independence and self-reliance was solidified and elaborated by the unique circumstances of a frontier society and later by industrialization and the celebration of emerging capitalism.

Protestantism in the sixteenth century must be understood as a rejection of the elaborate bureaucracy of the Catholic church and its doctrine that a Christian was able to achieve salvation only through the auspices of the church. Reformers such as Martin Luther and John Calvin emphasized individuals' responsibility for their own actions and their own fate. They also made work a key feature of individuals' social and moral obligations. Prior to the Reformation, all work except religious endeavors was perceived as a burden to be endured as a means of survival. Martin Luther elevated the value of every occupation by arguing that all forms of work played an integral part in God's worldly plans. Influential ministers demanded relentless industriousness in pursuit of a person's occupation, no matter how menial. Hard work offered countless rewards; it was intrinsically worthwhile but also was a way of serving God and a protection against the temptations of the secular world. More than one Calvinist theologian defined lack of employment as a crime or a sin. The unemployed were, in several colonies, actually subject to imprisonment or whipping (Feagin, 1975: 25).

Puritanism also gave religious sanction to social inequality, because economic success, or the lack of it, came to be associated with personal character. Calvinists proclaimed that wealth was a worldly sign of God's grace, for God would certainly not allow the immoral to prosper. He rewarded only the virtuous. Hence, individual failure was an indication of some personal flaw, not a consequence of family background and structural limits on opportunity. Some groups, such as the Quakers, spoke out against this view, but without much impact, and the powerful emphasis on individual responsibility for financial success or failure was established.

Benjamin Franklin was one of the chief advocates of the Puritan ethic. Writing in 1726 he resolved, "To apply myself industriously to whatever business I take in hand, and not divert my mind from my business by any foolish project of growing suddenly rich; for industry and patience are the surest means to plenty" (Franklin, 1761: 183). It was this link between industriousness and wealth that attracted the attention of Max Weber, who argued that Protestantism fostered the spirit of capitalism.

The Frontier and the Land of Opportunity

The American ideology of individualism was encouraged and reinforced by an abundance of open land on the western frontier. The frontier was much more than a distant geographic boundary, it was a symbol of unlimited opportunity (Turner, 1920). The image of plentiful land on the western frontier nourished a convenient mythology for the nation. There was no reason for anyone to fail, because there was always the vast untapped land to the west, with prosperity in forestry, farming, or fishing awaiting the strong and talented willing to seize the opportunity. This image was furthered in the mid-nineteenth century with discovery of gold in California, and in 1862 by passage of the Homestead Act that guaranteed cheap land to virtually everyone. The inherent risks—uncharted land, an indigenous population that sought to protect its lands, and lack of law and order—merely emphasized the rewards awaiting the adventurous and self-reliant. This led to the celebration of the rugged individualist, symbolized even today by the cowboy.

It was an ideology that could flourish in a largely agrarian economy with a broad expanse of open land and lacking traditional class barriers to success (with the notable exception of slaves). The flourishing of industrialization in the nineteenth century presented a different kind of opportunity—paid work in the factories, mills, and mines. There was also the opportunity for wealth through personal ingenuity, and early capitalism created millionaires out of those who invented or perfected production techniques, people such as Henry Ford and Thomas Edison. As the nation and individuals prospered, America became defined as the "land of opportunity." The image of a nation of apparently limitless economic opportunity attracted waves of immigrants fleeing poverty, famine, or oppression in their native lands. Most non-English immigrants met with discrimination and open hostility and were typically relegated to the least rewarding work in the factories. Yet their economic status was often much better than it would have been in the lands they abandoned, and there were opportunities for those from humble origins to prosper and support the belief system. The success of individual immigrants fueled the myth. Andrew Carnegie, for example, came to America from Scotland as a poor boy of 13 and eventually amassed a fortune in the iron and steel business. Those who did not themselves prosper were sustained by the notion that their children would enjoy the benefits of a better life.

Social Darwinism

People like Carnegie and J. P. Morgan amassed great wealth in the nineteenth century, and toward the end of the century a new variation of the dominant ideology emerged, one that created a link between science and affluence. Charles Darwin published *On the Origin of the Species* in 1859, and it soon became the basis for a social and economic ideology. Themes such as the "struggle for survival" and "survival of the fittest" were appropriated from a biological theory of evolution and grafted onto economic theories to explain and justify inequalities in wealth and power. John D. Rockefeller, speaking to a church school, explained,

> The growth of a large business is merely a survival of the fittest . . . This is not an evil tendency in business. It is merely the working out of a law of nature and a law of God (Feagin, 1975: 35).

Soon thereafter, sociologist William Graham Sumner lent academic legitimacy to Social Darwinism with his view of the rich:

> Millionaires are a product of natural selection, acting on the whole body of men to pick out those who can meet the requirement of certain work to be done. . . . They may fairly be regarded as the naturally selected agents of society. . . . There is the intensest competition for their place and occupation (and) this assures us that all who are competent for this function will be employed in it (Sumner, 1914: 90).

Therefore, he concluded, there should be no attempt to redistribute wealth or interfere with the evolutionary process. He believed that hard work could triumph over the most humble circumstances; hence, he had these words of advice for impoverished urban workers:

> Let every man be sober, industrious, prudent and wise, and bring up his children to be so likewise, and poverty will be abolished in a few generations (Sumner, 1914: 57).

The Great Depression

The themes of individualism, self-reliance, and boundless opportunity became difficult to sustain during the Great Depression of the 1930s. More than 6 million workers were thrown out of work between 1929 and 1930 alone, and a record 14 million were displaced in the mid-1930s. It is commonly estimated that unemployment stood at 25 percent of the labor force at the peak of the Depression. It became evident that no amount of individual effort could protect even the most diligent worker from joblessness as businesses failed and factories closed. The economic chaos of the period stimulated two dramatic changes in public policy. There was, first, a dramatic increase in governmental intervention in the functioning of the economic system. Government spending practices were used to stimulate the economy. Massive public works projects were undertaken to expand the infrastructure and create jobs. Regulatory agencies such as the Securities Exchange Commission were created to monitor the stock market. At the same time, the government began to fashion a safety net to assist individual victims of unbridled capitalism. For example, the Social Security Act of 1935 provided payments to the unemployed and established retirement benefits, and minimum wage legislation (1938) created a floor under wages for some workers. Such mechanisms were an open acknowledgment that capitalism was not benign and that individuals at the mercy of the system deserved some protection and aid from their government.

Further challenges to the emphasis on individual achievement surfaced during the turmoil of the 1960s. The civil rights and women's movements and the rediscovery of persistent structural poverty left little doubt that discrimination and structural barriers placed artificial limits on opportunities for significant segments of American society. Social scientists marshaled evidence that located at least some of the blame for poverty on the weaknesses of institutions such as the schools and subsistence wage jobs that failed to provide the income to support families. These developments challenged exclusive reliance upon individual success or failure and focused on social, political, and economic factors beyond the direct control of individuals, however highly motivated they might be.

Contemporary Class Ideology

The ideology of opportunity and individualism that shaped American society and culture for much of its history survives. The majority of white Americans still generally see America as a "land of opportunity" (Kluegel & Smith, 1986), and two out of three people insist that "hard work" is the key to economic success (Mitchell, 1996). Contemporary perceptions of individual chances for success are weakening in response to the well-publicized threat of worldwide economic competition and downsizing that is displacing countless workers. In addition, it reveals an awakening (or perhaps a public acknowledgment) of the fact that structural barriers to access prevail, especially for minorities, women, and the poor.

However, the causal link between individual effort and economic success remains strong. Although ideologies are complex social phenomena, they can sometimes be highlighted by a single issue, a single topic, or a single question. Many social scientists believe that inviting people to define the causes of wealth or poverty is such a focal issue. The poor occupy the bottom of the class structure, and perceptions of the cause of their situation demand that people distill their feelings and attitudes into a single response.

When confronted with this question, Americans divide into three almost equal categories (Exhibit 4.1). One segment of the population is most willing to blame the poor themselves for their plight due to a lack of effort, and another third locate the causes of poverty in circumstances beyond the control of the poor such as background, education, and the availability of jobs. The remaining one-third feel that both must be considered. It must also be noted that this is not a neutral issue, for very few people lack an opinion on the matter.

The ideology of individualism clearly flourishes more powerfully among some segments of the population than others. Men are somewhat more likely to subscribe

EXHIBIT 4.1 Perceptions of the Causes of Poverty

GROUP	LACK OF EFFORT	CIRCUMSTANCES	BOTH	NO OPINION
Overall:	33%	34%	31%	2%
Sex:				
Male	36	31	30	3
Female	29	37	31	3
Racial/Ethnic Group:				
White	35	30	33	2
Nonwhite	15	67	16	2
Hispanic	11	44	38	7
Social Class:				
Upper Middle	36	32	31	1
Lower Middle	41	36	23	<1
Working	29	36	31	4
Not in Labor Force	31	37	31	4

Note: Data are based on a national sample of 1505 adults. The question was worded as follows: "In your opinion, which is more often to blame if a person is poor—lack of effort on his own part, or circumstances beyond his control?"

Source: Gallup Poll. "Blame for poverty." *The Gallup Report* # 234, (March, 1985), p. 24. Copyright © 1985 by The Gallup Report.

to the importance of individual responsibility than women. As would be expected, the more advantaged segments of the population give more weight to personal effort, while blue-collar workers and racial and ethnic minorities are more sensitive to structural rather than individual sources of poverty.

More detailed analysis of individualist responses reveals the survival of the traditional values of Ben Franklin. The major causes of poverty are identified as the absence of some positive personal trait such as lack of thrift or proper money management, lack of effort, lack of ability and talent, or loose morals and drunkenness (Kluegel & Smith, 1986: 79). In contrast, when asked to explain the sources of great wealth, a majority favor factors such as personal drive, risk-taking, hard work, and initiative, although it is conceded that inherited wealth is some advantage. Those who emphasize social structure see the sources of wealth or poverty, success or failure originating with social barriers or in the circumstances that individuals confront in their own backgrounds. They assign the greatest weight to factors such as discrimination, exploitative wages, or failures of the school system.

The ideology of individualism is also evident in the tendency of Americans to make a distinction between the "deserving" poor and the "undeserving" or "unworthy" poor. The worthy poor are those who are hard-working but are the victims of circumstances and hence deserving of compassion and aid, while the unworthy are responsible for their own problems and do not deserve respect. The convergence of these various elements forms an ideology of individualism that stresses individual responsibility for the rewards that people enjoy and their place in the stratification system. This is evident in the aversion to the term "social class" in American society (DeMott, 1990). Acceptance of social class admits that society is divided into groups whose opportunities and rewards are enhanced or limited by the workings of the economic system.

RACE, ETHNICITY, AND STRATIFICATION

Members of racial and ethnic groups are often concentrated at the lower levels of stratification systems. Mexican-American men illustrate this situation. Seventy-seven percent are in service or blue-collar work, compared to 49 percent of non-Latino white men (del Pinal & Singer, 1997: 38). Consequently, 15 percent of Mexican families earn less than $10,000 a year, compared to 5 percent of white families. There are several different approaches to understanding the concentration of minorities at the lower levels of society, and they can conveniently be divided into three basic categories (Feagin & Feagin, 1996). One approach focuses on competition among groups for scarce resources; a second emphasizes deliberate systematic coercive exploitation of minorities; and assimilation theorists emphasize the sociocultural characteristics of minority group members that place them at a disadvantage in a system dominated by members of a different culture.

Competition Theory

Competition theory focuses on the clashes that occur when two or more groups pursue the same limited resources. Those resources are usually land, jobs, housing, education, or political power. The history of relations between Native Americans and Europeans must certainly be seen as a struggle for land, minerals, and natural resources. A different form of competition centers on jobs. Organized occupational groups frequently limit minority access. For example, the legal profession during the 1920s and 1930s erected barriers to limit the number of African Americans and Eastern European immigrants (Auerbach, 1976). Competition is usually stimulated by some broad geographical movement of groups. In the United States this was caused by the westward expansion of Europeans, foreign immigration, and internal migration from the south to the north and from rural to urban areas.

During the post–Civil War period the dramatic and relatively sudden competition for working-class jobs between African Americans and whites, set in motion by emancipation, ushered in the Jim Crow era. One estimate suggests that 100,000 of the artisans in the south in 1865 were African American (Brooks, 1971: 243), and it is not surprising that some white artisans worried about the threat to their jobs posed by the newfound freedom of skilled African-American carpenters, blacksmiths, and tailors. The situation was, of course, more complex than just a struggle between working-class whites and African Americans for skilled jobs. Other groups had vested interests. Large landowners also stood to benefit from the presence of a large pool of African-American workers excluded from skilled blue-collar work and thus available as a cheap labor force.

Some proponents of this approach emphasize that competition stimulates a strengthening of ethnic identity that encourages greater antagonism among groups. The reasoning is that competition and the presence of hostile groups encourage a sense of solidarity on both sides, and that, in turn, leads to mobilization and open conflict (Olzak, 1996; Nagel, 1995). Others note that racial and ethnic groups are often initially separated by preexisting feelings of **ethnocentrism,** the tendency of a group to view its own standards and perspectives as superior (Noel, 1968). Religion can be the basis of ethnocentrism, because most religious belief systems define their creed as "the one true faith," thus establishing an unequivocal basis for judgments of inferiority. Cultural values—by virtue of defining what is "right"—operate in the same manner. Ethnocentrism thus emphasizes social differences among groups and exacerbates the potential for conflict.

The subordination of one racial or ethnic group by another is ultimately resolved by the ability to control access to such valued resources. Not infrequently, competition is settled by violence—either actual or threatened. European expansion at the expense of Native Americans was eventually decided by the superiority of weaponry and military personnel. However, exclusion of African Americans from jobs also took less extreme forms. For example, white-controlled unions systematically excluded African Americans from membership and apprenticeship programs and prohibited their members from working with nonunion members, thus pressuring employers to exclude African Americans (Foner, 1964). Such practices were part of some union constitutions between the 1880s and the 1940s.

The validity of competition theories is supported by historical analysis that shows antagonism tends to increase when immigration expands and puts pressure on competition for jobs and during economic downturns when there are fewer jobs (Nagel, 1995). Although the focus of competition centers on the exclusion from jobs, it is not limited to the occupational sphere alone. It takes place within the larger context of exclusionary practices designed to keep minorities poor, uneducated, and powerless, thus discouraging competition and assuring another generation of workers.

Internal Colonialism

Political scientists use the term "colonialism" to describe the political control and economic use of weaker nations and groups at the hands of more powerful nations. This pattern can also be used to describe processes that occur within the borders of nations, and hence social scientists use the term **internal colonialism** to identify the political domination and economic exploitation of racial and ethnic groups by more powerful groups (Blauner, 1972). The thesis is embedded in economic imperatives, and it is argued that vulnerable (usually non-native) groups are explicitly exploited as a pool of low-wage workers to generate profits for agricultural landowners or industrial employers. This approach illuminates the American experience of a number of nonwhite groups, starting with the forced importation of Africans as slaves beginning in the seventeenth century, continuing in the midnineteenth century with the importation of poor Chinese workers to work the mines and build the railroads, continuing in the twentieth century with the influx of Mexicans to do field work and harvest the crops in the Southwest. Today, internal colonialism is likely to be found in urban sweatshops (see accompanying Case Study).

Not all exploited racial and ethnic minorities labor in sweatshops. Many are migrant farm workers, toiling in the fields. It is estimated that there are 2.2 million paid farm workers, 85 percent are foreign born, and nearly one-half (46 percent) live below the poverty level (Potok, 1996). Most are legal and illegal immigrants attracted by wages much higher than could be earned in their native lands. Some remain in the United States, migrating around the country as work becomes available, while others are "shuttle" migrants, working in one area during harvesting and then returning home for the rest of the year.

CASE STUDY:
Sweatshops Reborn

Sweatshops are firms, usually small, employing workers at low wages for long hours under poor working conditions. Sweatshops grew up in urban areas in the early stages of industrialization. They prospered in many industries in the United States during the Civil War, but particularly in the apparel business (Wong, 1983). Large clothing manufacturers hired small entrepreneurs to do some of the tailoring. Subcontractors' profits were the difference between what they earned and what it cost to produce the garments. They subdivided the various stages of the process into simple relatively unskilled tasks such as cutting, stitching, and sewing that could be mastered by children and unskilled adults. Money devoted to higher wages or better working conditions reduced profits, hence the margin was "sweated" from workers by paying them as little as possible for long hours in the most unsanitary and unsafe conditions. Sweatshops were located in tenements, over saloons or stables, in basements or attics or lofts, wherever rent was cheap. There were no restrictions on hours and workdays stretching from 5 A.M. to 9 P.M. were common. It is estimated that there were at least 20,000 sweatshops in tenements in New York City in 1901 (Adams & Sumner, 1985). "The workers, all immigrants, lived and worked together in large numbers, in a few small, foul smelling rooms without ventilation, water or nearby toilets" (Seidman, 1942: 56). The disreputable conditions were highlighted by a fire in the Triangle Shirtwaist Factory in 1911, when 146 girls and young women died, many because doors were locked to keep workers in and union organizers out. That tragedy helped to prompt legislation regulating hours and wages and working conditions.

The origins and proliferation of sweatshops in the nineteenth century reflected the convergence of three factors, labor intensive industries (such as apparel, cigar making, and meat processing), the practice of subcontracting work among many small producers, and the availability of a pool of vulnerable and exploitable workers (children, poor women, immigrants, and rural migrants). Unfortunately, the same conditions are repeated today. In 1991 twenty-five people were killed in a Hamlet, North Carolina, poultry processing plant fire that revealed crowded conditions and padlocked doors reminiscent of the Triangle Shirtwaist tragedy. The major change is that the Italians, Jewish, and Polish garment workers of the nineteenth century have been replaced by Asians and Latinos (U.S. General Accounting Office, 1988).

It is estimated that 2000 sweatshops operate in New York City alone, and they are also common in other cities where there is a ready pool of immigrant labor, such as Los Angeles, Miami, and El Paso, Texas (Hedden, 1993; Finder, 1995). Most are small operations employing twenty to thirty people, mostly young females, that open and close so frequently and so quickly that they easily evade the efforts of understaffed government inspection agencies. Children as young as ten spend up to sixty hours a week toiling at sewing machines for less than minimum wages. One undercover investigative reporter in New York City was paid 96¢ an hour for eighty-four hours of work per week (Lii, 1995). Some are illegal immigrants who cannot complain about pay or working conditions and who may owe huge sums to the smugglers who helped them enter the country. There are even instances of immigrants being held against their will. In 1995, for example, federal agents found 72 Thai workers in virtual slavery in a walled garment factory in El Monte, California, forced to work for less than $2.00 an hour (Chandler, 1995).

The Thai case underscores the longstanding problem of sweatshops in the garment industry. Although some garment workers enjoy decent wages and working conditions, it is estimated that one-half of all women's garments made in America are produced in whole or in part at factories that flout wage and safety laws (Hedden, 1993). To illustrate, a random check of sixty-nine garment makers in California found 93 percent guilty of health and safety violations, 68 percent refusing to pay overtime rates, and 51 percent paying less than the minimum wage (Chandler, 1995).

Sweatshops are a global problem, and at least some of the clothing sold by well-known American designers and retailers is produced in sweatshop conditions in developing nations such as the Dominican Republic, the Philippines, Malaysia, Thailand, and Vietnam. These are nations in which massive segments of the population—sometimes one-half—live in poverty. In 1997 major American firms agreed to a code of conduct for subcontractors that prohibits child labor and demands minimum work and safety standards, guarantees the right to unionize, and insists that workers be paid the prevailing minimum wage. The code of conduct is not without its critics, because the minimum wage in some developing nations is below the poverty level, and because it permits workweeks of up to sixty hours (Greenhouse, 1997a). The major obstacle will be developing a system for monitoring and enforcing the code in those nations. The problem of sweatshops will continue as long as the availability of highly vulnerable workers makes it possible for unscrupulous manufacturers to rank profits over human dignity.

Assimilation Theory

Assimilation theory is strongly influenced by the American experience. During the nineteenth century the United States was populated by succeeding waves of immigrants. It began with the Irish and later included Germans, Chinese, Scandinavians, Poles, Austrians, Czechs, Hungarians, Slovaks, and Italians. Most were driven from their homes by economic and social conditions—poverty, political unrest, and overpopulation. Each succeeding wave of immigrants tended to be concentrated at the lowest levels of the stratification system due to a combination of hostility by members of the dominant group and their own characteristics (lack of marketable job skills, absence of educational credentials, language barriers, and different cultural and religious traditions) that handicapped them in the competition for jobs and promotions. However, succeeding generations were usually able to improve their position by adopting the social and cultural attributes of the host society, a process called **assimilation.** The assimilation perspective emphasizes the erosion of the salience of racial and ethnic differences as the basis of inequality over time as immigrant groups surrender their cultural background and adopt the attributes and perspectives of the dominant culture (Gordon, 1964).

Assimilation theory is an optimistic approach, suggesting that as succeeding generations of immigrant groups adopt the dominant culture (language, values, customs) they are able to compete educationally and economically, leading to a weakening of prejudice and discrimination. Assimilation occurs because the racial and ethnic differences that originally set them apart and disadvantaged them are blurred. The experience of German, Scandinavian and Irish immigrant groups confirms the operation of the process. However, acceptance is gained at a price, the cost of **Anglo-conformity,** rejection of their identity, and acceptance of the values and perspectives of the prevailing English and Protestant culture. Ultimately, assimilation has not worked equally well for all groups, especially African Americans (Williams & Ortega, 1990).

Ideological Racism: Legitimizing Racial and Ethnic Inequality

Discriminatory and exclusionary practices are supported by values and belief systems that legitimize such practices. Almost all forms of subordination are shaped by some variation of ideological racism.[1] **Ideological racism** is a system of ideas that divides the world population into groups (races) based on physical traits that are, in turn, claimed to be unalterably linked to intellectual and psychological characteristics (Feagin & Feagin, 1996: 7).[2] Not surprisingly, the group controlling the ranking is always

---

[1] It must be emphasized that ideological racism as used in this context has a specific meaning distinct from the word "racism" as it is commonly employed in popular usage. In the media and elsewhere "racism" is used as a generic term to refer to any negative attitude or hostile act directed toward members of minority groups.

[2] Historically, the term "race" was used to identify groups of people distinguished by any number of observable physical or social characteristics. The basis for such classifications could be religion (*e.g.*, Jewish race), language (Arab race), nationality (Irish race, Mexican race), or physical characteristics (white race). Race is thus ultimately a social construct, not a biological reality.

at the top of the intellectual hierarchy. The inferiority imputed to subordinates by the dominant group thus justifies disparate treatment and unequal rewards.

The emergence of the European concept of races as groups of people with distinctive physical, attitudinal, and behavioral characteristics is associated with expansion into the Western Hemisphere beginning in the seventeenth century. Indigenous peoples and imported Africans were enslaved to perform heavy physical labor. For example, by 1700 somewhere between 500,000 and 600,000 African slaves had been brought into Brazil to work on the sugar and tobacco plantations and in the mills and mines (Russell, 1994: 42). African slaves were characterized as an inferior race as a way of justifying their servitude, even by people such as Thomas Jefferson, who championed political democracy for whites.

The eighteenth and nineteenth centuries witnessed countless efforts by scientists and others to sort people into groups on the basis of physical characteristics such as skin color, hair, and facial structure and to assert their inferiority. Many elaborate pseudoscientific theories flourished. There was, to illustrate, the theory of "polygenesis," which held that the various human races evolved at different times, and Africans, who were claimed to be the first to evolve, were the most intellectually primitive. Moreover, since culture and civilization were the product of biological capacity, the less advanced races could never create cultures comparable to those of higher races. Consequently, it was argued that although Africans were incapable of developing civilization on their own they had to be segregated and concentrated in menial tasks. In a sarcastic twist of ideological racism, it was argued that their importation and exposure to white culture was actually a privilege.

Racial and Ethnic Stereotypes

Racial and ethnic stereotypes play a key role in legitimizing discriminatory treatment by attributing inadequacies or negative traits to subordinate groups. They buttress inferiority in subtle and invidious ways. The experiences of African Americans and Mexican Americans illustrate the dynamics of the process. In both cases stereotypes center on the failure to conform to the standards of the ideology of individualism that demand talent and industriousness.

Stereotyping African Americans.   The moral ambivalence of Thomas Jefferson is well known; he opposed slavery but was a slave owner; he argued that blacks should be free but stereotyped them as mentally inferior. By the middle of the eighteenth century it was common to stereotype African Americans with terms such as "careless," "lazy," and "childlike." Such stereotypes had dual implications. First, it meant that blacks did not have the characteristics demanded by the ideology of individualism—dedication, hard work, and thrift. Second, because they lacked those traits it was logical and acceptable to exclude them from positions of authority and responsibility. They were, in short, deserving of relegation to the bottom of the system.

Sexual imagery also played a significant role in the process of stereotyping and subordinating African Americans. African-American men were cast as sexual

---

CASE STUDY:
Sports and Ideological Racism

Sports is sometimes referred to as the great equalizer. Ideological racism may survive in society and even in locker rooms or front offices, but on the field or on the court race is irrelevant; it is talent that counts. Consequently, African-American athletes achieve fame and fortune in professional sports, earning millions of dollars in salaries and endorsements.

Most Americans see this as a positive development, but there is also another perspective on African-American athletic success. It can, in subtle and destructive ways, perpetuate stereotypes and hinder the progress of future generations of African Americans (Hoberman, 1997). Hoberman argues that supremacy in sports celebrates physical prowess, strength, violence, and ferocity, and these traits resonate with nineteenth-century images of primitive and savage African-American men. Moreover, success in athletics can easily be interpreted as confirmation that African Americans are incapable of intellectual achievements. In short, it resurrects the slavery-era notion of biological inferiority that took so long to discredit.

In addition, the immense rewards that go to the small number of superstars can undermine the opportunities of future generations of African Americans. Fixation on sports by some African-American youth encourages them to concentrate on athletics and neglect the academic efforts that can be translated into advanced education and occupational careers.

---

aggressors, thus justifying oppressive measures to protect white women. In contrast, African-American women were cast as seductive and promiscuous, which offered justification for their sexual exploitation by white slave owners. Some African-American artists believe that the degraded sexual imagery imposed on African Americans has long limited the ability of writers and artists to explore African-American erotica for fear of providing confirmation of the stereotype (Marriott, 1997).

There were, in addition, subcategories for women of color. One was the myth of the aggressive and domineering "strong black woman," having more masculine than feminine traits, which can be twisted to explain racial inequality (hooks, 1984). The reasoning follows this logic: The strength of the African-American women violates broader social expectations of women and consequently emasculates African-American men, contributing to the breakup of the family, which in turn causes poverty. The function of the stereotype is, thus, to locate the causes of the problem with the personality of victims rather than in ideological racism and the structural problems that produce poverty.

Stereotyping Mexican Americans. The characteristics attributed to African Americans are repeated in relation to Mexican Americans. Allegations of laziness, incompetence, and backwardness abound. The origins of stereotypes reflecting ideological racism directed at Mexicans can be traced to the middle of the eighteenth century through selective perception and distorted interpretation of events (Feagin & Feagin, 1996). The defeat of the Mexican army, in the struggle for territory, in the 1840s became the basis of stereotypes that attributed cowardice to them rather than recognizing defeat at the hands of a superior military force. The period of internal turmoil that accompanied the Mexican struggle for independence was transposed into political incompetence. In the 1850s one observer invoked the usual claim that Mexicans lacked the abilities that Europeans did, describing them as "thoroughly debased and incapable of self-government, and there is no latent quality about them that can ever make them respectable" (Feagin & Feagin, 1996: 297). Media images of Mexican Americans during most of the twentieth century emphasized unclean sombrero-wearing caricatures who were either having a siesta or engaging in criminal behavior.

Stereotypes are a powerful force in American society, shaping the way people think about members of minority groups. Well into the 1960s, at least one-third of

---

CASE STUDY:
Ethnic Jokes

"Did you hear that their national library burned down? Not only were both books destroyed, but they hadn't finished coloring them."

Ethnic jokes and one-liners such as this are found in many societies, but those focusing on the alleged stupidity of ethnic minorities are characteristic of Western industrial democracies, although now mostly shared in private rather than in public (Davies, 1982). The following patterns of victimization are common:

COUNTRY	ETHNIC VICTIMS
Australia	Tasmanians
Canada	Icelanders
Denmark	Norwegians
England	Irish
France	Belgians
Sweden	Finns
United States	Poles

The enduring popularity of ethnic jokes and their place in the popular culture of these societies suggest they serve important social functions.

The most obvious feature of ethnic jokes is the blatant ignorance of all members of the group. Thus, the jokes reaffirm the legitimacy of the stratification system by showing that the concentration of these people at the lower ends of the hierarchy is both deserved and fair. Ethnic jokes also emphasize the social and moral boundaries between the dominant and subordinate groups. By projecting negative traits to ethnics they reinforce their separation from them and elevate their own status.

Californians endorsed the notion that Mexicans were "shiftless and dirty" (Brink & Harris, 1967). Such overt and open manifestations of ideological racism began to dissipate under the pressures of the civil rights movement in the 1960s and 1970s. However, negative stereotypes of Mexican Americans persist. In 1997 a major airline used a manual warning pilots that Latin American passengers are often unruly and drunk and call in false bomb threats when running late for a plane (Alexander, 1997). A national survey showed that one in five whites feels Latino/as lack the ambition and drive needed to succeed (Feagin & Feagin, 1996: 299).

GENDER AND STRATIFICATION

Anthropologists and historians have developed comprehensive analyses of work and gender that document a sexual division of labor as a common feature of human societies, in the sense that at least some tasks are typically assigned to either men or women. Biological or physiological differences between the sexes ultimately contribute little to the explanation of the division of labor because responsibilities allocated to men in one society may be the province of women in another, or vice versa. Sales work is, for example, dominated by women in the Philippines (69 percent female), but almost exclusively a male occupation (99 percent male) in the United Arab Emirates (Jacobs, 1989). There are also countless examples of shifts in the gender composition of occupations in one society over time. Men were the telephone operators and clerks in nineteenth-century offices in the United States and Britain until such jobs became women's work over the course of the twentieth century. The sexual division of labor is best understood as the outcome of the social, economic, and political forces that feminist theory seeks to explain.

Varieties of Feminist Theory

There are three main strands of feminist thought that focus on the social, political, and economic subordination of women: liberal feminism, social feminism, and radical feminism (Andersen, 1997). Liberal feminism is not strictly a theory of gender inequality but rather may be best described as a reform movement that attracts both women and men who advocate societal reforms aimed at creating equality of opportunity. It is grounded in the liberal tradition that emphasizes individual autonomy and choice and locates the main sources of inequality in gender socialization and patterns of discrimination that are based on traditional gender roles.

Socialist feminism tends to locate the origins of women's subordination in the nature of capitalist economic systems. The profit motive inherent in capitalism acts as an incentive to exploit the labor of vulnerable groups. Women have, for example, historically often been used to displace male workers or pitted against men to reduce wages. Social feminism has its origins in the thinking of Marx and Engels but moves beyond them to argue that the situation of women cannot be fully explained by capitalism and class relations.

Radical feminism emphasizes that inequality and the allocation of women to the lower ends of the stratification system are facets of a system of institutionalized control over women by men. The subordination of women is evident in countless areas: the sexual division of labor, law, domestic relations, and the political sphere. The concentration of power in the hands of men is referred to as **patriarchy.** Patriarchy thus interprets the allocation of women to inferior jobs, the gender gap in pay, and the glass ceiling as forms of maintaining control. Violence and sexual harassment are the most invidious ways of maintaining patriarchy.

The Division of Labor In Agricultural Society

Women have always been in the paid labor force, but the most dramatic increases in labor force participation in the United States date from the 1940s. The rate of female participation has increased steadily since and is expected to stand at over 60 percent at the turn of the century. Female participation rates vary around the world, ranging from about 56 percent in China to less than 25 percent in Peru (Exhibit 4.2). Overall rates of participation mask important demographic differences, with poor women, urban residents, and women of color always likely to be found working for wages. It is conventional to divide the history of the role of gender in the workplace into several broad periods, beginning with the period prior to industrialization (Kessler-Harris, 1982; Bose, 1987; Anderson, 1988).

From colonial times to the beginning of the nineteenth century, the individual household was the basic unit of production and consumption for the majority of the free white population. There were, of course, wealthy landowners and urban merchants at one extreme and slaves and sharecroppers at the other extreme. It appears that some labor in family enterprises was generally divided along gender lines, at least on modest family farms, with men having primary responsibility for agricultural production and women responsible for the inner economy—food, clothing, child care (Anderson, 1988). However, members of both sexes easily crossed these lines, with husbands involved in the socialization of children for adult community and religious roles and being particularly active in preparing sons to follow agricultural pursuits. Wives participated in production through keeping inventories, caring for livestock, and overall supervision of workers as well as helping with planting, cultivating, and harvesting during peak periods. Households were largely self-sufficient, but cash was needed for the purchase of tools and services (such as the milling of grain), and wives often produced the products and services that generated extra cash income, either by weaving, growing food on small plots, or even working as midwives (Jensen, 1980). Some elements of that pattern survive on contemporary family farms.

Industrialization, Gender, and Work

The first stirrings of the industrial transformation and the creation of a large urban working class began around the beginning of the nineteenth century with the proliferation of mines, factories, and mills. Displaced rural men, women, and children provided the bulk of the labor force for those early factories. A large share of the first

EXHIBIT 4.2 Labor Force Participation Rates for Women

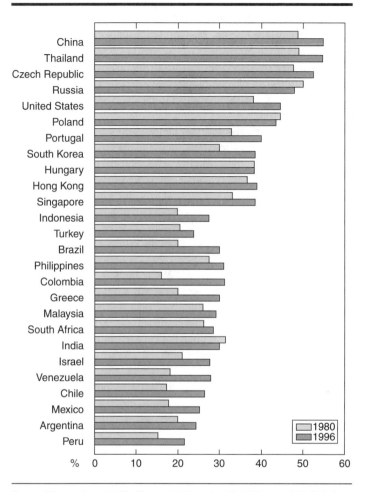

Source: "Women in work," *The Economist*, November 29, 1997, page 110. *Data from* International Labour Office.

workers were the daughters of rural families who contributed to household income through paid work, but they were soon supplemented by foreign-born immigrants (Kessler-Harris, 1982). The first major wave of immigrants were the Irish Catholics who first began to reach this country in large numbers in the 1840s. The men worked the docks and the textile mills, built the railroads, dug the canals, and supplied farm labor. Wives, daughters, and single women were most likely to end up as domestic servants for the wealthier classes. To illustrate, in 1855, 75 percent of all domestic workers in New York City were Irish women (Feagin, 1984: 93).

The most rapid and explosive industrial growth occurred between the Civil War and World War I. One measure of the scale of industrial transformation is the fact that within two decades after the Civil War industrial workers outnumbered farm workers for the first time in American history. The family farm did not disappear, but there was a shift toward commercial production for the market. This was a decisive period in the evolution of gender and work, for it was during this period that a number of forces combined to solidify a dichotomous separation of men's and women's social and occupational roles. It is an extraordinarily complex period, because a number of different forces were at work.

A most obvious difference between agrarian and urban industrial economies was that the workplace became physically separated from the place of residence. That made it more difficult for women with child-rearing obligations to combine domestic responsibilities with full-time paid work. Some continued in various forms of income-producing work at home. Lower-middle- and working-class women were doing laundry at home or taking in boarders as a means of supplementing family income well into the 1920s and 1930s (Kessler-Harris, 1982; Jensen, 1980). Countless others did industrial "home work," jobs such as sewing clothing, making lace or buttons, or even rolling cigars that were decentralized in private homes on a piecework basis. The home work practice was eventually banned in the 1940s because it was used by unscrupulous employers to avoid minimum wage and child labor laws.

Many women were thrust into the paid labor force on a more or less full-time basis during this period, often to supplement family incomes. Rural African-American women did field work, while urban African-American women, their options severely limited by overt discrimination, were typically relegated to domestic service. Factory work was largely the province of young single white women, usually immigrants or the daughters of immigrants. This was the period of massive Italian immigration. They toiled under some of the worst working conditions in disgraceful sweatshops, and as a result women were active in fighting for improved working conditions, both in the larger trade union effort and in organizing along gender lines with groups such as the National Women's Trade Union League (Bose, 1987). In 1881, 3000 African-American women participated in a washerwomen's strike (Hunter, 1997). Although occupational data of the time is unreliable, it appears that at least one in four workers in the paid labor force was a woman in 1900.

Some enduring patterns of gender segregation in occupations emerged during this period. The segregation of occupations along gender lines was legitimized and fostered by a configuration of gender beliefs and attitudes that defined the appropriate social and occupational roles of men and women (Deaux & Kite, 1987: 97). These ideas did not emerge during this period but were thrown into strong relief by the process of industrialization.

Gender Stereotypes.   In some cases, women and men were channeled into different jobs on the grounds that physical and mental skills are gender based. A common version of that justification for the division of labor was that women had more skilled and delicate hands and more patience for tedious work. Assembly-line work

CASE STUDY:
Gender Stereotypes and Management Careers

Gender stereotypes can contribute to important insights into the dynamics of the workplace. One consistent pattern that emerges is the perception that gender involves two distinct clusters of traits. Men tend to be viewed as stronger and more active, with potent needs for achievement, dominance, autonomy, and aggression. Women are seen as less strong and less active, with powerful needs for affiliation, nurturance, and deference. Research on gender stereotypes is typically approached through the use of lists of adjectives. Perceived male traits in the United States tend to cluster around terms such as independence, self-direction, and control, while perceived female traits cluster around caring, expressiveness, and sensitivity to interpersonal relations. The following listing of adjectives, summarized from a broad body of research, provides an outline of the perceived attributes of women and men (Schein, 1973; Deaux & Lewis, 1984; Brenner, Tomkiewicz, & Schein, 1989; Williams & Best, 1990). Attempts to capture the essence of the these clusters in a single word or phrase has popularized expressions such as "instrumental," "competency," "task-orientation," or "agency" for men and "expressive," "social orientation," or "communion" for women. Moreover, there is a general consensus (among both men and women) on these configurations of characteristics, and some indication that a number of these traits show up in other cultures (Williams & Best, 1990).

MALE TRAITS	FEMALE TRAITS
active	affectionate
aggressive	changeable
confident	emotional
courageous	gentle
daring	helpful
forceful	poised
inventive	sensitive
rational	sophisticated
stable	submissive
unemotional	sympathetic
unexcitable	warm

Such popular beliefs can work to the advantage or disadvantage of men and women in the occupational sphere in more than one way. People who are persuaded of the salience of stereotypes can disqualify themselves from the pursuit of specific occupations. It is more likely that they are held back or disqualified as they encounter barriers based on the assumption that they lack the traits necessary to function in certain fields or at certain levels. The link between occupational attainments and stereotypes is highlighted by considering the characteristics, attitudes, and temperaments *believed to be* necessary for success in certain kinds of jobs. Management careers present a clear illustration.

It is more common to associate male characteristics (aggressive, self-reliant, stable) than female characteristics (helpful) with success in management, at least among men (Schein, 1973; Brenner, Tomkiewicz, & Schein, 1989). This discontinuity between female sex-traits and managerial success means that women are perceived as less likely to have abilities to compete in the high-powered world of administration. The perceived characteristics of successful management may also be stereotypical, but their existence has the potential to place women at a disadvantage.

in electrical products and the auto industry illustrates the process. The assembly of light bulbs and small appliances began as, and tends to continue as, women's work. Eighty percent of light bulb assembly work was female in 1910 when it was still a hand operation (Milkman, 1983). Women were recruited because it was felt that they naturally excelled at the precise operations required in assembling electrical components: speed, dexterity, endurance, and attention to detail (Milkman, 1983).

In contrast, it was argued that women lacked the physical strength to handle the heavy manual labor of building cars. Consequently, auto manufacturing became men's work after initially being open to both sexes. Women were gradually displaced, and by 1929 over 99 percent of Ford Motor Company employees were men and 88 of the 110 auto factory job classifications were exclusively male (Milkman, 1983; Lewchuk, 1993). This pattern prevailed until temporarily disrupted by World War II, when large numbers of women were drawn into the plants, but as soon as the war began to wind down, women were again displaced by men.

It is interesting to note that Henry Ford was compelled to redefine the very concept of masculinity in order to convince men to accept the monotonous and repetitive work of the assembly line (Lewchuk, 1993). "There is one thing that can be said about menial jobs that cannot be said about a great many so-called more responsible jobs," he claimed in his autobiography, "and that is, they are useful, respectable and they are honest." His goal of replacing a craft model of masculinity emphasizing skill, pride, and autonomy with one based on brawn was nourished by arguing that only the "manly" could handle the strenuous demands of assembly work. This was encouraged by segregating women and creating a men's-club atmosphere in the factory. The debate over differences in men's and women's skills continues into the present, especially in jobs in the military, despite evidence that "women are capable of being trained to perform most very heavy military tasks" (Peterson & Manning, 1996).

Paternalism.   Paternalism was used in many different ways to limit and constrain occupational and educational opportunities. The ideology of **paternalism** defines women as less capable than men, and in need of protection and guidance (Reskin & Padavic, 1994). Paternalism was supported by "scientific" research on sex differences in intelligence and ability. Nineteenth-century craniometrists used the observation of average sex differences in stature to support claims of lower intellectual capacity among women. Social psychologist Gustave LeBon concluded that, "All psychologists who have studied the intelligence of women recognize today that they represent the most inferior forms of human evolution and that they are closer to children and savages than to adult, civilized men" (Deaux & Kite, 1987: 93).

This doctrine is highlighted by the rationale used to rebuff women who sought to surmount occupational barriers. When, for example, Myra Bradwell sought a license to practice law in Illinois in the 1870s, she was rejected by state courts and the United States Supreme Court. Her suit was denied on Constitutional grounds, but Justice Bradley located the decision in broader historical and social context:

> Law, as well as nature herself, has always recognized a wide difference in the respective spheres and destinies of man and woman. Man is, or should be, woman's protector and defender. The natural and proper timidity and delicacy which belongs to the female sex evidently unfits it for many of the occupations of civil life. . . . The paramount destiny and mission of women are to fulfill the noble and benign offices of wife and mother. This is the law of the Creator. And the rules of civil society must be adapted to the general constitution of things (*Bradwell v. Illinois,* 1873: 141-142).

The male protector and defender ideology also had an economic dimension. It was used to support labor unions' struggle for higher wages for men. Unions fought for a "family wage," on the grounds that it was the husbands' responsibility to provide financial support for their families. Samuel Gompers, speaking in 1905, proclaimed, "In our time, . . . there is no necessity for the wife contributing to the support of the family by working" (Foner, 1964: 224). There is a remnant of this idea in contemporary society among some men at all class levels who resist working wives as coproviders.

Paternalism also contributed to protective legislation that was introduced to protect women from hazards of the workplace. Protective legislation limited women's hours, strenuous activity, and exposure to hazardous substances. In retrospect, it is noted that considerations other than health were at stake, because the protected jobs were usually traditional male jobs and often the highest paid. In 1908 the U.S. Supreme Court ruled in *Muller v. Oregon* that special legislation for women was appropriate because women were not as strong as men, were dependent upon men, and were the mothers of future generations. Perhaps the key feature of that decision was that it placed all women in a separate legal classification because all women were potential mothers. Protective legislation excluding women of child-bearing age from jobs on the grounds of "fetal protection" was not finally eliminated in the United States until 1991. It is apparent from the perspective of the twentieth century that the family wage, protective legislation, and occupational segregation benefited some men by excluding women from competition for the more lucrative jobs in the paid labor force.

Competition for Jobs.   There was also an economic dimension to exclusionary practices. Women were sometimes exploited as pawns in the struggle between employers and workers. For example, early working class solidarity between men and women in the printing industry was eroded over the course of the nineteenth century when unskilled women were used to displace skilled male printers or were employed as strikebreakers (Barron, 1980). Skilled printers worried that the "petticoat invasion" threatened to depress their wages and undermine the skilled traditions of their craft. Consequently, gender cooperation faded in this and other areas, and women came to be perceived as competitors for scarce jobs. It was a pattern repeated in many other crafts unions leading to exclusionary practices that made the crafts the province of white males.

Men's and Women's Work in the Twentieth Century

While segregation along gender lines was occurring in the occupational sphere, households were also changing, at least among the upper middle class. Among the most important developments was the shift away from production for the family. The introduction of mass-produced clothing and foods combined with new-found affluence made home work less necessary, creating a "domestic void" for middle-class women, stripping them of meaningful work in the form of goods and services for the family; and they were caught up in the emergence of a home economics movement that transformed housework into an unpaid occupation (Ehrenreich & English, 1979). The home economics movement itself represented the convergence of several broader trends—wider availability of single-family homes; concern with the breakdown of the traditional, tightly knit family; the rise of scientific child-rearing; and medical science's discovery of the germ theory of disease (making wives responsible for cleanliness). Advocates of Frederick Taylor who were seeking to rationalize the workplace also turned their attention to the home, encouraging housewives to carefully study and analyze the best way to perform tasks such as peeling potatoes, maintain household records, and hold to rigorous schedules. Out of this emerged a new social ideal for upper-middle-class women, often called the "cult of domesticity." This ideal demanded dedication to home decoration, cleanliness, nutrition, meal planning, and child rearing. The cult of domesticity served to legitimize certain patterns. One was that it located the male role in the paid labor force (the public sphere) and the female role in the home (the private sphere). It is not at all clear how many women were actually able to realize this ideal, because many working-class wives, immigrants, and women of color continued in the paid labor force.

Trends in occupational segregation that had been set in motion earlier intensified during the period between the two world wars, along with the intensification of gender stereotyping of work. A whole range of occupations proliferated during this period, and they tended to split along gender lines. The professions—law, medicine, science, engineering—proliferated, but along sex lines. The feminization of clerical work began at the end of the nineteenth century; women outnumbered men by the 1920s and by the 1990s held over 90 percent of jobs such as bank teller, secretary, and typist. It has been suggested that men abandoned clerical work at least in part because it did not enable them to demonstrate masculine traits (Lockwood, 1958), but they may also have been influenced by the lack of mobility opportunities.

The power of gender stereotypes of work was powerfully demonstrated during the decade of the Great Depression (Milkman, 1983). It might be expected that the high rates of unemployment in manufacturing would constrain men to attempt to displace women from jobs, but that did not generally happen. Apparently neither employers nor unemployed men were willing to see men move into female-typed work such as nursing, teaching, or secretarial jobs, even in the face of joblessness. Thus, for example, although more men moved into schoolteaching, it remained an overwhelmingly female occupation. The flourishing middle-class ideal for housewives took on new meaning and new responsibility during this period. Aided by technological innovations directed toward work in the home (vacuum cleaners and washing machines) and prompted by mass advertising and the proliferation of women's magazines, upper-middle-class wives were expected to attain new heights of cleanliness, creative cooking, and neatness in the home. The more affluent could afford domestic servants, relegating unpleasant physical tasks to a corps of African-American women (Palmer, 1989). All during the first half of the century and continuing into the 1960s, housewives devoted increasing hours to housework. More importantly, wives' income and social status came to be defined by their husband's occupational attainments, and the expectation was that their personal success and satisfactions were subordinated to those of their spouses and children.

Work and Ideology Since the 1940s

World War II had a profound impact on women's situation. The influx of women into the civilian labor force, to replace men in the military, set the stage for the eventual blurring of the distinction between the public and private sector. Women filled jobs of all kinds (in both civilian industry and the military), including those that they presumably lacked the psychological traits to master. As the war wound down, an overwhelming majority expressed a desire to remain in the workforce. Although many were eventually displaced to make room for returning servicemen, the rate of participation of women in the paid labor force began an increase that has become permanent. An expanding economy created hundreds of thousands of new jobs. Older (over 45) married women with diminished child-rearing responsibilities were the first group to seek work in larger numbers, and since the 1970s younger married women have followed suit. Today, more than 60 percent of mothers with young children are in the paid labor force.

Social and legal change weakened many occupational barriers and opened opportunities in the upper middle class. Law schools, once an almost exclusively male domain, now enroll 40 percent women, and women make up more than 70 percent of the enrollments at veterinary schools. However, the segregation of jobs along gender lines that emerged during earlier phases of industrialization often continues. For every woman architect in 1997, 8 worked as domestics, 35 waited tables, 63 operated factory machines, and 100 were secretaries. Some of the most striking examples of occupations segregated by gender are shown in Exhibit 4.3.

EXHIBIT 4.3 Gender Segregation in Selected Occupations

OCCUPATION	PERCENTAGE FEMALE
Auto mechanics	.7%
Carpenters	.8
Welders	4.4
Engineers	8.4
Clergy	11.1
Sewing machine operators	85.7
Registered nurses	93.1
Teachers, K and Pre-K	98.2
Secretaries	98.5
Dental assistants	99.4
Secretaries	99.1

Source: "Employed civilians by detailed occupation, sex, race, and Hispanic origin." *Employment and Earnings* 43 (January, 1996), Table 11.

CONCLUSION: AMERICAN DILEMMAS

In the 1940s Swedish sociologist Gunnar Myrdal's study of the situation of African Americans exposed a moral contradiction that he called an **American dilemma** (Myrdal, 1944). He noted that the United States was a nation founded on democratic and individualist principles and yet simultaneously maintained social and legal barriers that openly discriminated against a sizable proportion of its citizens. In fact, the American dilemma can more accurately be traced much further back in time, to the colonial period. And it was never just African Americans who suffered. Barriers based on class, race and ethnicity, and gender had long been common. It must, for example, be noted that women, Native Americans, slaves and former slaves, and the propertyless were all denied the right to vote at some point in American history.

Ideologies legitimize and sustain the dilemmas. Ideologies resolve the apparent contradiction between ideals and reality by offering justifications for unequal treatment. The tenets of individualism, paternalism, or ideological racism legitimize inequality and offer justifications by explaining that members of subordinate groups lack some key attributes or are in some way inferior—biologically, socially, behaviorally.

There has certainly been much progress in the half-century since Myrdal's book, but the dilemmas linger. Most of the formal barriers have been reduced or eliminated. There is, then, cause for some optimism because the evidence of progress is everywhere. Medicaid buffers the poor from catastrophic illness, women once denied the right to even vote now hold political offices at all levels, ideological racism is discredited, and a solid African-American middle class has emerged. But undercurrents of hostility persist. Minorities continue to encounter discrimination in competition for jobs (Cross, Kenny, Mell, & Zimmerman, 1990). Women in the military and elsewhere continually confront strongly entrenched sexism. The poor are still blamed for their misfortune by some segments of society. Perhaps the most invidious side of the dilemma is the fact that the poor, women, and people of color continue to encounter countless everyday humiliations, indignities, and disrespect that continue the American dilemma. "The American Dream is about dignity, respect, connectedness, belonging," explains Professor Hochschild; African Americans might succeed financially and earn middle-class status, "but they still can't get a cab at midnight in New York City" (Coughlin, 1995).

KEY CONCEPTS

American dilemma	**ideological racism**	**internal colonialism**
Anglo-conformity	**ideology**	**legitimation**
assimilation	**ideology of individualism**	**paternalism**
competition theory	**institutionalization of**	**patriarchy**
ethnocentrism	**inequality**	**sweatshops**

SUGGESTED READING

FERGUS M. BORDEWICH, *Killing the White Man's Indian.* New York: Doubleday, 1996. A revealing exploration of the problems of contemporary Native Americans as they seek to establish control over their own lives and culture.

ELLIS COSE, *The Rage of the Privileged Class.* New York: HarperCollins, 1994. The author describes the everyday humiliations that infuriate members of the African-American middle class.

JENNIFER L. HOCHSCHILD, *Facing Up to the American Dream: Race, Class and the Soul of the Nation.* Princeton, NJ: Princeton University Press, 1995. An instructive discussion of the ways in which African-American and white perceptions of the American Dream converge and differ.

RICHARD HOFSTADER, *Social Darwinism in American Thought.* Boston: Beacon, 1955. The classic work on the impact of this powerful idea.

ALICE KESSLER-HARRIS, *Out to Work.* New York: Oxford University Press, 1982. Among the best historical discussions of women in the labor force.

JAMES R. KLUEGEL AND ELIOT R. SMITH, *Beliefs about Inequality.* New York: Aldine De Gruyter, 1986. A comprehensive analysis of Americans' perceptions of the class system.

CATHERINE A. MACKINNON, *Only Words.* Cambridge, MA: Harvard University Press, 1993. An outspoken feminist lawyer argues that pornography degrades women and bolsters gender inequality.

BARBARA RESKIN AND IRENE PADAVIC, *Women and Men at Work.* Thousand Oaks, CA: Pine Forge Press, 1994. A useful overview of the role of gender in the world of work.

JOHN E. WILLIAMS AND DEBORAH L. BEST, *Measuring Sex Stereotypes: A Multination Study.* Newbury Park, CA: Sage, 1990. A rich and rewarding investigation of gender stereotypes around the globe.

PART THREE

Patterns
of Inequality

Social class position has broad implications for individuals and groups, and economic, social, and political inequalities are among the most profound. Chapter 5 reviews trends in the distribution of earnings and wealth in industrial societies, ranging from the extraordinary wealth concentrated in the hands of a small number of people to the millions living in poverty. Chapter 6 explores social evaluations and rankings including occupational prestige and the dynamics of class, race and ethnicity, and gender in interpersonal relationships. Chapter 7 investigates access to positions of power and authority in the political system and the ability of class-oriented groups and organizations to influence the actions of the state.

CHAPTER 5

The Dynamics
of Economic Inequality

THE DISTRIBUTION OF WEALTH AND POVERTY

Computer wizard Bill Gates earned a fortune in computer software and is generally conceded to be the wealthiest person in America, worth over **15 billion dollars!** Despite his wealth, his is not the largest fortune ever accumulated. That distinction belongs to Sam Walton, the founder of Wal-Mart stores, who amassed more money than any other single individual, with an estate valued at $22 billion when he died in 1992. But even he does not qualify as the richest in American history when individual wealth is placed in the context of the nation's economy (Klepper & Gunther, 1996). John D. Rockefeller, with an estate of $1.4 billion at his death in 1937, held an amount equal to $\frac{1}{65}$ of the total gross domestic product of the entire nation in that year. Using that criterion relegates Bill Gates to Number 41 on the all-time ranking of the wealthiest Americans.

While Bill Gates and Sam Walton have billions of dollars, some 30 million people live in poverty, and another 25 million hover near poverty (O'Hare, 1996). For them, financial considerations are a matter of survival, touching upon such fundamental matters as hunger and basic nutrition, medical care, and housing. The most visible segment of the poor are the homeless. Somewhere between 200,000 and 600,000 people are without shelter at any given time, and about one-third are families with children (Moss & Dickson, 1994).

There is a broad range of middle-income families ranged between these two extremes, and they are able to develop a reasonable standard of living that includes home ownership, consumer goods, health care, and provision for the education of their children. However, it is not an income that is secure. Most people depend upon their jobs for the bulk of their income, and the ongoing restructuring of the workplace results in the continual loss of some jobs. In 1995, for example, 3.47 million workers saw their jobs eliminated (Lohr, 1996). Consequently, just about one-half of all Americans worry that someone in their household will be laid off in the foreseeable future.

There are two basic ways of looking at the overall distribution of financial inequality in a society, annual income and net worth (the value of all wealth and possessions), and both confirm the existence of a wide gulf between the privileged and the disadvantaged in the United States and other industrial nations.

ANNUAL INCOMES

One means of visualizing the scope of economic inequality is to focus on **annual income** and calculate the earnings of different segments of the population. The most common way of doing this is to divide the population into quintiles (fifths) and calculate the income characteristics of each group. The household must be the unit of analysis in calculating income to accommodate families with multiple earners.

In 1993 the average annual income for the lowest paid one-fifth of American households was $7411, while the average income of the top 20 percent was $98,589, and the highest-paid 5 percent averaged $163,228 (Exhibit 5.1). These numbers show the discrepancy between the best and worst in pay for the year, but the extent of income inequality is more clearly displayed by considering the share of total income earned by each fifth of the population. This criterion shows that the poorest fifth earns less than 4 percent of the total income while the highest-paid 20 percent earns about

EXHIBIT 5.1 Average Annual Income, United States, 1993

INCOME GROUPS	MEAN INCOME	PERCENTAGE SHARE OF TOTAL EARNINGS
Poorest fifth	$ 7411	3.6%
Second fifth	18,647	9.0
Third fifth	31,260	15.1
Fourth fifth	48,572	23.5
Wealthiest fifth	98,589	48.9
Highest 5 percent	163,228	21.0

Source: Paul Ryscavage, "A surge in growing income inequality," *Monthly Labor Review* 118 (August, 1995), Tables 1 and 2, pages 54 and 55.

49 percent of the total money income. The 60 percent of the families in the middle divide the remaining 47 percent of income.

Notable among the people in the top quintile are sports and entertainment figures and corporate executives who form a part of an institutional elite of multimillionaires. Corporate executives are at the core of the economic elite. A recent survey of compensation packages (salary, bonus, stock options, golden parachutes) shows that at least two dozen business executives earned $25 million, and for one it was over $100 million (Reingold, 1997). The five with the highest pay were:

Lawrence Coss (Green Tree Financial)	$102,449,000
Andrew Gove (Intel)	$ 97,590,000
Sanford Weill (Travelers Group)	$ 94,157,000
Theodore Waitt (Gateway 2000)	$ 81,326,000
Anthony O'Reilly (H. J. Heinz)	$ 64,236,000

The average compensation for CEOs at the largest American businesses was $5,781,300, an increase of 54 percent from the year before and 30 percent over the year before that.

This compares with an average increase of 3 percent for factory workers and 3.2 percent for white-collar workers, further widening the gap between the people at the top and bottom of firms that has been developing for two decades. It is estimated that in 1980 top executives earned 42 times the income of the average factory worker, but that ratio had escalated to 141 times that of average factory workers by 1995 and reached a multiple of 209 times in 1996 (Bryne, 1996; Reingold, 1997).

The Earnings Gap: Lower Pay for Women and Minorities

There is a persistent and enduring **earnings gap** between the earnings of women and men, and among whites, African Americans, Latinos, and other minority groups (Tomaskovic-Devey, 1993a; Bianchi & Spain, 1996). To illustrate, median earnings for women are about $22,500, compared to $31,500 for men. The magnitude of the earnings gap has narrowed from about 60 percent in 1960 to about 75 percent in the 1990s, although there are conspicuous differences among women of color (Exhibit 5.2). African-American women's earnings are $20,700 compared to $24,400 for men; Latina women earn $17,200 compared to $20,400 among men; and Asian women's earnings stand at $24,900 as opposed to $31,600 among men. Although the gender gap is narrowing in most industrial nations it has yet to be fully eliminated anywhere. For example, a comparison of wages in manufacturing industries in twenty-seven nations shows that women's pay in the early 1970s stood at 67 percent of men's and had improved to only 74 percent in the 1990s (Sivard, 1995). The situation prompted women in Switzerland to call a national one-day strike in 1991 to protest gender-based discrepancies in wages and benefits (Kalette, 1991).

The earnings gap compares the wages of year-round, full-time workers and therefore masks important variations in the size of the earnings gap at different class

EXHIBIT 5.2 Women's Earnings as a Percentage of Men's Earnings, by Race and Ethnicity: The United States, 1960–1994

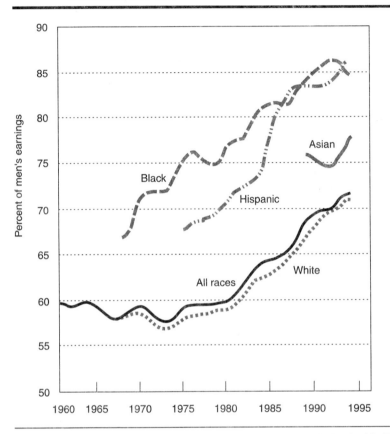

Source: Suzanne M. Bianchi and Daphne Spain, *Women, Work and Family in America*, Washington, DC: Population Reference Bureau, 1996, Figure 5 and Table 8, pages 24 and 25.

levels and in different demographic groups (Exhibit 5.3). The earnings gap is, for example, narrower for younger females than older women (Nasar, 1992). Younger women have higher educational credentials than older workers, which makes them more competitive, but it also suggests that women beginning their careers now are rewarded more equitably than those who entered the labor market earlier. The most pronounced earnings gap is found in sales work, where women earn only 57 percent of what men earn. Occupational segregation plays a major role in explaining this situation because women are concentrated in retail sales while men are much more likely to be in more lucrative fields such as insurance and securities. The gap is also wide in working-class jobs, where women earn about 70 cents for every dollar earned by men. A similar discrepancy shows up in upper-middle-class managerial work,

EXHIBIT 5.3 Median Weekly Earnings by Gender, United States, 1995

All workers	$538	$406	75%
Upper middle class			
Managerial	833	570	68
Professional	827	632	76
Lower middle class			
Technician	641	480	75
Sales	579	330	57
Clerical	489	384	79
Working class			
Crafts	534	371	69
Operatives	421	296	70
The poor			
Service	300	264	88
Laborers	328	284	87

Source: "Weekly earnings in 1995." *Employment and Earnings,* January, 1996, Table 39.

where men dominate higher levels in the managerial hierarchy. The gap is narrowest at the bottom of the stratification system in service workers and laborers where women average between 85 and 90 percent of men's earnings.

When median earnings for African Americans and whites are compared over time it is clear that measurable progress has been made since the 1950s. That was a decisive period, because it signaled the beginning of the collapse of patterns of overt discrimination stretching back to the days of slavery. Exclusionary and discriminatory practices combined to exclude African Americans from white-collar work and the more highly paid professional and crafts occupations, as well as producing unequal pay scales within similar jobs. Until that point African Americans averaged less than half the earnings of whites. The data for 1939, the first year for which there are comprehensive statistics, documents the burden of racism. African-American men earned an average of 45 percent of what white males did, and African-American women 38 percent of what white women did (U.S. Bureau of the Census, 1979: 136).

The earnings gap for African-American men narrowed to about 60 percent in the 1960s and reached 72 percent in 1979, but gains have been extremely sluggish since, currently standing at about 75 percent (Bennett, 1995). The situation for African-American women has improved more rapidly, reaching about 90 percent of white women's earnings by the end of the 1970s, but has stagnated since. Moreover, they too are still burdened by the gender gap, meaning that they earn only about 85 percent of what African-American men earn.

No single factor explains the earnings gap. It is rather the result of a combination of conditions. Among the most significant are occupational segregation, education, job tenure, and demographic considerations. Statistical analysis makes it possible to estimate the amount women and minorities would earn if they had comparable education and employment patterns, but such studies always reveal that there is an unexplained difference that must be interpreted as the result of discrimination—both overt and unintentional—which produces lower pay and hinders opportunities for advancement.

Occupational Segregation.   A major factor explaining the earnings gap is employment patterns, accounting for one-quarter to one-third of the difference by some estimates (Sorenson, 1989). Despite the erosion of barriers that historically excluded women and people of color from some fields of endeavor, these groups still do not hold the same jobs. Both groups continue to be underrepresented in the better-paid professional, managerial, high-skill crafts jobs, and overrepresented among low-paying clerical, retail sales, and service occupations. For example, a tabulation of the principal occupations of women shows that four out of ten women are concentrated in just ten occupations (*e.g.,* traditional women's occupations such as secretary, elementary school teacher, and nurse, as well as low-paying clerical jobs such as cashier) (Reskin & Padavic, 1994: 53). This pattern holds true for Latina, Asian, and African-American women as well.

Occupational segregation is even more invidious than it might appear because not only do workers enter these occupations at low entry-level salaries, but they are less able to improve their earnings over time by the personal strategies that American ideology proclaims to be the means to upward mobility—education and work experience. Economists are fond of referring to this as "returns on human capital," measuring the income increments associated with more education or longer work experience. The fact is that clerical work, service and sales work, and less-skilled blue-collar work do not yield significant financial returns to people who have formal education or longer work experience. In large part this is due to the fact most of these are low-ceiling careers, lacking in meaningful promotion opportunities to higher-paying positions.

Education.   Formal educational credentials are a prerequisite to gain access to most higher-paying jobs in management and the professions. The earnings gap encompasses workers of several generations, and up until the 1970s fewer women earned college and professional degrees than men. Although women currently earn more than one-half of the bachelor's degrees, they still lag behind in professional degrees and Ph.Ds (necessary for careers in academics and the sciences). Advanced education opens doors to better-paying occupations but is no guarantee of more equitable wages, because the earnings gap for women in the United States persists at every educational level. To illustrate, college-educated women earn $34,400 compared to $50,330 for men. In short, despite diminishing differences in educational attainments, more formal education simply does not translate into better pay for women.

Differential educational attainments also handicap African-American workers (Tomaskovic-Devey, 1993b). African Americans generally bring lower levels of formal educational attainment to the labor market and are thus more likely to be channeled toward lower-paid work. However, it also important to emphasize that African Americans simply do not earn the same economic rewards for education that whites do. It has long been observed that African Americans are destined to earn less at every educational level compared to white workers. Some attribute this to an inferior quality of preparation in the schools attended by African Americans, but it has also been argued that it may have less to do with the actual value of the education credentials and may be attributed to the assumption of inferiority on the part of employers. This may be a disguised form of racial discrimination used as a rationale for limiting the promotion opportunities or not paying wages similar to those for whites in comparable positions.

Intermittent Careers.   Also to be considered is the fact that women are more likely than men to interrupt their careers, usually to assume responsibility for young children or aging parents. Disruption of work careers can be costly. One study that compared American women with steady employment histories and comparable women with irregular careers, indicated those returning to work initially earned about 33 percent less than women who never left the labor force (Jacobsen & Levin, 1995). Moreover, this gap persists for decades. Women experiencing a hiatus in their careers earn about 5 to 7 percent less twenty years later.

Many reasons account for this pattern. Women's intermittent work careers mean that men accumulate more seniority and job-specific experience, which translate into higher wages. Loss of seniority also renders workers more vulnerable to layoffs under "last hired, first fired" rules. There is also the potential for job skills to atrophy during absence from the workplace. Many white-collar occupations, such as banking, which employs large numbers of women, are undergoing dramatic changes flowing from the introduction of electronic data processing, placing returning workers at a competitive disadvantage. Finally, absence from a job can penalize workers by the simple fact that they are not physically there to be considered for salary increments or, more importantly, promotions to better positions. It is no coincidence that the peak years of child-bearing and child-rearing (twenty-five to thirty-five) coincide exactly with the years in which employers are making fateful decisions about the futures of their younger employees (Kanter, 1977). There may also be a subtle form of employer bias at work in that supervisors may view gaps in work history as a sign that women may leave again and thus supervisors are less willing to promote them into positions with greater responsibility and rewards.

Demographic Factors.   Some of the earnings differential has its origin in the demographic characteristics of the African-American and Latina/o populations. Age is one consideration, because they are on the average younger; and youthful workers, regardless of race or gender, earn relatively less. The geography of residence also seems to work against African-Americans. A large percentage reside in the South where earnings are, on the whole, lower than in other regions. In fact, some of the overall income gains reflect patterns of migration out of the South beginning in the 1960s, leading to some degree of optimism for the future. Urban residence also puts

African Americans at a disadvantage as job opportunities in the better-paying manufacturing sector are lost, being replaced by poorer-paying service work.

Earnings for African-American women have been approaching parity with that of white women much more rapidly than among male workers. In fact, in some areas median income is actually balanced in their favor, something almost never found among their male counterparts. Among recent college graduates (one to five years on the job) African-American women earn an average wage of $11.41 an hour compared to white women's $11.38 and African-American men's $11.26 (Roberts, 1994). As more and more African-American women have been able to break the barriers that held them in the traditional domain of domestic work in favor of blue-collar and lower white-collar jobs, their overall position has improved.

It is possible that, by a sad and ironic twist, the improved position of African-American women may have its origins in the sociocultural heritage of American racism and discrimination. Young African-American women attach great importance to work as a part of their adult roles and anticipate lengthy working careers, probably because they can anticipate low earnings for themselves and their future husbands (Hudis, 1977). In the face of anticipated discrimination, women develop a powerful commitment to work and the income-producing aspects of labor, thus expending considerable effort to find jobs that can be translated into greater rewards.

Discrimination.   Discrimination against women in the workplace, as elsewhere in society, has its origins in attitudes and beliefs prevalent in the larger society. One salient attitude is the very fundamental issue of whether or not women, especially those with young children, should even be in the labor market. It is a question that involves both money and social roles. The traditional division of labor that prevailed during much of this century imposed responsibility for the family on women and responsibility for providing economic support on men. This can have negative consequences for women if it causes employers to doubt the appropriateness of working females. It can mean that men will be given preference for jobs and promotions on the grounds that they must support families. The other dimension is parental, the belief that maternal employment detracts from time for the family and is a factor in the breakdown of the family. Studies confirm that many people believe that having a mother in the labor force is detrimental to their children (Greenberger, Goldberg, Crawford, & Granger, 1988).

Another form of bias relates to the question of the correspondence between gender traits and occupational requirements. Simply put, traits attributed to women are assumed to be inconsistent with the traits necessary for success in the field. Such thinking generalizes to all members of a social category, ignoring individual differences and abilities. Moreover, it is often based on unverified assumptions about the traits needed to succeed in an occupation. Male police academy recruits, for example, preparing for the hazards of their work, often equate their own personal safety with physical strength. Consequently, there is some reluctance to accept women as partners, despite the fact that the record shows that injury or death is seldom a matter of physical prowess but rather a failure to follow established procedures (Remmington, 1981).

NET WORTH: MEASURING HOUSEHOLD ASSETS

An alternative way of measuring monetary inequality is to focus on the distribution of the finances and other resources of households. **Net worth** refers to the total value of privately held assets, including money in bank accounts; real estate; stocks, bonds, and securities; personal property in the form of cars, homes, and furnishings; the value of pension plans and life insurance; and equity in a business or profession. An average household in the United States controls about $37,000 worth of assets. For most families, the largest share of their net worth (44 percent) is based on the equity in their homes. The household is also the unit of analysis in calculating private wealth because resources are typically held jointly between spouses.

The Distribution of Assets

The U.S. government periodically estimates the net worth of its citizens, and the distribution of economic resources is dramatic (Exhibit 5.4). The highest one-fifth of households based on income hold 44 percent of the total private assets in the society! Their net worth stands at approximately $119,000. In contrast, the bottom one-fifth of the society has but 7 percent of the total assets, worth an average of less than $4,000. Private wealth is more equitably distributed among the middle groups, but is still skewed toward upper-end families.

The distribution of assets among minority households reveals even more stark contrasts. The median net worth of all households is only $4418 for African Americans and $4656 for Hispanics, compared to $45,740 for white households. The lowest quintile among African Americans has a median net worth of just $250 and Hispanics $499. When it is noted that these numbers represent medians it is evident that many families have no tangible assets or are in debt.

The number of households with great wealth is small, but the amount of wealth concentrated in their hands is extraordinary. Other estimates of wealth, based on alternative measures of assets, suggest a much greater concentration of wealth in the

---

EXHIBIT 5.4 Distribution of Household Assets, United States, 1993

QUINTILES	ALL HOUSEHOLDS	PERCENTAGE SHARE OF ASSETS	WHITE	AFRICAN-AMERICAN	HISPANIC
Lowest fifth	$ 4249	7.2%	$ 7605	$ 250	$ 499
Second fifth	20,230	12.2	27,057	3406	2900
Third fifth	30,788	15.9	36,341	8480	6313
Fourth fifth	50,000	20.6	54,040	20,745	20,100
Highest fifth	118,996	44.1	123,350	45,023	55,923
Net Worth	$ 37,587	100%	$ 45,740	$ 4418	$ 4656

Source: U.S. Bureau of the Census, Current Population Report P70-47. *Asset Ownership of Households, 1993.* Washington, DC: U.S. Government Printing Office, 1995, Table B (p. 95) and Table F (p. 9).

hands of a small number of households. One estimate claims that 10 percent of families own over 70 percent of the total wealth, including about half the value of all real estate and over 90 percent of corporate stocks and bonds (U.S. Congress, 1986: 35). Within this 10 percent there is an even smaller, more privileged group. The very wealthiest—the top one-half of one percent (about 420,000 households)—hold a minimum of $2.5 million each and average $8.9 million in assets. Together, these are the **super-rich,** who own 35 percent of the total private wealth in America. Moreover, it appears that the concentration of wealth is increasing, for the super-rich controlled only 25 percent of the wealth a generation ago in 1963. Thus, it is possible to isolate a small segment of the society who have been able to amass great wealth, on the basis of their own efforts, through inheritance, or some combination of the two.

POVERTY

In 1962 Michael Harrington published *The Other America,* a scathing exposé of poverty in the midst of prosperity. The sad fact is that the book continues in print even today, decades later, standing as a stark reminder of the persistence of poverty in industrial nations. The number of the people living in poverty fluctuates over time, and specific individuals escape impoverishment, but the conditions that produce poverty seem intractable, because those who break out of poverty are replaced by others.

In an abstract sense, the word **poverty** implies the lack of resources necessary to maintain a decent standard of living. However, it is difficult in practice to establish a dollar amount that defines poverty because it is an issue shaped by personal values and obscured by ideology and politics. One social scientist, for example, estimates that a family of four in the late 1990s needs an income of $27,000 for a minimally acceptable standard of living (Schwarz, 1997). Some European nations have attacked the problem by calculating a **decency threshold** that seeks to set a monetary value on sustaining a decent standard of living, including proper food, clothing, shelter, and an occasional movie. It is set at 68 percent of average earnings and leaves 3 million British working women below the decency threshold (Hill, 1996).

The most widely used measure of poverty in the United States is the poverty threshold. **Poverty thresholds** are a continuation of original federal poverty measures first established in the 1960s by the federal government and updated annually to accommodate inflation.[1] This is the figure that shows up in official estimates of the number of Americans in poverty each year. The calculation of the poverty threshold

---

[1] A number of other terms are frequently encountered in discussions of the nature and scope of poverty. *Poverty guidelines* are a simplification of poverty thresholds and are used for administrative purposes such as determining eligibility for certain federal programs (*e.g.,* Head Start). The *near poor* are people with incomes between 100 and 150 percent of the poverty level. They are the group most vulnerable to falling into poverty. *Extreme poverty* refers to those 15 million Americans (40 percent of the poverty population) with incomes of less than 50 percent of the poverty threshold. Children, people in female-headed households, and minorities are most likely to be living in extreme poverty (O'Hare, 1996: 29).

began with the cost of a minimal, nutritionally adequate, food budget and multiplied that figure by three (poorer families typically devoted one-third of their income to food) to allow for nonfood items. It was based on an original plan developed by the Department of Agriculture as an emergency budget for families short of money, not one that would be satisfactory over long periods of time. A higher, alternative food budget was considered but rejected, in part because it would elevate the number of poor to a politically unacceptable level (Fisher, 1992). Poverty thresholds and guidelines are adjusted annually for increases in consumer prices, and in 1996 stood at $7740 for a single individual and $15,600 for a family of four.[2]

The threat of poverty in America reached its peak in the Depression years of the 1930s when upwards of 25 percent of the labor force was unemployed. Estimates suggest that as many as two-thirds of the nation were mired in poverty in 1939 because the economy had not yet recovered from the worldwide depression that threw millions of people out of work (Ross, Danziger, & Smolensky, 1987). World War II and post-war prosperity steadily reduced the proportion of poor Americans to less than 25 percent in 1959. It is in that year that official government data begin, and these data show that the numbers of poor declined steadily during the 1960s and stabilized at about 25 million during the 1970s, reaching an all-time low of 23 million people in 1973 (11.1 percent). Unfortunately, poverty began to rise in the early 1980s and again in the early 1990s (Exhibit 5.5).

The Many Faces of Poverty

Virtually no one is exempt from the threat of poverty. Any number of critical life transitions can suddenly thrust people into poverty. Joblessness is the most obvious cause, and the 1990s were a period of major restructuring and downsizing that caused millions of jobs to disappear. Births and drastic family disruptions brought about by death, divorce, or abandonment are the other major factors that can tip the balance between abundance and impoverishment. An analysis of the characteristics of the poor is revealing because it dispels many myths and misconceptions (Exhibit 5.6).

Minorities.   It is often assumed that most of the poor are people of color, and although many minority group members are poor, the majority of the officially poor are white. Two-thirds of the poor are white. African Americans make up about one-quarter of the poor population, and Latino/as (who can be of any race) 22 percent. However, focusing on the rates of poverty for these groups reveals that people of color are much more likely to be poor than whites. Approximately one in ten non-Latino/a whites is poor, compared to about three in ten African Americans; Latino/as and Native Americans have a poverty rate three times that of whites. Even more dramatic is the incidence of "extreme poverty" (incomes of less than the official poverty level) among minorities, where the rate is 3 percent for whites but 12 percent for Latino/as, 13 percent for Native Americans, and 15 percent for African Americans (O'Hare, 1996: 29).

---

[2]Up-to-date poverty guidelines are available on line at: http://aspe.os.dhhs.gov/poverty/poverty.htm.

EXHIBIT 5.5 Trends in Poverty, United States, 1959–1994

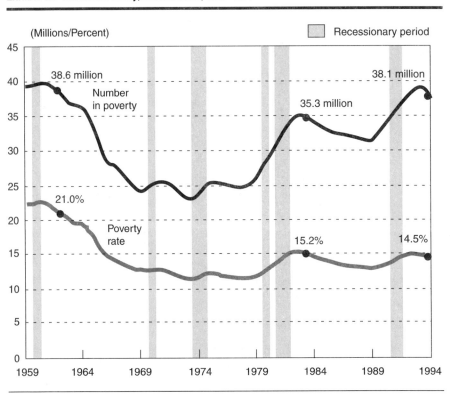

Shaded areas = Recessionary periods

Source: U.S. Bureau of the Census, Current Population Reports, Series P60-189, *Income, Poverty and Valuation of Non-cash Benefits, 1994.* Washington, DC: U.S. Government Printing Office, 1996. Figure 3, page xv.

Gender and Poverty.   More of the poor in America are women (57 percent) than men (43 percent), and that proportion has not changed significantly over the last several decades. This situation is repeated in most industrial nations, although the discrepancy is narrower (Casper, McLanahan, & Garfinkle, 1994). Women are at greater risk because the burden of changes in family status such as births, divorce, or separation fall more heavily on them. Births increase the vulnerability to poverty by imposing additional financial burdens on parents, as well as causing some women to drop out of school or the labor force to assume child-care responsibilities. Divorced women usually suffer greater financial hardship than divorced men. Typically, the household income (per family member) of women declines by about 24 percent, while that for men drops by only 6 percent (Bianchi & Spain, 1997: 2). Many different factors produce this discrepancy. Wives not in the paid labor force during the duration of the marriage are handicapped when subsequently seeking work, while husbands enjoy the financial benefits of work experience and seniority accumulated

EXHIBIT 5.6 Characteristics of People Living in Poverty, United States, 1994

CHARACTERISTIC		PERCENTAGE OF POOR PERSONS
Race/Ethnicity:	White	67%
	African American	27
	Hispanic	22
Sex:	Male	47%
	Female	53
Age:	Under 18	40%
	18 to 64	50
	65 and over	10
Residence:	Central cities	42%
	Suburbs	36
	Rural areas	22
Work status:	Worked 50 weeks	20%
	Part of the year	28
	Did not work	52

Source: U.S. Bureau of the Census, Current Population Reports, Series P-60, No. 189, *Money Income and Poverty Status of Families and Persons in the United States, 1994.* Washington, DC: U.S. Government Printing Office, 1995.

during marriage. Those in the paid labor force, or who enter it after divorce, confront the earnings gap that means they will earn approximately three-fourths as much as men. The death of a spouse also increases the risk of poverty for women. The chances are greater because they earned less on average during their working lives and because they are less likely to have private pension plans. Moreover, it is very difficult for older women to escape poverty through reemployment or remarriage.

The large number of female-headed families is another factor. While most will eventually marry, they must assume major responsibility for child care for some period of time. Moreover, many single mothers are teenagers, and the presence of children can increase the chances of terminating their education, thus limiting their futures and channeling them to lower-paying work. Women who do not finish high school have a much greater chance of being poor (38 percent) than men (27 percent). Single mothers with limited education often cannot find work that covers the cost of child care (O'Hare, 1996).

Alimony and child-support programs were, in part, originally designed to alleviate the financial burdens on nonemployed spouses after divorce. The program in practice falls short of its original goal because not all former spouses meet their financial obligations. Approximately one-half of all spouses receive full payment, but one-quarter get partial payment and one-quarter get nothing from absent fathers (U.S. Bureau of the Census, 1993). Mothers living with children of an absent father have a poverty rate of 35 percent, more than four times the rate for married couples with children.

Children and the Elderly.   A frequently overlooked characteristic of the poor is the fact that less than half are of working age. About 40 percent of the poor are children and youths aged 18 and under. This translates into 15 million youngsters living in poverty, including 5.9 million under age six. Poverty exacts a heavy toll on children. Studies have shown that children raised in continual poverty have lower vocabulary and reading achievement and exhibit more behavior problems than the nonpoor or even those who experience shorter episodes of poverty (Duncan, Brookes-Gunn, & Klebanov, 1994; Korenman, Miller, & Sjaastad, 1995). Thus, childhood poverty weakens the chance of acquiring the cognitive skills necessary to succeed in school and the workplace.

The presence of children increases the risk of poverty for the family. The obvious reason is that children increase the financial burdens on families, but there are also child-care problems that cause many parents to leave the workforce. Quality child care is difficult to find for low-income people and can consume as much as 20 percent of their incomes. Thus, affordable child care is often the decisive factor in preventing low-income mothers from participating in the labor force (U.S. General Accounting Office, 1994).

About 10 percent of those living in poverty are aged 65 or older. In contrast to the problem of persistent poverty among the young, there has been a pronounced decline in the proportion of the aged among the poor from 15 percent in the 1960s to 10 percent in the 1990s, despite the fact that more Americans are living longer. The expansion of federal programs such as Social Security and Medicare is responsible for much of the progress, along with the expansion of private pension plans. The risk of poverty among the aged has not been eliminated but reduced.

Rural Poverty.   It is also evident that although urban, center-city poverty is the most visible, poverty is not exclusively a metropolitan problem but also reaches small towns and rural areas (Duncan, 1992). In fact, rural areas have a very large share of poverty (22 percent), considering the relatively small number of people living in such areas. The reason is that many rural communities lack competitive educational systems and stable employment opportunities. Those jobs that do exist tend to be in low-paying manufacturing, service, and agricultural work.

The Working Poor.   The poor are repeatedly perceived as lacking the will to work or take the actions necessary to escape poverty. Actually, it is clear that many of the poor are either too young or too old to work, are disabled, or have child-care responsibilities. Focusing on the adult working-age poor (ages twenty-two to sixty-four) shows that about one-half worked at some point during the year. Twenty percent of poor adults worked at year-round jobs, and 28 percent worked for at least some part of the year. These are the **working poor**, people in the labor force who do not earn enough to lift themselves or their families out of poverty. The working poor include those unable to find regular, stable jobs and those who earn below poverty-level wages. The minimum wage (currently at $5.15 per hour) is a handy symbol of the problem for the working poor. Working forty hours a week for 52 weeks a year yields only $10,712, just about the poverty threshold for a two-person family.[3]

The Dynamics of Poverty

People do climb out of poverty—about one-third escape every year—but they are replaced by others who slip into poverty. Thus, poverty in America must be understood as a complex structural problem; the problem of poverty endures, although there is a continuous circulation of specific poor individuals and families (see accompanying Case Study). For example, between 1992 and 1993, 6.3 million people rose out of poverty, but they were replaced by 6.5 million who slipped into poverty (U.S. Bureau of the Census, 1996b).

If there is any optimism in the poverty picture it is that most episodes of poverty are relatively short. Detailed analysis of the experiences of people in poverty shows that the majority are poor for less than a year (Duncan, 1984; Gottschalk, McLanahan, & Sandefur, 1994). This means that most people are able to confront the problems that produced their poverty and reestablish their lives. Displaced workers find new jobs, the disruption of families is overcome, and child care is arranged. Unemployment insurance and social welfare programs such as AFDC can facilitate the process.

For the remainder of the poor, poverty is a long-term problem. Seventeen percent are poor for up to two years and another 13 percent for between three and four years. A small group of the poor are trapped in long-term poverty. The term **persistent poverty** is often used to describe those who remain poor for long periods of time, usually five continuous years. This phrase highlights the fact that some people face the bleak prospect of unremitting poverty.

Social Welfare Programs

Federal, state, and local governments sponsor a wide variety of programs aimed at helping the poor and low-income Americans.[4] The first major wave of social welfare programs emerged out of the turmoil of the Great Depression in the 1930s with plans such as Aid to Families with Dependent Children and unemployment insurance. Medicare and other programs came later as part of the war on poverty in the 1960s. By the mid-1990s the federal government devoted over $200 billion to some seventy welfare programs. Most federal money was designed to support people who are poor rather than help them out of poverty. Only 10 percent of means-tested money went to education and training programs that could foster self-sufficiency (O'Hare, 1996: 33).

---

[3]Only about 5 percent of hourly workers' wages are at or below the minimum wage, and a large proportion of those are young single workers, but this group also includes many single parents, people over sixty-five, and spouses supplementing family incomes.

[4]Programs specifically focused on low-income people are called "means-tested," because recipients must meet minimum income tests in order to qualify for benefits. For example, families with incomes 130 percent of the poverty threshold are eligible for food stamps.

CASE STUDY:
Escaping Poverty

Every year some people living in poverty are able to rise above the poverty threshold. The chances of escaping poverty are not equal and reveal some interesting patterns. Minorities have less of a chance of leaving poverty than whites, as do the young and the old, who are more likely to be mired in poverty than middle-aged people (the nineteen to sixty-four age group). The group with the greatest chance of escaping poverty are young adults (eighteen to twenty-four), most of whom are completing their education and seeking employment. And, as might be expected, employment is a major factor in understanding the dynamics of poverty. Over one-half of the adults who remain in poverty from one year to the next are unemployed in both years. Fifteen percent of those unemployed in both years escaped poverty, usually as the result of a change in family status or increased earnings by another family member, but the most significant exit rates are found among those who worked, either by getting a better-paying job or working more hours.

The Chances of Escaping Poverty

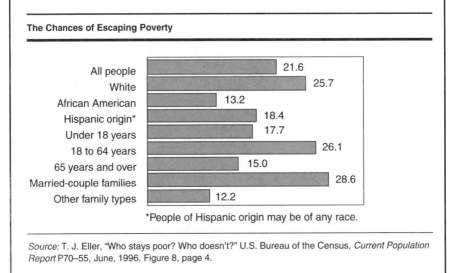

*People of Hispanic origin may be of any race.

Source: T. J. Eller, "Who stays poor? Who doesn't?" U.S. Bureau of the Census, *Current Population Report* P70–55, June, 1996. Figure 8, page 4.

By the 1990s the welfare system had lost its legitimacy with major segments of the public and legislatures, resulting in strong political pressure to cut government spending. Many people doubted that the existing system could solve the problem of poverty, and some worried that it even perpetuated poverty and dependency. The result was the Personal Responsibility and Work Opportunity Reconciliation Act of 1996. The legislation cut spending, granted more responsibility to the states, and set restrictions on eligibility. Among the most notable restrictions are time limits on cash assistance, such as two years for able-bodied adults and a five-year lifetime limit for 80 percent of a state's welfare recipients. One obvious goal was to move people off welfare and into the labor force, and therefore states are required to enroll 50 percent of welfare families in job training by 2002.

The welfare reform act generated much debate. On one side are those who believe it will motivate the poor to take the initiative and lift themselves out of poverty. Those who oppose it worry that the lack of meaningful opportunities will mean that the poor will be further impoverished. The full impact of welfare reform will not be felt for years as programs are developed and restrictions phased in, but it is clear that less money will be devoted to social welfare programs in the future. That could mean more people will fall below the poverty level and that others could have their modest living standards further reduced. One estimate suggests that 2.6 million more people, including 1.1 million children, will fall below the poverty thresholds (Zedlewski, Clark, Meier & Watson, 1996).

HOMELESSNESS: LIFE ON THE STREETS

The most touching aspect of poverty is **homelessness.** There is some debate over the specific number who regularly go without shelter, with estimates ranging up to 600,000 persons living in shelters or on the street on any given night (Jencks, 1994). In addition, some advocates for the homeless warn that millions more are living on the edge, "one paycheck or one domestic argument from the streets." Whatever the exact number, the homeless qualify as the poorest of the poor, for "not only do they lack material resources, but they lack human resources as well—friends or family who will take them in" (Piliavin, Sosin, & Westerfelt, 1987–1988: 20).

What is striking about the street people is their diversity—young and old, black and white, families and individuals, women and men are without homes. The homeless population is somewhat different in each locality, a response to local social, economic, and political conditions, but it is possible to sketch some broad overall patterns based on multiple city surveys done by the United States Conference of Mayors (Puente, 1993; Moss & Dickson, 1994).

The largest single group among the homeless are single adult males. In some cities they make up more than half the homeless population. Many of them are Vietnam-era veterans, and many suffer from problems ranging from mental illness to substance abuse. About 10 to 15 percent are women, a large proportion of whom are abused or battered women, evicted or seeking to escape from violent domestic arrangements. Most are middle-aged or younger. There are very few older people— men or women—among the homeless for two reasons: first because the elderly qualify for Social Security, Medicaid, and other age-related benefits; and second because the mortality rate for the long-term homeless is so high that few survive to old age.

About one-third are families with children. Many are single parents, and a large group are young, lower-blue-collar families, typically thrown onto the streets by joblessness. The children in these families are at risk for psychological distress, unusually high rates of depression, anxiety, and reduced self-esteem. Most children are members of family units, but there is also a core of unaccompanied children (about 4 or 5 percent, with equal numbers of boys and girls) counted among the homeless. They are typically runaways or "throwaways" (abandoned or evicted children) fleeing abusive homes, all-too-often reduced to crime or prostitution to survive. There are also high rates of pregnancy and substance abuse among these youths.

African Americans are dramatically overrepresented among the homeless. Overall, more than one-half of the homeless are African American, but the rates are even higher in some cities. In New York City, African Americans are seventeen times more likely to be homeless than whites, while in Philadelphia it is a factor of twenty-one (*The Economist,* 1997c). In New York, African-American children under five are thirty-three times more likely to end up in a shelter than white children.

Sources of Homelessness

Homelessness is the result of the interplay among a number of social and economic forces. Among the most important are poverty, unemployment, increases in the incidence of troubled individuals, abusive and broken families, and the limited availability of low-income housing (Jencks, 1994; O'Flaherty, 1996).

As would be expected, poverty and unemployment drive many people onto the streets. However, some of the homeless (one in five) are the working poor, employed, but unable to find or afford housing. Another segment is driven to the streets and shelters by domestic circumstances. These are usually female single parents and teenagers. Divorce, abandonment, or the need to escape domestic abuse throws them on their own resources. Research shows that those most likely to become homeless are socially isolated, lacking supportive social relationships with family or friends who might be able to aid them. For example, an unusual proportion have spent some period in foster care during their childhood (Piliavin, Sosin, & Westerfelt, 1987–88).

A substantial proportion of the homeless do have psychological or behavioral problems that contribute to their plight. Vietnam-era veterans are overrepresented, some suffering service-related disabilities. Substance abuse is frequent, with almost half misusing drugs and alcohol or some combination of substances. About one-quarter of the homeless have a history of mental illness. Their plight represents an ironic twist in the evolution of the care of the mentally ill, a process called **deinstitutionalization** that opened the doors of mental institutions but failed to provide alternative sources of care (Dear & Wolch, 1987). Several factors contributed to this situation. First, the assertion of patients' civil rights has made it virtually impossible for police, psychiatrists, or family members to hold people in hospitals against their will, unless they are very seriously impaired. Second, reforms in the treatment of chronic mental patients shifted the emphasis from institutional care to the idea of returning patients to the communities where they must live. Although a worthy idea, governments failed to provide the necessary community-based outpatient facilities to help those released from institutions. Those not able to successfully adapt are left to fend for themselves on the streets.

Ultimately, the most obvious problem is inadequate affordable housing for low-income people. Gentrification and urban renewal raze low-income housing and low-rent hotels to make way for middle-class homes, roads, and shopping centers. In other cases, property owners in inner cities allow buildings to deteriorate to a point that sets in motion the decline of whole neighborhoods. Neither governmental efforts nor private construction has kept pace with the demand for low-income housing since the 1970s. It is estimated that there was a shortage of 4.7 million low-rent homes (6.5 million units for 11.2 low-income renters) in the United States in 1993 (Barry, 1996).

Responses to the Homeless

Americans exhibit contradictory and ambivalent attitudes toward the homeless. Compassion and caring are unmistakable in efforts to alleviate the suffering. Most Americans agree that homelessness is a serious problem and worry that the problem is getting worse (Taylor, 1996). Less than one person in ten believes the situation is improving, and 80 percent feel there is something fundamentally wrong with a society with so many homeless people. Cities open shelters, and governments devote millions of dollars to the creation of affordable housing for the homeless. Much of the work being done on their behalf represents the work of private and religious charitable institutions and individuals. Nine out of ten shelters for the homeless are operated by community groups or churches, and at least 80,000 volunteers work in these shelters (Whitman, 1989).

In contrast, there is also a mean-spirited streak. Affluent suburbs around the world are accused of transporting their homeless to city centers (Barbanel, 1987). During 1995, two dozen communities enacted limits on activities associated with homelessness (Ybarra, 1996). Among them were bans on sitting on sidewalks, begging, standing too near cash machines. In Toronto, where three homeless men froze to death on the streets, a political leader generated public outrage by asserting that people on the streets were there voluntarily (Crary, 1996).

There is no single explanation of the sources of such negative responses to the impoverished, but several factors seem to operate. At the deepest level it may reflect the pervasive effect of the dominant ideology of individualism that locates responsibility for such problems in personal failings rather than structural problems. It is, for example, not uncommon for one-third of the population to invoke individual explanations for poverty and homelessness (personal choice, aversion to work, laziness) rather than structural explanations (bad luck, economic forces such as downsizing) (Lee, Jones, & Lewis, 1990).

There are also a number of practical considerations that arouse negative feelings. Business owners complain that beggars clog the sidewalks and deter potential customers. And aggressive begging or soliciting at cash machines, especially after dark, is admittedly intimidating within an environment of widespread urban violence. In the courts this issue has become a clash between the public order and the rights of the homeless to occupy public parks and abandoned buildings, to sleep on the streets, to beg in the streets.

WIDENING THE GAP BETWEEN RICH AND POOR

The majority of households occupy a broad middle-income range that allows families to enjoy a comfortable standard of living that includes home ownership, consumer goods, health care, and education for their children. However, the overall position of middle-income groups has actually declined as the share of income earned by the top earners has increased (Phillips, 1990). In addition, the gap between the incomes of the wealthiest and the poorest segments of the population in the United States has been widening steadily since the late 1960s (Weinberg, 1996). As shown in Exhibit 5.7, the share of income earned by the most affluent groups is expanding at the expense of the rest of the population. The top 5 percent earned 21 percent of the total earned income in 1994, up from 16.5 percent two decades earlier. Between 1974 and 1994 the income share of the highest quintile rose from about 43 percent to 49 percent. The share of each of the other groups shrank. For example, the share of the poorest fifth shrank from 4.3 percent to 3.6 percent during the same period.

Thus, 20 percent of the households earn just about one-half the total aggregate income of the whole nation. The process has continued through periods of expansion and recession and during successive Republican and Democratic administrations, suggesting that the widening gap is grounded in fundamental shifts in the economic system. Moreover, this pattern is being repeated around the world, in Britain, Brazil,

EXHIBIT 5.7 Trends in Shares of Household Income, United States, 1974-1994

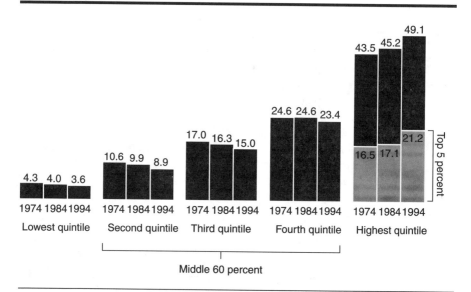

Source: U.S. Bureau of the Census, Current Population Reports, Series P60-189, *Income, Poverty and Valuation of Non-cash Benefits, 1994.* Washington, DC: U.S. Government Printing Office, 1996, Figure 2, page xv.

Guatemala (Crossette, 1996). This trend is the product of a changing class structure. A disproportionate share of new jobs being created are either upper middle class—high-skill professional and managerial work—or lower-end service and white-collar work. The wages for jobs demanding high skills and low skills are diverging. To illustrate, wages for male high school graduates *declined* by 17 percent between 1979 and 1992, while earnings for college graduates increased by 5.2 percent during the same period (Kilborn, 1995). Female workers fared somewhat better, with college graduates' incomes rising by 19 percent and high school graduates improving marginally by .9 percent. In both cases wages for the better educated are rising much faster than the least educated.

The discrepancy between the extremes in the economic hierarchy is also accentuated by the emergence of dual-income families with both spouses in professional and business positions. The expansion of occupational opportunities for college-educated women is a major consideration in this area. Women once excluded from well-paying careers by discrimination now hold a significant proportion of such jobs. They are often married to men in similar lucrative positions, creating very-high-income households.

CONCLUSION: FAVORING GREATER EQUALITY

Financial resources are, by any criteria, unequally distributed across the society. A few hundred thousand citizens enjoy substantial wealth at the same time that more than 30 million people live in poverty. Most Americans express some reservations about the current distribution of money and wealth. A full 62 percent of Americans feel that money and wealth "should be more evenly distributed among a larger percentage of the people" (Gallup Poll, 1985; 1990; 1996). In contrast, about one-third (33%) feel that current economic patterns are "fair" while about 5 percent have no opinion.

As would be expected, opinions on the fairness of the current system are shaped by class, race, and gender. Women are somewhat less likely to endorse the fairness of the current situation, as are minorities. Judgments of fairness are directly related to the size of income, with one-half the people in families earning more than $40,000 seeing the distribution of financial resources as fair, with the percentages declining to only 16 percent of those in the $10,000 or less income bracket. It is not surprising that perceptions of the fairness of the stratification system are defined by location in that system.

KEY CONCEPTS

annual income	**homelessness**	**poverty thresholds**
decency threshold	**net worth**	**super-rich**
deinstitutionalization	**persistent poverty**	**working poor**
earnings gap	**poverty**	

SUGGESTED READING

DENNY BRAUN, *The Rich Get Richer: The Rise of Income Inequality in the United States and the World,* 2nd ed. Chicago: Nelson-Hall, 1997. A critical analysis of the widening gap between rich and poor around the world and the threat to the basic fabric of societies that accompanies this development.

CYNTHIA M. DUNCAN, ed., *Rural Poverty in America.* Westport, CT: Praeger, 1992. An analysis of the breadth of rural poverty and the special problems that arise in attempting to deal with it.

MICHAEL HARRINGTON, *The Other America: Poverty in the United States.* New York: Macmillan, 1962. This is the book that was instrumental in bringing the problems of poverty into the national spotlight and helped to stimulate President Lyndon Johnson's war on poverty in the 1960s.

CHRISTOPHER JENCKS, *The Homeless.* Cambridge, MA: Harvard University Press, 1994. Professor Jencks' book stresses the structural sources of homelessness—deinstitutionalization, the drug culture, and the loss of low-income housing.

MICHAEL B. KATZ, *The Undeserving Poor: From the War on Poverty to the War on Welfare.* New York: Pantheon, 1989. An examination of divergent attitudes toward the poor in American history.

WILLIAM P. O'HARE, *A New Look at Poverty in America.* Washington, DC: Population Reference Bureau, 1996. An up-to-date and comprehensive overview of the nature and scope of poverty and the implications of recent welfare legislation.

CHAPTER 6

Social Evaluations and Social Relations

CLASS AND SOCIAL JUDGMENTS

Individuals and families, social classes and occupations are ranked on hierarchies of social status in all contemporary societies. Synonyms commonly used to describe the same phenomena are prestige, social standing, social honor, or esteem. **Social status** is a collective social judgment of relative superiority or inferiority, respectability or disdain, desirability or rejection. Status represents the subjective evaluation of members of society by other members of that society using contemporary values and beliefs.

Some evaluations are based on personal performance. American society, for example, places great emphasis on musical talent and athletic prowess. Individuals with these skills earn huge salaries and become cultural icons. Social evaluations are also based on structural position (occupation, social class, family) and social attributes (race, ethnicity, gender, age). It is fair to conclude that occupation is the most salient source of social status in urban industrial societies (Nock & Rossi, 1979). This is because occupation is used to anticipate a wealth of information about a person or family—income, education, lifestyle, and personal attributes. Such projections prevail despite the fact that they may very well be based on assumptions, stereotypes, or inappropriate generalizations.

The subjective evaluation of others is important because people are sensitive to the judgments of those around them and prize the admiration and positive evaluation of others. Therefore, social status has the ability to influence the way people perceive themselves and how they feel about themselves. It is obvious that people strive to improve their social status in subtle and not-so-subtle ways. The most transparent is conspicuous consumption in cars, clothes, and accessories in an attempt to impress others, and advertisers are quick to exploit the status value of their sneakers, pens, wristwatches, and designer clothing.

The implications of social standing extend beyond the mere approbation of others, although that is important in and of itself. Social status is also an important factor in social relations. People who occupy a similar rank on status hierarchies tend to define themselves, and be defined by others, as social equals. Therefore, in a number of situations social interaction is segregated by social status, with association concentrated among people at the same social level. This shows up in friendships and marriage patterns as well as residential choices and membership in social clubs. This is in part voluntary, but it is also the outcome of deliberate attempts to exclude people judged to be lower in the status hierarchy. In extreme cases people at the same class level will attempt to form exclusive communities, limiting all forms of social contact to others at the same level. Such behavior stands as a reminder that status is ultimately a judgment of social superiority and inferiority.

SOCIAL CLASS AND SOCIAL STATUS

Americans tend to divide members of society into three, four, or five social classes, depending on the way in which the question is posed. The public will often spontaneously respond with three—wealthy, middle class, and poor—when asked how many social classes there are (MacKenzie, 1973; Coleman & Rainwater, 1978). Others think in terms of four classes, inserting the working class between the middle class and the poor, or five by making a distinction between an upper and a lower middle class. Income, occupation, lifestyle, and other factors are the basis of these class distinctions (Jackman, 1979). These classes are ranked in terms of increasing social status from the poor at the bottom to the wealthy at the top. The feelings of people at the upper levels toward lower classes confirms this ranking. Members of more advantaged classes may be indifferent to the less affluent or feel sympathetic and compassionate toward them, but seldom do they envy people at the lower reaches of the stratification system. Two major considerations influence social status based on social class, the ideology of individualism and type of work.

The Ideology of Individualism

The ideology of individualism is a major factor underlying social status. The idea that economic and occupational success is related to individual effort enhances people's social standing. In addition, economic success means material rewards that allow the more affluent to live a comfortable and desirable lifestyle. At the very top of the system are the "rich and famous" whose lives are celebrated in the media. By the same standard, members of the middle and lower classes have been relatively less successful and are denied access to the material rewards that could enrich their lives and enhance the opportunities of their children. Many of the negative attitudes toward the poor are embodied in the phrase "poor white trash" (see accompanying Case Study).

CASE STUDY:
Blaming the Poor for Being Poor: Poor White Trash

The phrase **poor white trash** combines racial and social class imagery in the form of a group of stupid and lazy families. It is a stereotype with a long history and is used to describe a number of different groups of people. It appears that the term originated early in the nineteenth century among African-American slaves who used the term to denigrate white domestic servants (Wray & Newitz, 1997). The point was that the African Americans' poverty was forcibly imposed by their servitude, but whites' destitution was due to their own failures, their own lack of effort. By the end of the century the term was used to identify the rural poor as degenerate hillbillies—promiscuous, lazy, violent, alcoholic, ignorant, and mentally defective due to incestuous sexual unions.[1] Eugenic researchers were actually successful in sterilizing poor rural whites on the grounds that they were "genetic defectives" (Duster, 1990).

In the 1950s the stereotype was enlarged to include the lower-middle- and working-class residents of trailer parks (Berube & Berube, 1997). Inhabitants were people with modest aspirations and limited occupational accomplishments, and deviance—sexual promiscuity, domestic violence, and substance abuse—was attributed to them. Consequently, many communities passed zoning laws that banished trailer parks to the remote outskirts of cities. Today, trailer dwellers' taste in home furnishings is the stereotypical velvet Elvis portrait, a choice readily ridiculed by the middle classes. One critic of President Bill Clinton's family's fondness for pizza, steaks, and burgers labeled it as an example of "the Clintons' trailer park tastes" (Sweeney, 1997).

Poor white trash is thus a handy stereotype for some members of the middle class. The poor are portrayed as victims of their own limitations and self-defeating behavior and structural limitations that inhibit the rural poor are ignored. The term conveys the idea that some whites are biologically defective and stupid. This, combined with their improvident behavior—substance abuse, indolence, lack of ambition—explains their position at the bottom of the stratification system. And it confirms the dominant ideology that rewards hard work and talent.

---

[1]There is perhaps no better characterization than that found in James Dickey's book and the film *Deliverance.* The 1990s comedy of Jeff Foxworthy parodies the lifestyle of the rural Southerner.

Manual Work and Mental Work

Another fundamental status distinction in contemporary American society is the line between blue-collar and white-collar work. The origin of these labels and their implications can be traced to the early stages of industrialization. Crafts workers, machine operators, and laborers who toiled in the factories and mills came to be identified symbolically by the sturdy dark clothing they wore. In contrast, the owners, managers, clerks, and record keepers worked in the offices and wore distinctive white shirts, which showed that they did not soil their hands or their clothing as they worked.

Blue-collar and white-collar thus came to signify a range of differences. Office workers enjoyed cleaner and safer working conditions than those who worked the land or operated machines. They were also likely to have more formal education because their jobs required communication skills. However, the most basic distinction then and now is the difference between manual and mental labor. Electricians, carpenters, janitors, auto mechanics, truck drivers, assembly line workers, machine operators, and laborers work with their hands; they perform manual labor. In contrast, managers, accountants, secretaries, lawyers, teachers, and salespeople perform mental or social tasks. Phrases such as "working with people" or "working with ideas or information" (rather than things) are commonly used to separate white-collar work from blue-collar work. An oil refinery worker has no problem making the distinction, "It's when you work with your hands rather than your brain. It's physical work, it's not mental work" (Halle, 1984: 210).

As a general rule, white-collar work enjoys higher status. Historians point out that the relative prestige of the two kinds of work is deeply embedded in Western cultural traditions (Tilgher, 1930). It originated with the ancient Greeks who believed that manual work was the curse of capricious gods. Physical labor was demeaning and inferior compared to the exercise of the intellect. Therefore, manual labor was, whenever possible, to be avoided and relegated to subordinate classes, peasants, or slaves. Work using the mind and the intellect became the cultural ideal, a claim to respectability, and ultimately the basis of powerful status distinctions.

This status distinction continues to have relevance for the way people think about social class and themselves. White-collar workers tend to depreciate those who do physical labor and feel that it is somehow demeaning to work with one's hands (Sennett & Cobb, 1977). Blue-collar workers depreciate white-collar workers who, they feel, do not work very hard or produce anything tangible or useful (LeMasters, 1975; Halle, 1984). Members of the working class are acutely aware of their relatively lowly position in the status hierarchy. Blue-collar workers tend to view themselves as doing decent, important, and honest work, but they are very sensitive to the fact that their work does not carry the same social prestige as white-collar work. There is not much question in their minds that office work carries more status than factory work. However, they are frustrated by a lack of respect for their work and by the derogatory stereotypes used to identify them.

People tend to prefer to interact with others at the same class level. This is, in part, because people feel more comfortable associating with others at the same social level. A comment by a manager's wife clearly reveals the relationship between social class and social relationships,

> I consider myself middle class. My husband works for a construction company in the office. Many of the construction workers make a lot more money than he does. But when we have parties at my husband's company, the ones with less education feel out of place and not at ease with the ones with more education. I think of them as working class (Coleman & Rainwater, 1978: 184).

OCCUPATIONAL PRESTIGE

Occupation is perhaps the most powerful status consideration in industrial societies. It is also the principal consideration in class placement, and social classes are thus composed of occupations of roughly similar social status. Members of occupations, sensitive to their public status, regularly devote themselves to improving or protecting the prestige of their work. For example, when the issue of lawyer advertising first reached the U.S. Supreme Court, opponents of professional advertising claimed that advertising would cause commercialization, undermine the lawyer's sense of dignity and self-worth, and tarnish the dignified image of the profession. This urge to protect status also shows up in groups' attempts to upgrade their prestige by inventing new titles for their work, as is evident in the evolution of names for those who handle the dead, from "undertaker" to "mortician" to "funeral director."

Occupational Prestige Rankings

The systematic study of occupational prestige originated in the 1920s among vocational counselors seeking to determine the relative social standing of different jobs (Counts, 1925). Today the literature on the subject is rich and comprehensive. This tradition of research confirms that occupations are located on relatively stable hierarchies of prestige. Despite some individual variation, there is a high level of consensus on the relative placement of most occupations within nations, even in those with markedly different religious, political, and cultural traditions (Treiman, 1977).[2] There are no major differences in ranking associated with gender, race, income, or geography in the United States. Admittedly, people do tend to inflate the social standing of their own occupations and those similar to it. There is also some variation in the relative weight given to different criteria, with, for example, economic rewards being a more salient criterion for people at the lower end of the stratification system while educational attainment is given more weight by those at the upper end.

---

[2]There are, however, conceptual and methodological considerations that demand that this research be approached with some caution. Some general titles actually encompass quite different circumstances. "Lawyer," for example, includes corporate lawyers and solo practitioners, public defenders, and costly celebrity attorneys. The question of comparability of occupations in different societies is also an important consideration. For example, the role of "judge" is often organized quite differently and carries somewhat different cultural meanings in different societies. There is, in addition, a potential sampling bias in these studies because urban and educated populations tend to be overrepresented.

A review of students' ranking of twenty-four occupations in the United States, Taiwan, and the People's Republic of China (PRC) is reported in Exhibit 6.1. Taiwan and The People's Republic share long cultural and religious traditions but have followed different political and economic systems over the last several decades. The People's Republic is based on a socialist system in which all workers earn similar wages, in the $30 to $60 per month range. Taiwan, in contrast, has built a more democratic and capitalist system upon the same cultural traditions and was strongly influenced by an American military presence.

Similarities among the prestige hierarchies in these three systems are most evident at the extremes. Highly educated professionals are consistently accorded the highest prestige. In all the three professions (law, medicine, engineering), along with banking, are the most prestigious occupations. Also, as in the United States, blue-collar jobs tend to be ranked by skill levels. And at the other extreme, there is cross-cultural consensus that unskilled jobs are the least prestigious. Ditch digger, janitor and hod carrier (an unskilled construction laborer) are near the last in all three.

EXHIBIT 6.1 Occupational Prestige Rankings: United States, Taiwan, and the People's Republic of China

AMHERST, MA	TAIPEI, TAIWAN	BEIJING, CHINA
Physician	Lawyer	Physician
Lawyer	Physician	Lawyer
School superintendent	Civil engineer	Banker
Civil engineer	School teacher	Civil engineer
Banker	Banker	Machinist
Army captain	Machinist	Army captain
School teacher	Army captain	School teacher
Electrician	School superintendent	Insurance agent
Insurance agent	Mail carrier	School superintendent
Carpenter	Insurance agent	Soldier
Soldier	Farmer	Barber
Plumber	Electrician	Mail carrier
Traveling sales	Carpenter	Bus driver
Machinist	Bus driver	Electrician
Mail carrier	Grocer	Traveling sales
Farmer	Soldier	Truck driver
Barber	Traveling sales	Carpenter
Grocer	Barber	Coal miner
Bus driver	Plumber	Plumber
Truck driver	Coal miner	Farmer
Coal miner	Truck driver	Janitor
Hod carrier	Hod carrier	Grocer
Janitor	Janitor	Hod carrier
Ditch digger	Ditch digger	Ditch digger

Source: Ronald H. Fredrickson, Jun-chih Gisela Lin, and Shaomin Xing. 1992. "Social status ranking of occupations in the People's Republic of China, Taiwan and the United States." *Career Development Quarterly* 40: 351–360, Table 2.

The similarities should not obscure the fact that there is also diversity, reflecting the unique cultural traditions of these societies. Among the most notable are those having to do with education. In Chinese societies, schoolteacher is rated at least as high as in the United States, reflecting the ancient Chinese reverence for education. But, in contrast to the United States, school superintendent ranks below that of teacher in China. This discrepancy reveals differences in the organization of the roles in China and the United States. While superintendent implies policy making and control of budgets in America, it is associated with more mundane record-keeping tasks in the PRC and with discipline in Taiwan.

The construction trades are also consistently ranked higher in the United States than in either other society. This reflects the fact that they do not enjoy a traditional position as skilled craftspeople but rather as self-taught general construction workers. Machinist, however, ranks higher in both Taipei and Beijing. American students perceive machinists as little more than machine operators, while the Chinese more accurately see them as members of a highly skilled trade playing a central role in the process of industrialization.

These hierarchies hint at both the diversity and the commonalties in occupational prestige around the world. Diversity is rooted in the unique values, beliefs, or history of a society. This is manifest in the agrarian ideology in Taiwan that serves to elevate the role of farmer while in PRC farming is still associated with demanding physical labor. But underlying such diversity is consistency. The professions always maintain high prestige. Medicine universally has very high prestige, even in societies where physicians do not earn as much as they do in the United States. Factory work tends to be ranked below crafts work. And finally, unskilled work is depreciated in every society.

The relative prestige accorded occupations by members of a society appears to be influenced by two analytically distinct processes. One is rooted in socialization experiences beginning in childhood and carrying on through the life cycle that teach each new generation that some occupations have more prestige than others. This is called **ascribed prestige**. In contrast, occupations also earn prestige on the basis of an evaluation process in which they are ranked on the basis of the perceived characteristics or rewards of the work. For example, as a general rule prestige is related to levels of income and education, indicating that people take these two factors into account in rating occupations. This may be labeled **achieved prestige.**

Ascribed Prestige

Occupational prestige hierarchies are part of the cultural traditions of societies and are transmitted during socialization. The power of ascribed prestige is unmistakable in the fact that very young children, with little direct contact with the nature and dynamics of social stratification, are sensitive to gradations of inequality and social status. It is no problem for preschoolers aged three to five or first graders to distinguish between "rich" and "poor" people based on visual clues (Tudor, 1971; Ramsey, 1991). Third graders give virtually the same rankings to jobs as adults do (Simmons

& Rosenberg, 1971). These findings suggest that children are exposed to clues to the ranking of groups in society very early in the socialization process. The culture of a society offers many clues to the relative worth of different occupations, clues embedded in everyday social interaction and media representations. The ascription of occupational prestige is, as is the case with other forms of social learning, a combination of both conscious and deliberate attempts to convey a particular point of view and the unintentional learning that evolves from exposure to the values and preferences shared among members of the society.

Interpersonal Contacts.   Children begin to meet representatives of many occupations very early in their lives. Jobs such as mail carrier, police officer, supermarket clerk, teacher, principal, garbage collector, and school janitor are a very real part of their social environment. Consequently, they are able to observe how people in such jobs are treated and at the same time see that they themselves are encouraged in direct and subtle ways to show more respect to some than others. People tend to exhibit deference toward members of some occupations but not others. Deference may take the form of exaggerated politeness, the use of courtesy titles ("Doctor," "Ms," "Sir," "Your honor"), providing favors, repressing disagreement, or acquiescence. In contrast, others are treated less well, conveying their relative social standing. Adults may, for example, be rude and demeaning to servers in restaurants but respectful and deferential to their religious leaders. The sum of these interpersonal interactions will tend to reproduce the existing hierarchy of prestige. An awareness of the prestige ascribed by others seems to exert a significant influence on subsequent personal judgments about prestige (Haug & Widdison, 1975).

It seems that adults are constantly posing the question, "What are you going to be when you grow up?" Parents, grandparents, teachers, peers, and even strangers always want to know what careers children aspire to when they are old enough to enter the work force. Adult reactions to choices such as prison guard, which might seem exciting to children, are less enthusiastic and are likely to be accompanied by lectures listing the disadvantages and handicaps of such work. The prestige of other occupations is enhanced by their definition as good career choices, typified by the cliché of the proud parent, "My daughter the doctor."

Television.   Children are exposed to many hours of television, and what they see molds their view of the world of work. In fact, television sometimes provides their only image of certain occupations. Most children have no direct personal contact with the work of judges, lawyers, reporters, military personnel, or corporate executives, yet these are among the roles most frequently found in TV programming, and there is some evidence that most occupational knowledge of these roles originates with television (Jeffries-Fox & Signorielli, 1978). Media portrayals thus have the potential to shape perceptions and stereotypes of jobs and shape characterizations of workers.

Much of the population is in blue-collar or service work, but such occupations are rarely seen, with their invisibility suggesting a lack of importance and value. Professionals and executives make up about one-quarter of the work force but are 60 percent of television characters (Gable, 1993). Moreover, those blue-collar and lower-white-collar workers who do appear look different—they are more likely to be overweight and behave differently—they drink more, commit more crimes, tell more lies. However, the real villains in television are business people (Lichter, Lichter, & Rothman, 1991). They are consistently portrayed as unsavory and engaged in criminal conduct.

The role of police in society may, more than any other single occupation, be shaped by the media, and polling data suggest an ongoing decline in respect for the police. This is in part a reflection of changing fictional portrayals of the police over the last several decades (Lichter, Lichter, & Rothman, 1991). Television police of the 1950s through the 1970s tended to be admirable characters. The police in "Adam 12," "Dragnet," "Kojack" and "The Streets of San Francisco" were honest, hard-working, bright, likable people. By the 1980s the image of law enforcement began to include more incidents of police misconduct and violations of civil rights. At the same time videotapes of apparent police misconduct surfaced in court cases and the news. Thus, television (via news and programming) helped convince the majority (68 percent) of Americans that police brutality is a frequent occurrence, despite the fact that only 20 percent have direct personal knowledge of anyone mistreated or abused by the police (Gallup Poll, 1991).

Achieved Prestige

Achieved prestige focuses on a more deliberate evaluative process in which jobs are compared on various standards such as income or working conditions. The underlying view is that occupations earn prestige on the basis of having desirable characteristics. This approach suggests that four broad kinds of criteria influence collective judgments. Some are self-evident and obvious, but others are more subtle and complex.

Prerequisites.   Several of the qualifications for admission to a particular kind of work are considered in determining prestige. The level of intelligence, the complexity and difficulty of training, and the amount of education all correlate directly with prestige. Educational requirements are the single most significant factor in prestige scores in industrial systems (MacKinnon & Langford, 1994). This helps to account for the high ranking of the professions, all of which involve lengthy formal education. Moreover, as a general rule professions that require graduate education or training (college professor, physician, scientist, and lawyer) are placed above those requiring a bachelor's degree (teacher, architect, accountant). The fact that in the United States most of the crafts involve apprenticeships or extensive experience contributes to their standing above those blue-collar jobs viewed as not requiring any extensive occupational training. Jobs not having any particular qualifications—unskilled and service work—have the lowest prestige.

The question of the scarcity of qualified personnel may also be a factor. It will be recalled that structural functional theory places considerable importance on this factor. Although it is difficult to assess scarcity in any objective sense, it may help to account for the generally high prestige of occupations perceived as demanding rare and special attributes such as the physical dexterity of the athlete, the analytic ability of the scientist, the humanitarianism of the social worker, or the creative impulse of the artist.

Rewards.   One consistent finding both in the United States and other countries is a very high correlation between earnings and prestige (Treiman, 1977). Income confers prestige because it can be translated into attractive lifestyles, but it also has symbolic value because money is sometimes taken as a rough guide to success. There are, of course, notable exceptions. Teacher and clergy have higher levels of prestige than could be predicted using income as the sole criterion, while butcher and garbage collector are lower than expected.

Characteristics of the Work.   Occupations earn prestige on the basis of the tasks involved, the social organization of the work, and working conditions (Marsh, 1971). Cleanliness and safety are factors. Physically dirty or unsafe work tends to be devaluated. Routine and repetitive work has less prestige than work that is interesting and creative. Level of responsibility and autonomy are also considerations. Jobs requiring the supervision, evaluation, and direction of subordinates place higher than those that are under the control of superiors and allow little individual discretion. Many authors would claim that power is a decisive factor in understanding prestige hierarchies, arguing that power is universally valued in all human societies (Treiman, 1977). This might explain high ranking of governmental roles, since all exercise unusual power.

There is a good deal of debate over the concept of the functional importance of jobs. Structural functional theory argues that certain types of occupations are essential to the survival and welfare of all societies (Davis & Moore, 1945). Clergy, for example, occupy a central role because religion serves to integrate members of a society through a common value system. Scientific and technical occupations develop the technique and hardware to achieve national goals such as the exploration of space or the eradication of disease. Functional theory claims that it is imperative that these roles be filled and that people are motivated to perform these essential services. Prestige is among the major rewards that can be used to motivate people, and thus it becomes one of the rewards attached to the more important positions in society. Prestige is thus an "unconsciously evolved device by which societies insure that the most important positions are conscientiously filled by the most qualified persons." It is not at all clear that people utilize this abstract concept of functional importance in considering the prestige of occupations, but they are able to rate occupations along a continuum of "importance to society" (Haug & Widdison, 1975).

CLASS, RACE, AND SOCIAL RELATIONSHIPS

One of the most common—and relatively obvious—characteristics of the social organization of societies is the tendency for people with similar attributes to associate with one another. Friendships illustrate this, because people usually group themselves on the basis of social qualities such as age, religion, occupation, ethnicity, and shared attitudes and beliefs. The same process is also evident among members of the same social class. People at the same class level are more likely to associate with other people in the same class than with people who rank above or below them in the stratification system. This pattern has long been documented in numerous social patterns including friendships, residence, social club membership, dating, and marriage (Warner & Lunt, 1941; Laumann, 1966; Fischer, 1982).

Class-based patterns of association are, in part, the normal outcome of sharing a common structural position. The work setting is a clear example of this. Formal and informal associations will be extensions of contacts in the work place. For example, workers, whether teachers or construction workers, often participate in special-purpose social clubs or unions that bring them together off the job. Informally they may congregate to socialize after work and discuss the problems of their work. Thus, in a very real sense bars, clubs, and other social situations are extensions of the work setting. This is also evident in residential patterns where housing costs will contribute to the sorting of neighborhoods on the basis of income. The segregation of social relationships is also the consequence of more deliberate attempts to create exclusive social networks.

Social Distance and Intergroup Contacts

Studies of social relations among diverse groups in societies often employ the idea of **social distance,** a concept originated by Emory Bogardus in the 1920s, to measure whites' willingness to accept racial and ethnic minorities into a number of social situations that suggest increasing degrees of social intimacy. Although this concept originated to explore association with minorities, it can be expanded to include social class. Social distance scales are designed to tap underlying attitudes by focusing on degrees of acceptance of people:

as residents in the country,
as visitors to the country,
as speaking acquaintances,
in the same work group,
into the neighborhood,
as very good friends,
as marriage partners.

Studies show that most people express the highest tolerance of minority groups that are the most similar and least accepting of peoples that are the most dissimilar. Americans, for example, are consistently most accepting of Canadians, a close geographic neighbor with a long history of peaceful relations and sharing many common socio-cultural, linguistic, and political elements. In contrast, there is the least acceptance of Chinese, Japanese, and Arabs, groups separated by geography, culture, religion, and language (Crull & Bruton, 1985). This holds true for both men and women, but as a general rule females are more tolerant than males in studies of social distance.

Social distance scales measure attitudes, a preference for maintaining physical and social separation. These attitudes contribute to observed patterns of social segregation in many different social contexts—interpersonal, organizational, neighborhood, residential, and educational—based on class and color.

Neighborhood Preferences

The dynamics of social distance are evident in segregation of neighborhoods because they reflect preferences for associating with members of the same class (Exhibit 6.2). For example, when asked to express neighborhood preferences, nine out of ten people give a class-based answer, and there is strong preference for a neighborhood composed of people of the same class or a higher class (Jackman & Jackman, 1983: 195). The expressed preference for living among people of the same class is most powerful among the working and middle classes. Not unexpectedly, it is weakest among the poor, who would probably rather escape areas that are often deteriorating and unsafe.

Residential Segregation

Class preferences are only part of the explanation of patterns of residential segregation. The practice of deliberately, physically excluding groups of people has a long history. The word "ghetto" appears to have originated with the sixteenth-century Italian practice of isolating Jews in certain parts of cities. The U.S. government relegated Native Americans to reservations and banished trailer parks to urban fringes; and immigrants congregated in Chinatowns, Little Italys, and barrios in urban communities. Residential segregation is a complex phenomenon because there are always financial constraints on the peoples' housing choices. In addition, some segregation has a voluntary dimension because immigrants may be attracted to the areas where their native language and culture are maintained.

As is well-known, there were separate churches, schools, bathrooms, restaurants, and places on buses for African Americans in the United States well into the

---

EXHIBIT 6.2 Social Class and Neighborhood Preferences

Class	PREFERENCE FOR A NEIGHBORHOOD WITH:	
	Own class only	Own/higher class
Poor	20.3%	68.3%
Working	52.5	35.1
Middle	57.3	13.2
Upper middle	40.5	5.5

Source: Mary R. Jackman and Robert W. Jackman. *Class Awareness in the United States.* Berkeley, CA: University of California Press, 1983, Table 9.1, p. 195. Copyright © 1983 by the University of California Press.

1960s. In fact, early in the 1940s four out of five urban whites openly endorsed separate sections of towns for "Negroes." One of the most bizarre remnants of the segregated system surfaced in 1996 in a small southern town when church deacons asked that a mixed-race infant be exhumed and removed from their graveyard because they wished it to remain exclusively white (Bragg, 1996). The request generated massive media attention, and church deacons subsequently relented and apologized publicly.

Exclusionary practices based on color continue to play a role in residential segregation. For a long time African Americans and whites lived in separate communities. Whites' racial attitudes have softened over the years, and blatant racial discrimination is prohibited by the Fair Housing Act of 1968, although enforcement is uneven, and the growth of the black middle class expands the economic options of more families. Consequently, residential segregation is slowly declining in major cities, but the rate and the magnitude of change is modest. The **index of dissimilarity**[3] for African Americans that measures residential segregation declined from 68 to 64 between 1980 and 1990 in major American metropolitan areas (Farley & Fry, 1994). As shown in Exhibit 6.3, neighborhood segregation is most common in the older manufacturing cities, such as Detroit, Cleveland, Gary, and Buffalo, and less typical in cities in the south and west such as Boulder or Jacksonville.

Dual Housing Markets.   Only a small portion of the racial segregation that occurs within suburban areas can be explained by African-American–white income differences (Stearns & Logan, 1986). Nor can it be explained by minority preferences for minority neighborhoods, for most African Americans favor integrated neighborhoods (Streitweiser & Goodman, 1983). Residential segregation has racial and class dimensions that interact. Social scientists point out that individuals' choices are limited by the workings of a **dual housing market**, in which a variety of agencies including realtors, lending institutions, and insurance companies channel the poor and racial groups—both overtly and subtly—into separate areas and communities. Class is a factor in the reluctance of banks, mortgage companies, and insurance companies to operate in poor neighborhoods because of higher crime rates and declining property values. Such decisions have a disproportionate impact on minority residents. But race cannot be discounted and is a factor when realtors and sellers attempt to exclude minorities from certain areas.

Two common practices perpetuate residential segregation. Both are prohibited by the Fair Housing Act of 1968 and other laws. "Redlining" refers to the unwillingness to grant loans or insurance for property in poor or minority neighborhoods. The term originated when banks physically drew red lines around such areas on community maps. A review of mortgage applications in 1995 showed that middle-income minority applicants in mostly minority areas were twice as likely to be rejected as middle-

---

[3]The index of dissimilarity measures how closely the racial and ethnic mix of neighborhoods matches the composition of the entire metropolitan area. If, for example, 25 percent of the people in a city are Latino/a and every neighborhood is also 25 percent Latino/a, the index is 0. But if all Latino/as live on exclusively Latino/a blocks and non-Latino/as exclusively on non-Latino/a blocks, the index is 100.

EXHIBIT 6.3 Residential Segregation in Metropolitan Areas, United States, 1990

| | | MINORITY INDEXES | | |
| | MINORITY | African | | |
RANK AND AREA	POPULATION	American	Latino/a	Asian
Most segregated				
1 Detroit, MI	25.1%	89	42	48
2 Cleveland, OH	22.5	86	57	42
3 Gary, IN	28.0	91	53	42
4 Buffalo, NY	15.1	84	60	56
5 Flint, MI	22.9	83	34	45
6 Birmingham, AL	28.2	77	37	53
7 Milwaukee, WI	19.1	84	58	47
8 Chicago, IL	37.7	87	65	47
9 Cincinnati, OH	14.6	79	36	47
10 St. Louis, MO	19.5	80	29	44
Least segregated				
209 Ft. Walton, FL	15.0	41	26	28
210 Chico, CA	13.1	48	30	42
211 Lawrence, KS	12.3	38	21	43
212 Cheyenne, WY	14.7	42	33	31
213 Yuba City, CA	27.4	41	29	37
214 Lawton, OK	30.8	37	23	28
215 Boulder, CO	10.5	32	33	30
216 Anchorage, AK	21.3	38	25	31
217 Bremerton, WA	11.5	46	22	28
218 Santa Rosa, CA	15.7	41	30	29
219 Jacksonville, FL	27.3	28	27	32

Note: Data were collected for 219 major metropolitan areas with at least a 10 percent minority population.

Source: Basic data: "By the numbers, tracking segregation in 219 metro areas." Patricia Edmonds, *USA Today* (November 11, 1991): 3A, and Reynolds Farley and William H. Fry, "Changes in segregation of whites from blacks: Small steps toward a more integrated society." *American Sociological Review* 59 (1994): 23–45.

income whites living in mostly white areas (Loeb, Cohen, & Johnson, 1995). For African Americans the rejection rate was 37 percent compared to 18 percent for whites. And in 1997 a major insurer agreed to a $13.2 million settlement with the Justice Department for allegations of redlining (Dugas, 1997). "Steering" identifies the practice of directing potential home buyers into neighborhoods dominated by members of their own class, ethnic group, or race. This is accomplished by real estate agents who fail to show residences in white neighborhoods to African-American potential home buyers. There is evidence that some degree of steering occurs in as many as half the encounters with realtors in some cities, both North and South (Glaster, 1990).

Most families prefer to move to neighborhoods with better resources (schools) and amenities (parks) as their class position improves. The predicament is that it is more difficult for African Americans to move out of segregated and low-income neighborhoods as their income rises. Consequently, African Americans at the same income level are more likely to live in neighborhoods with fewer resources for themselves and their children (Massey, Condran, & Denton, 1987).

Educational Segregation: Separate but Equal?

Separate schools for African-American and white children was official policy or informal fact in many areas prior to the 1954 Supreme Court ruling in *Brown v. Board of Education*. Court-ordered desegregation plans that included bussing students were implemented in many places, but the popularity of neighborhood schools combined with the continuing reality of residential segregation raises the question of the success of public policy initiatives in eliminating school segregation. Studies of the composition of schools indicate that segregation has declined but persists, especially in the northeast (U.S. Commission on Civil Rights, 1987: Edmonds, 1994). There is, as shown in Exhibit 6.4, still a large proportion of minority children in public schools that have more than 50 percent minority enrollments. Eight out of ten African Americans favor greater efforts to integrate the schools, and two-thirds of both African Americans and whites feel that integration has improved the quality of the education of African-American children.

Marriage Patterns

Some people argue that intermarriage among people of different classes and racial and ethnic groups is the best measure of the breakdown of invidious status distinctions. It is clear that marriages are sorted by social class, even in a heterogeneous and geographically mobile urban society. To illustrate, a study in Detroit showed that a majority (58 percent) of people married someone in the same social class (Whyte, 1990). A conspicuous part of this is that parents generally prefer that their children marry someone of the same or higher social class. People often express such feelings very directly. Speculating on future marriage partners for a child, an upper-middle-class parent comments,

---

EXHIBIT 6.4 Segregation in the Public Schools

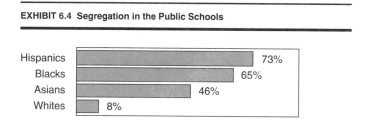

Note: Percentage is of students attending public schools that have more than 50 percent minority enrollment.

Source: Patricia Edmonds, "Have schools really changed?" *USA Today* (May 12, 1994): 2A.

What sort of a husband would a carpenter be? . . My viewpoint would not jibe with a carpenter. Marriage is based on equals. I would want my daughter to marry in her own class. She would go to college and would want her husband to be educated. I would want to be able to mix with in-laws and converse with them (Laumann, 1966: 29).

This quotation points to an underlying dimension of class and social relations, the common belief that members of different social classes have different perspectives and values. All other things being equal, many people simply feel more comfortable with others having similar styles of life.

The gradual weakening of residential segregation tends to reduce barriers between groups. People attend school together, become friends, and eventually date and marry. It is therefore possible to anticipate rates of intermarriage on the basis of residential segregation. The link between residential segregation and intermarriage is evident when Britain and the United States are compared. Urban residential segregation for African Americans in the United States is twice that for Britain (*The Economist,* 1997d). One reason is that wealthy British people are more comfortable living near poorer neighbors than are Americans. In turn, a dramatic 31 percent of married sixteen- to thirty-four-year-old British Afro-Caribbean men have a white partner, and 21 percent of women have a white husband. American data is not broken down by age, but overall approximately 4 percent of African-American men and 2 percent of African-American women have a white spouse.

The Capitalist Class: An Elite Social Network

Perhaps the most dramatic instance of exclusionary social relationships developed during the nineteenth century among members of the emerging capitalist class in the United States (Baltzell, 1958; 1964). In the 1880s, wealthy, white, British-descended Protestant industrialists and bankers, prompted by concern over the mass immigration that was bringing literally millions of foreign workers to the United States, began a conscious attempt to formalize an exclusive social network. Exclusive country clubs sprang up, expensive boarding schools such as Groton (1894) proliferated, and groups such as the Sons of the Revolution (1883) that traced their ancestors to the colonial period were formed. Members of this class soon congregated in exclusive neighborhoods and in 1887 published the *Social Register*, a volume that listed the names (and addresses, alma maters, country homes, club memberships, and yacht names) of socially acceptable families in major American cities. Members of this self-defined, social elite lived and partied together and sent their sons and daughters to exclusive Ivy League and Seven Sisters colleges and universities (Yale and Harvard) where they dated and eventually married the children of other elite families. Members of the social elite dominated business, industry, the arts, and politics during the early decades of the twentieth century.

The *Social Register* continues to be published, and the 1998 edition contains some 30,000 names (Sargent, 1997). However, the boundaries of the original capitalist social elite are blurred. It has been impossible for members to maintain their exclusive domain in the face of dramatic social changes. New millionaires are being created, marriage across social class lines is more common, and although members of this social elite are still influential, power is more widely distributed. That does not mean that the new rich institutional elite are all readily accepted by members of the old capitalist elite. All of Donald Trump's money could not, for example, gain him access to their homes or clubs (Kunen, 1990).

The Contact Hypothesis

It is often predicted that interpersonal contacts among members of diverse groups will promote positive attitudes and reduce intolerance and prejudice, an idea called the **contact hypothesis** (Allport, 1954). This belief supports attempts to integrate jobs, neighborhoods, and schools. The lack of social contacts produced by various

---

CASE STUDY:
Melting Pot or Multiculturalism

In 1909 a Jewish immigrant authored a play called *The Melting Pot* that affixed a new identity to the United States. The imagery of a **melting pot** defines America as a crucible in which the various immigrant nationalities blend to create a unique new American culture. In practice, generations of immigrants during the nineteenth and twentieth centuries usually adopted and reinforced the dominant Western European Protestant culture. Thus, they **assimilated** the prevailing culture, rather than dramatically recasting it, although many third-generation white Americans do retain some elements of their ethnic heritage.

An increasing tolerance of racial and ethnic difference and a new appreciation of cultural diversity began in the 1960s, as a reaction to the discrimination and exclusionary practices that were then common. This has evolved into an alternative societal model—**multiculturalism,** the image of a nation of many racial and ethnic groups maintaining their unique identities and enjoying mutual acceptance and respect. Bilingual education to assist the children of immigrants, laws that protect non-Western religions and customs, and classroom programs that emphasize the social and political contributions of minorities in American history are tangible manifestations of multiculturalism.

Proponents of multiculturalism or pluralism emphasize that it encourages understanding and appreciation of the values and beliefs of the many groups that contribute to the creation of the nation. Critics of multiculturalism feel that it threatens the social cohesion of the nation by fostering divisions among peoples. Many critics favor integration and assimilation. They worry that multiculturalism might foster the social and physical resegregation of racial and ethnic groups. They recall extreme instances around the world where racial and ethnic divisions led to wars and ethnic cleansing. Debates about multiculturalism are also about political power, because the growth of racial and ethnic identity can be translated into political power and shows up in the form of the increase in the number of minority candidates for office and the need to respond to the needs of groups that form cohesive voting blocks.

forms of segregation allows ignorance to flourish and stereotypes to prevail. The contact hypothesis proposes a self-perpetuating process of intolerance where isolation separates people from the interpersonal contacts with the potential to disconfirm stereotypes. Among both African Americans and whites, prejudice is more likely among the less educated, lower and working classes (Sigelman & Welch, 1993; Farley, Stech & Krysan, 1994). Research has produced mixed results, but interracial social contacts generally do contribute to more positive racial attitudes, especially among whites (Sigelman & Welch, 1993; Smith, 1994). Although the magnitude of results is sometimes modest, the weakening of negative attitudes is cause for some optimism on the future of race relations in America (see accompanying Case Study).

CLASS AND CHARACTER JUDGMENTS

The public may never know what, if anything, happened at the Excelsior Hotel in Little Rock on May 8, 1991. Paula Jones, a lower-middle-class, white-collar worker, claimed that Bill Clinton, then governor of Arkansas, made improper sexual advances, which he denied. Her allegations were ridiculed by members of the press who quickly fastened on her modest social class position to attack her character. She was dismissed as "some sleazy woman with big hair coming out of the trailer parks" by a columnist at a major news magazine (who later apologized). "Drag a $100 bill through a trailer park and there's no telling what you'll find," added a high-profile political consultant.

This is not an isolated incident, but merely one manifestation of the fact that people may construct judgments about the character of people on the basis of location in the class system. Americans are likely to believe, for example, that traits such as intelligence, competence, and responsibility increase at each higher class level (More & Suchner, 1976; Jackman & Senter, 1982). One study reveals that college students feel that mothers in low-prestige occupations are less competent than higher-status mothers (Etaugh & Poertner, 1991). A major sneaker company used that strategy when it claimed that buyers at a discount store could not distinguish their brand from a similar-looking, less expensive model. The judge rejected the claim as "elitist," and added, "the fact that a consumer may prefer to purchase low-price footwear (or have no other option) does not transform them into an unsophisticated, careless shopper" (Pines, 1994). It may be assumed that such character judgments help to explain certain patterns of interaction, such as mock jury deliberations where it is consistently found that people at the bottom of the stratification system—unskilled workers—have the least influence on deliberations and are viewed as least helpful and least likely to be chosen as foreperson (Berger, Fisek, Norman, & Zelditch, 1977).

The link between class and character is ultimately embedded in the ideologies of class, race, and gender. The dynamics of the ideology of individualism lead members of society to attribute generally negative character traits to members of the lower classes and more positive traits to higher classes, reasoning that location in the class structure is the outcome of individual abilities and effort. For example, research in the 1960s suggested that a majority of Americans held the poor individually responsible for their own plight, specifically as a result of a lack of thrift or effort (Feagin, 1972).

While such judgments identify specific traits they do not necessarily solidify into totally positive or negative stereotypes (Skafte, 1989). Higher-class persons may be rated smarter, more intelligent, healthier, and happier than the poor, but they are also thought of as more self-centered and selfish. The poor may be judged as less intelligent, to be more likely to steal and have lower self-esteem, but are also seen as hard working, generous, and handling money wisely. In short, although the poor may be perceived as less able this does not extend to the notion that they are lazy and unmotivated. Rather it suggests recognition that social position shapes character rather than the notion that character determines position. This may be interpreted as further evidence of the weakening of the salience of the ideology of individualism and opportunity.

CONCLUSION: CLASS AND SELF-ESTEEM

The existence of occupational and class hierarchies of social status has the ability to influence the way that people think about and evaluate themselves. Social scientists ordinarily use the generic term "self-concept" to describe individuals' overall thoughts and feelings about themselves (Rosenberg, 1989). Self-concepts are complex phenomena and include several different dimensions, but the one that has received the most attention in recent years is self-esteem. **Self-esteem** is a person's self-evaluation of his or her social or moral worth. Self-esteem is shaped by many factors, and it is, at least in part, a product of social interaction. People's feelings about themselves are strongly influenced by their judgment of what others think of them. Those in the least prestigious work typically seek to counter judgments of inferiority, reflected in these words of a grave digger:

> Not anybody can be a grave digger. . . . You have to make a neat job. . . . A human body is goin' into this grave. That's why you need skill when you're gonna dig a grave. . . . It's like a trade. It's the same as a mechanic or a doctor. . . . A grave digger is a very important person (Terkel, 1972: 658–660).

Unfortunately, such claims that their work is good and useful and meaningful can neither erase nor neutralize broader social judgments.

There is a clear relationship between social class and self-esteem (Rosenberg & Pearlin, 1978).[4] The poor, usually the most socially depreciated members of society, exhibit the least positive self-concepts (Faunce, 1989). Social class position is associated with other indications of psychological well-being, including "happiness" and

---

[4]The issue of identity and self-esteem among minorities has received insufficient theoretical or empirical attention (Porter & Washington, 1993). Consequently, it is impossible to untangle the relative impact of race and class.

generalized "satisfaction with life" (Gallup Poll, 1995). Such measures of quality of life may represent the interplay between the multitude of consequences of class—social as well as economic. People are sensitive to their social environment, and social hierarchies include many judgments with the potential to harm or enhance self-image. The very concepts of status and prestige mean inferiority and superiority. This basic fact and related issues such as judgments about class, character and preferences for including or excluding people from social relations combine to influence self-concepts.

The link between class and self-esteem is strongest among adults, but it is also present in adolescents (Rosenberg, Schooler, & Schoenbach, 1989). Adolescent self-esteem is the subject of a great deal of concern because low self-esteem is often associated with poor grades, psychological depression, and juvenile delinquency. All are factors that have serious long-term implications. Bad grades in school or a record of delinquency can limit the occupational options of these youngsters later in life, relegating them to the lower rungs of the class system.

KEY CONCEPTS

achieved prestige	dual housing market	poor white trash
ascribed prestige	index of dissimilarity	self-esteem
assimilation	melting pot	social distance
contact hypothesis	multiculturalism	social status

SUGGESTED READING

E. DIGBY BALTZEL, *The Protestant Establishment.* New York: Random House, 1964. The primary study of the origins and wide-ranging influence of the capitalist elite in the first half of the twentieth century.

ROBERT D. BULLARD, J. EUGENE GRIGSBY III, AND CHARLES LEE (eds.), *Residential Apartheid.* Los Angeles, CA: CAAS Publications, 1994. A collection of essays that explores the many dimensions of residential segregation.

WILLIAM J. GOODE, *The Celebration of Heroes: Prestige as a Social Control System.* Berkeley, CA: University of California Press, 1978. The idea of cultural heroes as the embodiment of society's basic values and ideals.

MELVIN L. KOHN AND CARMI SCHOOLER, *Work and Personality.* Norwood, NJ: Albex, 1983. A broad-based discussion of the subtle and less-than-obvious ways that work and class shape thinking and behavior.

EDWARD O. LAUMANN, *Prestige and Association in an Urban Community.* Indianapolis, IN: Bobbs-Merrill, 1966. One of the most thorough and comprehensive analyses of the ways that social class shapes social relationships.

DONALD J. TREIMAN, *Occupational Prestige in Comparative Perspective.* New York: Academic Press, 1977. This survey of research on occupational prestige around the globe is dated but remains the best single source on the topic.

MATT WRAY AND ANNALEE NEWITZ (eds.), *White Trash: Race and Class in America.* New York: Routledge, 1997. An intriguing collection of essays that explore the nature of the "white trash" stereotype, including several papers by people who grew up in modest circumstances.

CHAPTER 7
The Shape of Political Power and Influence

POLITICAL POWER: CONCENTRATED OR DISPERSED?

Developments in democratic industrial nations over the course of the twentieth century have concentrated enormous power and authority in the hands of national, state, and local governments. Among the most conspicuous governmental responsibilities are: policing and prosecution of criminal behavior; collecting taxes; building and maintaining public works (roads, public buildings); regulating the professions, business, and industry; educating children; sustaining social insurance programs (Social Security, Medicare); and protecting and defending the nation's vital interests around the world. Thus, the activities of government touch every facet of the lives of its citizens.

The broad reach of government raises the question of how that authority is exercised and who exercises it. A long-standing debate over the distribution of political power divides observers of contemporary American society. One side argues that the interests of the elite class generally overwhelm all others in the political arena. This perspective is labeled "elite theory." Another group of scholars, the "pluralists," emphasize the distribution of power among different groups.

Elite Theory: Mills and the Power Elite

The basic parameters of **elite theory** were first laid out by C. Wright Mills (1956). Mills, writing in the 1950s, pointed out that three institutional sectors—corporations, the federal government, and the military—had grown to the point that they exercised unusual influence over society. He emphasized that their growth signaled a major transformation in industrial societies. The growth of capitalism fostered the emergence of large corporations that displaced small businesses. The Great Depression and World War II expanded the scope of the federal government and created a massive military bureaucracy. He envisioned three levels of power. Singular power was thus vested in the people who directed these structures—corporate executives, the president, his staff and cabinet, and generals and admirals. This group of people was called the **power elite.**[1]

Mills argued that the power elite exercised largely uncontested control of decisions in two key areas, establishing economic policy and the conduct of foreign policy. Political activity at the next level involved various interest groups seeking to influence Congress. Those groups—labor unions, professional associations, environmental groups—competed with each other, but it was impossible for any one to really succeed. The majority of people at the bottom of the system were impotent because the power elite were beyond their reach, and hence they became passive witnesses to the flow of events.

Mills also felt that the members of the power elite formed a single more or less unified elite. These people shared a common perspective because, he argued, they were overwhelmingly recruited from similar backgrounds and went to the same small circle of colleges and universities. Not only did they share a common value system, but there was a constant interchange of people circulating among the military, industry, and the government. Dwight Eisenhower was, at the time, the epitome of the process because he had left the military to become a college president (Columbia) and then President of the United States.

Contemporary advocates of elite theory often disagree over the composition of the controlling elite and the details of the exercise of power, but they are united on the key points that an inordinate amount of power and influence resides in the hands of a narrow and unrepresentative segment of society; and, that the majority of the population has minimal influence over political events (Mills, 1956; Domhoff, 1990; Dye, 1995). The goals of the upper class center on the expansion and protection of individual and corporate wealth and power.

Pluralists: The Dispersion of Power

In contrast, **pluralists** claim that the ability to influence the government is widely distributed among different groups and at different levels of the stratification system. Pluralists argue that governments in democratic industrial societies respond to countless different pressure groups, each pursuing their own agendas (Dahl, 1958). Working-class trade unions, farmers, business groups, upper-middle-class professional associations, and broadly based environmental advocates are among the groups that press for legislation that promotes their interests, but no one group is ever able to prevail in all

---

[1]President Dwight Eisenhower was discussing the same process when he warned of the emerging influence of the "military-industrial complex" as he left office in 1961.

cases and on all issues. Thus, although trade unions may be able to win increases in the minimum wage level, business interests can limit the size of the raise.

Pluralists usually concede that representatives of the wealthy and business interests dominated politics in the early years of the republic but insist that paths to success are increasingly open to merit and that no one class dominates all institutions. Rather, society is characterized by shifting combinations of groups that temporarily join together on specific issues. Moreover, although business groups are influential, they lack a common focus because there are major differences among business groups; high-tech telecommunications firms obviously have much different interests than banks or retailers.

Individuals and groups influence the political process in democratic societies in several ways. They participate directly in the political process by joining political parties, voting, and holding political office. Moreover, they have the right to try to determine policy by influencing their representatives by active lobbying (either individually or through interest groups), public demonstrations, petitions, letter-writing campaigns, making financial contributions to political candidates, and other forms of behind-the-scenes persuasion.

THE ELITE: PATTERNS OF INFLUENCE

Political influence is exercised in different ways in democratic societies. There is the open and public dimension that includes holding public office and making financial contributions to candidates. Such activities are a matter of public record and commented on in the media, but political influence is also regularly exercised away from public scrutiny. It is exerted in private meetings, in quiet lobbying and the activities of obscure special interest groups, and in the circulation of individuals between government and industry. Many people believe that exercise of influence by the upper class must be shrouded in secrecy because that is the only way to maintain the legitimacy of the political system in the minds of the rest of the population. The subtlety of the exercise of upper-class control means that it is sometimes difficult to document, but it cannot be underestimated or ignored.

Direct Participation in Government

It is not uncommon for members of the elite class to hold high political office, and it is logical to assume that they are more responsive to the interests of people like themselves than others whom they do not know or understand. The earliest American presidents such as Washington, Adams, and Jefferson were drawn from the wealthy land-owning classes, and more recent presidents (and contenders) such as Franklin Roosevelt, John F. Kennedy, George Bush, and Malcolm Forbes were born to privileged upper-class families. Once elected, Presidents often bring members of the elite into their administrations. Studies of cabinet-level appointees from the 1890s onward followed this pattern (Mintz, 1975). Well over one-half, and possibly two-thirds, of the appointments went to people with links to the upper classes. Even judicial appointments tend to go to people of unusual wealth. It is estimated that 34 percent of President Clinton's nominations for federal judgeships and 32 percent of George Bush's selections were millionaires (Willing, 1997). To illustrate, twenty-five people with average assets of $1,798,000 were nominated in 1997, and fifteen were millionaires. Those with wealth enjoy lifestyles that distance them from the rest of society, as is suggested by the fact that one candidate earned $13,800 renting her luxurious home as a location for filming Hollywood movies.

Campaign Financing: Soft Money and Political Action Committees (PACs)

The cost of seeking political office rises with each election, with the bulk of it going to buy television time. Therefore, fund-raising is a constant concern. "Money is," as political consultants like to say, "the mother's milk of politics." House and Senate candidates spent an estimated $660 million in 1996, and the total cost of elections at all levels is estimated at $3 billion (*The Economist,* 1997e). Calculations suggest that the average Senate race costs about $4.5 million. That means a candidate must raise $14,000 a week every week of a six-year term to finance a reelection campaign. Campaigns in some large states cost even more, as is evidenced by the fact that Michael Huffington spent $30 million on an unsuccessful Senate campaign in California in 1994.

Soft Money.   Wealthy individuals and families were once the major contributors to election campaigns, but a series of campaign financing reforms enacted in the 1970s weakened the influence of wealthy citizens and radically altered campaign financing. Individuals' donations are currently limited to $1000 per candidate per election, and there is a ceiling of $25,000 annually for all national elections. There are, however, no real limits on so-called **soft money** contributions to political parties to be used for "party-building" activities. The original idea behind soft money was that the money would be used for nonpartisan political activities such as citizen education or voter registration drives. Approximately $235 million in soft money was donated to political parties in 1996, often in exchange for the chance to make personal contact with decision-makers. Large soft-money donors to the Democratic campaign could, for example, spend a night in the Lincoln bedroom in the White House or enjoy coffee or a meal with the President. One dinner with the President for a select group of sixteen people raised $488,000 (Keen, Hasson, & Squitieri, 1997). Nine hundred and thirty-eight White House guests contributed $10,176,840, an average of $10,849 apiece, although many were long-time friends who gave nothing (Bennet, 1997). Contributors to the Republican side could, for $6000, attend the Super Bowl with powerful House members or, for $5000, enjoy a golf weekend with some twenty members of Congress (Wayne, 1997). Ambassadorships to foreign nations are a good example of political favors for large donors. An ambassador to France under President Clinton was a New York City investment banker who contributed some $600,000 to the party.

Donations of money in exchange for the opportunity to try and influence office holders is not a new development in American politics, but the 1996 election produced an unprecedented number of allegations that soft money was used illegally for clearly partisan purposes in violation of the law (Drew, 1997). In one exchange of partisan charges, soft money was used to sponsor ads that accused Republicans of endangering Medicare, which in turn inspired an equally partisan ad that charged that Democrats were controlled by labor bosses.

PACs.   Campaign financing reform legislation also endorsed **Political Action Committees** (PACs) designed to encourage smaller donors to pool their money and thus have more influence than they could individually. Any group or organization may form a PAC, and virtually all major labor unions, corporations, and interest groups support them. Corporations or unions may not contribute directly to PACs, but they can organize them and facilitate contributions by their members. Each PAC is limited to donations of $5000 per candidate per election. There were, in 1996, 4000 PACs, and they accounted for one-third of all contributions (*The Economist,* 1997e). Political Action Committees are thus a critical source of funds for politicians.

PAC contributions are distributed in different ways. Sometimes they are used to bolster the candidacy of a specific individual or a particular party based on the belief that they will pursue a specific political agenda once in office. Business leaders, for example, tend to favor the Republican party because they anticipate more favorable treatment from them. However, PACs are usually much more pragmatic; they tend to target incumbents because nine out of ten typically retain their seats, and more often than not money is spread among all major candidates to assure supporting the candidate who eventually wins. To illustrate, the largest corporate PACs in a recent election distributed 53 percent of their money to Republicans and 47 percent to Democrats (Clawson, Neustadtl, & Scott, 1992). In that way contributors guarantee themselves access to whoever is the office holder. It is very simple: "The PAC gives you access. It makes you a player," explains the chair of a business PAC (Clawson, Neustadtl, & Scott, 1992: 1).

Corporations are aware that they can not ordinarily prevent legislation that is popular, even if it is detrimental to their interests. For example, things like corporate taxes, occupational safety, and clean air are too popular with American voters to ever be eliminated entirely. Rather, the usual goal of corporate PACs is to win special benefits for their particular company or industry (see accompanying Case Study). They seek to weaken legislation that is costly or cumbersome or win exemptions, extensions, or exclusions from laws that they cannot prevent. Such exemptions are often hidden or buried in obscure sections of bills and thus escape public scrutiny. For example, a 1986 law increasing corporate tax rates is 880 pages long; Section 739, subsection J, paragraph iii, contains an exemption that limits the tax liability of one company. The firm is identified only as "a corporation incorporated on June 13, 1917, which has its principal place of business in Bartlesville, Oklahoma" (Clawson, Neustadtl & Scott, 1992: 91).[2]

---

[2]The only firm that fits this description is Philips Petroleum.

CASE STUDY:
Corporate Welfare

The success of business groups in the political sector shows up clearly in **corporate welfare,** the tangle of tariffs, subsidies, laws, regulations, tax breaks, and exemptions that benefit business and cost taxpayers millions of dollars each year in lost revenues or higher prices. It is difficult to know the precise cost of corporate welfare, but the tab is high by any estimate. One research center calculates corporate welfare at about $60 billion in industry-specific tax breaks, and another $75 billion in government spending that directly benefits business (Borrus, 1997). The extent of corporate welfare shows up in things such as higher drug prices, television channel giveaways, subsidies for foreign advertising, and the federal census of the population.

Drug Prices. Pharmaceutical companies face the prospect of price competition from generic drugs when the patents on their patented products expire. Consequently, they engage in extensive lobbying campaigns to extend their patents and thus prevent competition. The absence of competition translates into higher prices for consumers. For example, in 1996 a quiet amendment to a budget bill extended the patent on the anti-inflammatory drug "Daypro" (with $280 million in annual sales), shielding the maker from competition for an extra two years (Glastris, Barnes, Jenkins & Shute 1997). The company's political contributions amounted to $256,875.

And 1994 witnessed a bureaucratic miscalculation that turned into a major windfall for pharmaceutical companies. A technical error in a trade agreement inadvertently granted a group of 109 drugs special protection from generic competition. Some senators sought to rectify the error when they realized that consumers and insurers would pay some $6 billion in higher prices. However, drug companies were able to convince enough senators not to correct the error. A spokesperson for a drug company that stood to gain $2 billion by maintaining high prices, and one that subsequently contributed $487,000 to the Republican National Committee, insists that lawmakers' votes were based on the merits of the bill, not politics (Glastris, Barnes, Jenkins & Shute 1997).

Television Channels. In 1997 the Federal Communications Commission allocated free broadcast channels to television stations that will allow them to transmit digital video in the future. The broadcast industry that benefited from this action had contributed more than $850,000 to political candidates. It was money well spent, because had the channels been auctioned off as public airwaves usually are, they would have cost broadcasters about $30 billion dollars, enough to grant a $260 tax refund to every household.

Foreign Advertising. American companies typically compete in the global marketplace. The government annually contributes about $100 million a year to help American companies advertise their products abroad. That means taxpayers are helping to subsidize the advertising budgets of corporate giants like McDonald's, Campbell's soups, Mars candy, Miller beer, and Gallo wine, among others. The companies who receive these subsidies defend them on the grounds that the money allows them to sell their products in the highly competitive foreign market for food and beverages, which translates into jobs for Americans. Critics argue that in a true market economy businesses should succeed or fail on their own merits rather than being supported by taxpayers.

The Census.   The Constitution mandates that the government count the population every decade to determine representation in Congress, and the results are also used for allocating various forms of federal aid. The census is strongly defended by corporate America because the census also collects a vast amount of information on consumer habits and demographic data that is very useful to retailers. In 1997 lobbyists for JCPenny, Sears, and other stores were able to frustrate attempts by the census bureau to cut costs by reducing the collection of such data (Peyser, 1997). The census costs taxpayers $4 billion and provides business with enormous benefits, free of charge.

Business Lobbies

There are also much more obscure but powerful business-sponsored groups such as the Business Roundtable, the Business Council, the National Chamber of Commerce, and the National Planning Association that seek to shape foreign policy and social welfare programs and forestall antibusiness legislation (Useem, 1983). The work of the Business Roundtable, founded in 1972, exemplifies the inner workings of political influence. It is composed of about two hundred top executives from some of the largest industrial corporations. The group works through a dozen "task forces" that develop policy recommendations that are distributed to members of Congress and the executive branch, and individual members personally lobby law makers. The Business Roundtable is generally credited with successfully obstructing attempts to create a federal Consumer Protection Agency that would have meant more regulation for business and industry. The American Conference of Governmental Industrial Hygienists is much less well known than the Business Roundtable, but it had a powerful impact on shaping regulations concerning toxic substances in the workplace (see accompanying Case Study).

Informal Forms of Influence

It does not always require campaign donations for members of the elite to contact government officials, because they often move in the same social circles as political decision-makers. There is, for instance, a network of national clubs and resorts where

---

CASE STUDY:
OSHA, ACGIH, and PELs

The Occupational Safety and Health Administration (OSHA) was created in 1970, and one mandate was to formulate rules to protect workers from exposure to hazardous substances. Scientists estimate that as many as 60,000 chemicals used in industry pose a potential health threat, and among the most notoriously dangerous are known carcinogens such as asbestos and benzene. Consequently, there are "permissible exposure limits" (PELs) for approximately 600 of the most dangerous substances. PELs define, for example, the maximum level of toxic substances that may be present in the air workers breathe. The current air quality standard for formaldehyde is one molecule per million molecules of air.

Permissible exposure limits for these 600 substances were most recently updated in 1989. Eleven different groups offered chemical exposure standards to OSHA. Ultimately the limits proposed by the American Conference of Governmental Industrial Hygienists (ACGIH) prevailed because they were "most suitable." The standards adopted by OSHA for 459 of the chemicals (79 percent) copied ACGIH guidelines exactly and in some cases adopted less stringent standards than this group recommended. In addition, OSHA declined to regulate another forty-two chemicals that its own scientists felt should be regulated.

It thus appears that ACGIH was instrumental in establishing the levels of exposure for 30 million American workers. Despite its formal name, the group is not a governmental agency or a public interest group of concerned scientists, but rather a private group linked to the chemical companies that are subject to the regulations it helped create. It is alleged that virtually every member of the small group that actually wrote the standards is an employee of the chemical companies that make or use the chemicals in the manufacturing process, either as a paid consultant or a worker on loan to ACGIH. The group holds no public meetings nor routinely makes its records public, and industry representatives are regularly consulted, but not trade union representatives. Consequently, it is suggested that employees of the major chemical companies wrote the safety standards for some of the chemicals their firms produce.

Critics fault the quality of the research the group does and argue that it is inappropriate for a group with ties to chemical companies to establish standards for industry. Representatives of OSHA point out that they have an obligation to strike a balance between protecting workers and creating standards that are technically and financially feasible for the chemical industry. Thus, the chemical industry has had a major influence on the shape of regulations, but the workers exposed to them have not (Bauers & Wallick, 1989).

---

the elite socialize informally with members of the government (Domhoff, 1974). Among the most well-known is the Bohemian Grove, an exclusive camp in northern California with a membership that includes corporate executives (officers of forty of the fifty largest) and bankers (twenty of the largest twenty-five). The guest list at one of their meetings suggests that these sessions create the opportunity for business people to mingle with other powerful segments of society; several major university presidents were there, as were two members of the President's cabinet, the Chairman of the Joint Chiefs of Staff, the president of United Press International, and the Governor of California.

Actually, the boundary between government and business is often blurred by the regular interchange of personnel between government, industry, and lobbying groups. This process of movement among jobs is referred to as the **revolving door** of power, money, and politics. The revolving door finds people leaving government jobs and moving into the private sector and sometimes eventually back into government. Federal law prevents them from lobbying Congress for one year after leaving government, but they are free to make contact after that point. To illustrate, soon after Bob Dole failed in his run for the Presidency, he accepted a $600,000 position with a major Washington law firm that lobbies the government on behalf of corporate clients (Lavelle, 1997). Other members of the same firm include former Treasury Secretary Lloyd Bentsen, former Texas Governor Ann Richards, and former Senate majority leader George Mitchell. Onetime governmental officials have sensitive information about pending legislation and a host of personal contacts that can prove useful in influencing the course of future government actions. It is also argued that the lure of potential high-paying jobs after retiring from politics could encourage government officials to be more cooperative with business and industry during their tenure in Washington.

WHITE-COLLAR AND BLUE-COLLAR POLITICAL ACTIVITY

The broad middle classes also seek to shape political policies by working for political candidates, contributing money, and joining organized interest groups. Some are active participants in government at the national, state, and local levels. Moreover, numerically this group holds the balance of electoral power in elections. There are, however, important class differences within this broad category, and the most consistent finding is that almost all forms of political activity and participation decrease at each lower class level.

The Upper Middle Class in Government

A very large proportion of the people who hold seats in Congress are upper middle class, joining the House or Senate from careers in the professions or private business. It has, for example, long been the case that members of a single upper-middle-class occupation—lawyers—dominate the Congress. Fifty-six members of the Senate (56 percent) and 174 members of the House (40 percent) in the 105th Congress are attorneys. People in upper-middle-class occupations have major advantages in the political arena—education, income, social prestige, lifestyle, managerial experience, and social contacts—all of which are factors that enable them to become active in local civic and political enterprises. Candidates for public office are recruited from this pool of people. One consequence of this situation is that upper-middle-class interests receive special attention in the Congress as reflected in some elements of the tax laws—such as the ability to deduct interest on mortgages for second homes and tax-sheltered retirement income.

Direct participation in the sense of holding political office is rare among members of the lower middle or working classes. Time and resources are a factor, but so too is the work situation. Clerical and blue-collar jobs seldom provide people with the opportunities to develop skills in directing and managing other people (Kohn & Schooler, 1983).

Lobbying and PACs

Many of the wealthiest PACs are organized around upper-middle-class or working-class occupations. For example, attorneys', teachers', physicians', automobile dealers', real estate brokers' and accountants' PACs all dispensed over one million dollars to candidates in 1996 and still have millions of dollars on hand for future campaigns (Exhibit 7.1). Over a million dollars was also disbursed by labor unions such as machinists and auto workers. The work of these groups enables them to protect and enhance the interests of their own members, and this often puts them in competition with one another on some issues. Trial lawyers and physicians are, for example, major contributors, because they often confront each other over the size of financial awards in medical malpractice cases. Physicians' groups regularly seek to impose limits on the size of penalties imposed on doctors and hospitals in malpractice cases, while attorneys whose fees are linked to the size of awards oppose such limits. Situations exactly like this lead pluralists to argue that no one group is ever able to prevail in all cases.

Trial lawyers also find themselves pitted against corporate interests because they pursue product liability cases against businesses. The President of the U.S.

EXHIBIT 7.1 Financial Disbursements, Political Action Committees, 1996

PAC	DISBURSEMENTS
Association of Trial Lawyers	$5,084,785
National Education Association	5,031,657
American Federation of State and Municipal Employees	4,307,997
American Medical Association	4,133,528
United Auto Workers	3,955,068
Machinists	3,615,292
National Automobile Dealers Association	3,248,147
Realtors	2,229,891
American Institute of Certified Public Accountants	1,848,826

Source: Federal Election Commission, FECInfo Page, *PAC Summary Totals, 1996.*
(On-line at: http://www.tray.com/cgi-win/pacsum.exe).

Chamber of Commerce, the nation's largest lobbyist on behalf of business, openly targets trial lawyers whose "main objective is to get money for themselves, not for the plaintiffs," he claims (Belton, 1997). And manufacturers point out that the cost of lawsuits against them is ultimately passed on to consumers in the form of higher prices. Lawsuits add $23 to the $120 price of aluminum ladders and $3000 to the $18,000 cost of heart pacemakers.

Labor Unions

Labor unions are among the largest contributors to political campaigns despite the fact that union membership in the United States has been declining, currently enrolling about 15 percent of the workforce. Teamsters, the United Auto Workers, and government workers are the best financed. Labor unions have had mixed results over the last decade in winning legislation benefiting members of the working class. Probably the most decisive defeat occurred with the passage of the NAFTA, which labor unions opposed because they believed that American jobs would be lost.

VOTING AND POLITICAL PARTICIPATION

It is estimated that one-half the world's population lives in countries that restrict voting rights in some way. Those people reside in nations at war or under the control of autocratic regimes that outlaw political parties or control the selection of candidates for elected office. Citizens in the rest of the world have the prerogative to elect lawmakers. The right to vote, to exert some influence over the course of governmental action by choosing among candidates for political office, does not mean that people will necessarily exercise that right. Despite its powerful democratic traditions, the United States has a relatively low level of participation in the electoral process when compared to other industrial democracies. Voter turnout is typically about 50 percent of all adults; that figure lags well behind nations such as Italy, the Netherlands, Belgium, Australia, Sweden, Germany, and Norway where voting averages above 80 percent (Jackman, 1987).

Many factors influence voter turnout, but class, gender, race and ethnicity are among the most salient. The data in Exhibit 7.2 report voting patterns in the 1994 elections in the United States, where only 45.6 percent of employed adults over eighteen went to the polls. Women (47 percent) were more likely to cast ballots than men (44 percent). There is also a clear relationship between social class and voting, especially at the upper and lower reaches of the stratification system. The highest rates of participation are found among the upper middle class, where approximately six out of ten people cast votes. Voting among members of the lower middle class stands at about 50 percent. Turnout slips to about one in three eligible voters among the working class. The lowest levels of voting are found among the unskilled segment of the poor, where only about 23 percent cast a ballot. The service sector of the poor has a higher level of participation, similar to that of blue-collar operatives.

EXHIBIT 7.2 Patterns of Voter Turnout, the Elections of 1994

CLASS/OCCUPATION	All	MEN			WOMEN		
		White	African-American	Latino/a	White	African-American	Latino/a
Upper middle class							
Managerial	59%	61%	56%	35%	59%	51%	46%
Professional	63	65	57	46	65	57	52
Lower middle class							
Technicians	49	55	47	38	47	37	32
Sales workers	45	52	35	22	43	27	25
Clerical	51	49	38	39	53	47	35
Working class							
Crafts workers	37	38	36	14	34	40	12
Operatives	28	29	32	10	28	30	8
Transportation workers	33	32	36	14	43	54	28
The poor							
Service	34	39	33	14	33	34	14
Laborers	23	23	21	10	29	30	15
All persons	46	46	37	19	49	41	26

Source: U.S. Bureau of the Census, *November 1994 Voting and Registration,* June 4, 1996, Table 11, "Voting and Registration of Employed Persons by Race, Hispanic Origin, Sex, and Major Occupational Group." (On-line at: http://www.census.gov/population/socdemo/voting/work/tab11.txt).

Voter turnout among African Americans (37 percent) lags behind that of whites (46 percent), but the overall pattern of class-related voting is repeated. One very interesting exception does stand out; African-American members of the working class (both women and men) are generally more likely to vote than are members of the white working class. Latino/as have a very low overall level of voter turnout, as shown in the 1994 elections where only about 21 percent voted. The low Latino/a vote is a complex phenomenon and has a number of sources (del Pinal & Singer, 1997). It must be remembered that approximately one-third of the Latino/a population in the United States are ineligible because they are not yet citizens. Latino/as are overrepresented among the poor and the less-skilled segments of the working class, and these groups always have lower rates of voter turnout than members of white-collar occupations. Language is a barrier for others, distancing them from involvement in the process, and in some cases literacy tests are conducted in English. In addition, a high proportion of Latino/as are young, and political participation is consistently low among younger people in all groups.

Party preference also reflects the interaction of class and ethnicity. Support for the Democratic party has been consistently stronger among those at the lower levels of the stratification system, and African Americans tend to identify themselves as Democrats by a margin of eight to one. Latino/as nationwide also tend to support

Democratic candidates, with the exception of Cubans, many of whom are political refugees who favor the stronger anti-Communist stance of the Republican party and have memories of the failure of the Kennedy administration to support revolutionaries at the Bay of Pigs. However, within the Latino/a population, more issues divide them than unite them (DeSipio, 1996).

Voter turnout is but one measure of involvement in the political process. Others include keeping abreast of political matters, contributing money, and becoming actively involved in political campaigns. All follow the same general pattern found in voter turnout, viz., the very lowest levels of involvement tend to be found at the lowest levels of the stratification system.

GENDER IN THE POLITICAL SPHERE

Organized women's suffrage movements date from the middle of the nineteenth century, and in 1893 New Zealand became the first nation to grant women the same voting rights as men. Scandinavian countries (Norway, Denmark, and Finland) followed early in the twentieth century and the United States in 1920. It took until the 1940s for women in France and Italy to win the right to vote and until 1971 in Switzerland. Today, women have the legal right to vote and hold office everywhere except in a few nations in the Middle East and Asia. Global data on voting by gender is not available, but in the United States women are currently somewhat more likely to vote than men, a trend that first appeared late in the 1970s. Prior to that point men were more likely to vote than women.

The Gender Gap in Voting

Since women vote in greater numbers than men, their votes can be decisive. In the 1996 Presidential election men divided their votes about equally between Democrat Bill Clinton (43 percent) and Republican Bob Dole (44 percent), but women clearly favored Clinton (55 percent) over Dole (38 percent) (Seltzer, Newman, & Leighton, 1997). About 7 percent of both women and men supported Ross Perot. This is but one facet of a broader pattern of female support for the Democratic party that has been evident in elections for national office since the 1960s[3] and is commonly referred to as the political **gender gap**. The gender gap is typically 6 to 9 percent in Presidential elections.

The gender gap has its origins in the differing attitudes of men and women toward government and political issues in general and the stance of the Republican party on specific social and economic issues of particular interest to women. To begin with, women in America, when compared to men, tend to be more critical of business, have greater economic worries, and are more favorably disposed to an

---

[3]Women have been more likely to support Democratic Presidential candidates since 1964 and consistently more likely to support Democratic Congressional candidates since 1982. Women have been more likely to identify with the Democratic party since 1964 (Seltzer, Newman, & Leighton, 1997).

active role of government in addressing social issues. This is an outlook that is generally closer to the political philosophy of the Democratic party than Republicans.

Moreover, the position of the Republican party on a number of specific issues contributed to the alienation of women. Many see 1980 as a watershed year, because that was the point at which the party adopted a platform that supported a constitutional ban on abortions and decided to oppose the Equal Rights Amendment, thus abandoning several decades of support for that goal (Melich, 1996). Although not all women favored either initiative, they did serve to separate many women (and men) from the party. The party also became identified with opposition to social programs that benefit many more women than men: Medicaid, Social Security, parental leave, nutritional programs for women and children. In contrast, the Democratic party has endorsed positions that resonate with women—gun control, environmental protection, women's health issues, and education and job training.

Gender and Class.   Women at the lower ends of the stratification system are, just as are men, more disposed to the Democratic party. Women at that level are plagued by economic insecurity, even in periods of prosperity, because they are more sensitive to the consequences of low wages and the threat of unemployment. Their concerns tend to focus on very basic issues—health insurance, child care, schools. It is the Democratic party that, over the years, has been identified with creating and protecting a safety net of social welfare programs for the more vulnerable members of society: the poverty program, Medicare and Medicaid, Social Security, unemployment insurance, and minimum wage laws. Consequently, women in general are more likely to support Democratic candidates, as shown in Exhibit 7.3, and the difference is much more pronounced at lower levels of the income hierarchy.

Gender and Race.   African-American women typically support Democrats by a margin of about nine to one. Race and class intersect for the large numbers of African-American women who hold (or whose husbands hold) low-paying blue-collar and service jobs. However, race is also an independent factor, because Democrats have long been identified with the interests of racial and ethnic minorities. This

---

EXHIBIT 7.3 Partisanship and Gender, Congressional Elections, 1990–1994 (percentage voting Democratic)

INCOME LEVEL	WOMEN	MEN	GAP
Overall	52.7%	41.6%	11.1%
Under $15,000	66.6	55.8	10.8
$15,000 to $30,000	54.1	47.2	6.9
$30,000 to $50,000	50.4	39.7	10.7
$50,000 plus	49.5	36.3	13.2

Source: Richard A. Seltzer, Jody Newman, and Melissa Voorhees Leighton, *Sex as a Political Variable.* Boulder, CO: Lynne Rienner, 1997, Table 3.10, pages 58–60.

dates from the coalition of working class and minority voters forged by Franklin Roosevelt in the 1930s. Therefore, the party is associated with support for civil rights legislation, voting rights, and affirmative action.

Women in Government

Individual women have gained leadership roles in government in the years since they won the right to hold political office. Margaret Thatcher in Great Britain, Golda Meir in Israel, and Gro Harlem Brundtland in Norway exerted a powerful influence over the affairs of their nations. However, women as a group hold a relatively modest share of positions in government compared to their numbers in the general population. Women around the world hold just 10 percent of the seats in national legislatures and 6 percent of their cabinet offices. The Scandinavian countries such as Finland and Sweden have the highest levels of women's political participation, while countries such as Japan and Jordan exhibit much more modest levels. Some examples of the proportion of political participation are shown in Exhibit 7.4.

These numbers confirm that women are underrepresented in government in the United States, but simultaneously signal significant progress since the 1960s when government was almost exclusively a male domain. Women have had to overcome a whole host of obstacles. There was, for one, the social division of labor between home and work that extended to the political arena. As late as 1972 a majority of Americans felt that women should concentrate their energies on the home and family and "leave running the country up to men" (Lipman-Bluman, 1984: 189). Gender stereotypes suggested they lacked the traits needed for political leadership. Then too, women's social class position worked to their disadvantage, with relatively small numbers of women holding the upper-middle-class occupations that are the traditional recruiting

EXHIBIT 7.4 Women's Role in Governments, 1994

COUNTRY	SHARE OF SEATS IN NATIONAL LEGISLATURES	FEMALE MAYORS	FEMALE COUNCIL MEMBERS	SHARE OF CABINET OFFICES
Canada	17%	—	18%	14%
Finland	39	16	30	39
Great Britain	7	—	25	9
Israel	9	0	11	9
Japan	7	0	3	6
Jordan	3	—	—	3
Netherlands	29	12	22	31
Russia	8	0	30	0
Sweden	34	—	34	30
United States	10	16	21	15

Source: United Nations Development Programmme, *Human Development Report.* New York: Oxford University Press, 1995, Table A2.4, pages 60–61.

ground for political candidates. Finally, it is difficult for newcomers (women or men) to unseat incumbents who are reelected about 90 percent of the time.

These disadvantages were challenged on a large scale beginning in the 1960s. Participation in the civil rights movement and the women's movement led to broader political involvement and political action (Lipman-Bluman, 1984). Women, for example, played a major role in grassroots attempts to revitalize communities and influence local governments on issues ranging from industrial pollution, poverty, the declining qualities of schools, deterioration of neighborhoods, and toxic waste activism (Brown & Ferguson, 1995). Such movements appear to have mobilized both middle- and working-class women.

By the 1970s a number of groups such as the National Women's Political Caucus were formed to promote and foster political participation. Women increased their involvement in party politics at the community and state levels and began seeking elective office in ever-greater numbers. The combination of grassroots experiences and success in local politics provided the seasoning and credibility necessary to seek higher political office. Money also entered into the calculus at that point with the creation of fund-raising groups such as EMILY's List (Early Money Is Like Yeast), formed to provide campaign funds to women very early in the electoral process when it is essential to sustain support. Interestingly, by 1996 the EMILY's List PAC was the largest single contributor to candidates, distributing over $13 million. Thus, during the 1980s women were able to show significant progress in gaining access to positions of political power, both elected and appointive. Women currently hold positions in Congress and in the Cabinet in Washington, in every state legislature, and are governors and mayors.

Gender in Elections.   As more women have entered the political arena, gender has lost some of its saliency as a factor in choosing among candidates. This is illustrated by public opinion polls. In 1937 this question was posed, "If your party nominated a woman for president, would you vote for her if she were qualified for the job?" At that point less than one-third (31 percent) admitted they would support a woman, but in 1994 the same question elicited agreement by over 90 percent of both men and women (Seltzer, Newman, & Leighton, 1997: 17).

Some reluctance to support female candidates for political office remains, and gender stereotypes play a role in explaining those attitudes. There is a tendency to believe that assumed female gender traits render women less suitable for the demands of higher political offices than men. Definitions of a "good" or "ideal" candidate for President still favor masculine traits (Rosenwasser & Dean, 1989; Leeper, 1991; Huddy & Terkildsen, 1994). Perceived male traits such as strength, self-confidence, determination, and decisiveness are considered more helpful in dealing with issues such as the economy, defense, or the military. Women's perceived strengths (warmth, gentleness, compassion) are viewed as more suitable for the needs of legislative or judicial posts. In contrast with typical male traits, those typical female traits are considered more suitable for lower, nonexecutive positions. Thus, women who contest for national office must confront bias among some voters.

There is also some indication that women are treated differently by the media (Kahn & Goldenberg, 1991; Kahn, 1992). Analysis of Senate races shows that women tend to receive less coverage than men, and the coverage is likely to remind voters of candidates' gender. The media tends to downplay issues and devotes its efforts to the process, *i.e.,* questions of the ability of women candidates to win, and emphasizes their effectiveness in stereotypical policy areas—education, health, poverty.

Obviously, polls and attitude surveys have limits, and the question of actual gender bias in the voting booth is much more difficult to measure. Comparing the success of women candidates pitted against men is never easy because so many factors impinge upon voters' decisions that it is difficult to apportion the exact influence of gender. There is some evidence that women voters are more likely to support women candidates (Huddy & Terkildsen, 1994). However, gender is not always the decisive factor for most voters. Party preference is a major factor in voting, but voters will cross party lines to vote for a candidate perceived as strong—woman or man—or against a weak candidate—woman or man (Zipp & Plutzer, 1985). On the whole it appears that men and women candidates are evaluated in the same manner and have an equal chance of being elected (Seltzer, Newman, & Leighton, 1997).

Gender and Legislative Policy.   Electoral victories place increasing numbers of women in positions where they are able to influence public policy through the introduction of legislation and by supporting or opposing statutes. Legislative decisions are complicated and shaped by many factors, including ideology, the characteristics of their constituencies, individual priorities, political party affiliation, and persuasion from interest groups. Gender is also one of the factors that enters into legislative behavior. Female legislators tend to have more liberal voting records and give higher priority to issues relating to women, children, and families[4] than males, who are more likely to focus on business and economic legislation (Thomas, 1994).

To illustrate, party affiliation is decisive on most votes in the U.S. Congress, with men and women voting with their parties on issues such as foreign aid, campaign reform, and governmental reorganization (Segal & Bruzy, 1995). However, on certain key pieces of legislation, women (both Democrat and Republican) vote much differently than men. They oppose the prohibition of publicly funded abortions, support handgun control, and endorse the Family and Medical Leave Act. Thus, gender becomes a salient factor on issues that focus directly on women's rights but also on broader issues that deter violence, promote health and safety, protect the environment, support the family and child care, and upgrade education. It suggests that the increase in the proportion of women in political office has the potential to produce a discernible impact on the shape of public policy.

---

[4]These are sometimes defined as "women's issues," but that is misleading because they transcend gender and include education, safety and health, and workplace matters that benefit all members of society.

Race, Gender, and Policy Priorities.   African-American women in legislatures stand with non–African-American women on most issues and with African-American legislators on minority issues. If there is any single difference it is that African-American women exhibit an unusual degree of consensus on policy priorities (Barrett, 1995). For African-American women policy makers, the most pressing issues are clear—education, health care, employment.

MINORITIES IN THE POLITICAL SPHERE

The 1960s are remembered for the violence that accompanied attempts to end barriers to African-American participation in government. Prohibitive poll taxes, stringent literacy tests, closed primaries, and outright intimidation were employed to deny the vote and access to public office. Massive voter registration drives supported by the Voting Rights Act of 1965 enfranchised hundreds of thousands of new voters. At the same time whites' attitudes toward African-American candidates softened. Tangible evidence of this is found in public opinion polls tracking attitudes toward an African-American candidate for President. In 1958, almost 80 percent of African Americans, compared to only 35 percent of whites, expressed readiness to support an African-American candidate, but by 1997 more than 90 percent of both groups expressed a willingness to endorse an African American for President (Holmes, 1997). The result is that African Americans, Latino/as, and other minorities now hold office at all levels of government ranging from local school boards to big-city mayors, from state legislators to state governors and cabinet officers in Washington; and in 1996 Colin Powell was courted by both major political parties. The election of minority candidates to public office is of inestimable symbolic value, validating the increasing openness of the political system.

Lower overall minority voter turnout has been noted, but that does not mean that these groups are not a significant political force, especially in those areas where they form a meaningful segment of the population. This is evident among the Latino/a population, where the six states with the largest Latino/a populations—California, Texas, Florida, New York, Illinois, and New Jersey—have over 170 of the 270 electoral votes needed to elect a President. Latino/a voters made up a full 20 percent of the voters in the 1997 New York City mayoral campaign (Levy, 1997). Consequently, both parties openly and aggressively court Latino/a voters. The growth of the Latino/a population in these states has the potential to give them even greater political leverage into the twenty-first century.

Race and Policy.   Political participation among minorities has positive benefits for minority citizens. One consequence is the expansion of minority businesses. Most elected African-American officials give very high priority to fostering African-American–owned business, and they are in a position to accomplish this through the distribution of contracts and government purchasing practices (Jaynes & Williams, 1989). In addition, some municipalities initiated set-asides for minority businesses. The result is that African-American–owned businesses tend to be larger and more successful in cities with African-American mayors than in those with white mayors (Bates & Williams, 1993).

Policing is also affected by African-American participation. Policing is an issue of long-standing concern to African-American citizens because some police departments, like many other organizations, once systematically discriminated against minority employment and were often socially distanced from minority communities. Moreover, incidents of white police mistreatment of African-American citizens continue to surface all too frequently. Hence progress in this area would seem to be a vital component in fostering interracial tolerance.

A comprehensive review of police department activities suggests that certain kinds of innovations in policing practices are more likely to emerge in communities with African-American political involvement (Saltzstein, 1989). For example, cities with large African-American populations of potential voters are more likely to have community outreach programs (storefront offices, meetings with African-American community groups) and a policy of measured responses (mediation as opposed to arrest) to disturbances of the peace. Communities with African-American mayors make more progress with minority representation on the police force and in the creation of civilian review boards that oversee police conduct. Thus, it appears that African-American political strength in the form of votes or elected representation does have the potential under the right circumstances to translate into specific programs.

CONCLUSION: CLASS AND POLITICAL ALIENATION

One of the more notable trends in the political sphere over the second half of the twentieth century is increasing **political alienation,** the erosion of public support and confidence in America's political system (Lipset & Schneider, 1983). Political alienation is caused by a combination of two perceptions of the workings of government. One could be called "estrangement," a lack of faith or trust in government. The decline in trust in government over the last half of the twentieth century is dramatic. Between the mid-1950s and the 1990s, the proportion of Americans who felt that "you can trust the government to do what is right most of the time" fell from 75 percent to 22 percent (Seltzer, Newman, & Leighton, 1997). The numbers are even more dismal when the question focuses on a specific branch of government. In the 1990s, only 7 percent of the public express a "great deal" of trust in Congress and 10 percent in the executive branch (Smith, 1997).

Estrangement focuses on feelings of trust, but there is also the more pragmatic issue of "efficacy," beliefs about the ability to have an impact on the political process or activities of government. A lack of efficacy means a sense of powerlessness to have an impact on the direction of public policy. Powerlessness is unmistakable in feelings that special interest groups have too much control or that political leaders are out of touch with the people. Americans tend to believe that special interest groups exercise disproportionate influence. Three of five people agree with this statement, "No matter what laws are passed, special interests will always find a way to maintain their power in Washington" (Gallup Poll, 1997).

The observed increases in political alienation are shaped by many factors, including some that touch all levels of the stratification system. Recurring public scandals (Watergate, Iran-Contra, Savings and Loan bailout, campaign financing) have a broad negative impact on faith in government. Moreover, specific governmental actions produce patterns of dissatisfaction among different segments of the population. Reductions in social welfare spending increase feelings of political disaffection among the poor, while members of the elite and upper middle classes are alienated by reductions in government subsidies to industry (*e.g.*, tax credits, grants of land or property). Political disaffection among the lower, middle, and working classes increases with corporate profits and levels of debt. Thus, government actions that bring benefits to one class are likely to engender dissatisfaction among other segments of society.

As would be expected, disaffection and efficacy tend to be linked, and the general pattern that emerges is that people at each lower level in the stratification system feel more alienated, with greater feelings of disaffection and lower perceptions of effectiveness (Verba, Nie, & Kim, 1978). Class position shapes alienation in many subtle ways. More education means greater familiarity with the dynamics of the political process, and having more money to contribute to candidates increases a sense of involvement and direction. It has also been suggested that the work of most people below the level of the upper middle class does not give them much experience with the exercise of power; the resulting lack of power in the economic sector may contribute to more general feelings of powerlessness in the political sector.

The irony is that political alienation is in part self-perpetuating in the sense that feelings of powerlessness can contribute to the failure to engage in the very activities—voting, political organization—that might have an impact and produce a feeling of having some control over the political process. Consequently, class position contributes to feelings of alienation and in turn reduces the effectiveness of the least-advantaged classes. At the other extreme, a sense of control can stimulate even greater political effort, which in turn produces a greater effect on the political process (Herring, 1989).

This is evidenced by the interaction between political participation of African Americans in cities with African-American mayors (Bobo & Gilliam, 1990). In those cities the levels of political knowledge and political participation among African Americans is higher than among African Americans in other cities and higher than whites at comparable class levels. This suggests that African Americans in leadership positions instill a greater sense of efficacy and stimulate greater involvement.

KEY CONCEPTS

corporate welfare	**Political Action**	**power elite**
gender gap	**Committees (PACs)**	**revolving door**
elite theory	**political alienation**	**soft money**
pluralists		

SUGGESTED READING

DAN CLAWSON, ALAN NEUSTADT, AND DENISE SCOTT, *Money Talks: Corporate PACs and Political Influence.* New York: Basic Books, 1992. A far-reaching analysis of the organization and operation of business PACs, including interviews with corporate officials.

ELIZABETH DREW, *Whatever It Takes.* New York: Viking Penguin, 1997. A disturbing portrait of the role of money in shaping the elections of 1996.

C. WRIGHT MILLS, *The Power Elite.* New York: Oxford University Press, 1956. Mills's original formulation of elite theory continues to be debated today.

JOSEPH S. NYE, PHILIP D. ZELIKOV, AND DAVID C. KING (eds.), *Why People Don't Trust Government.* Cambridge, MA: Harvard University Press, 1996. A collection of essays (suitable for advanced students) that explore the sources of political alienation.

RICHARD A. SELTZER, JODY NEWMAN, AND MELISSA VOORHEES LEIGHTON, *Sex as a Political Variable.* Boulder, CO: Lynne Rienner, 1997. This broad analysis of voting for and by women in the United States dispels a number of misconceptions about the role of gender in the political process.

PHILIP M. STERN, *Still the Best Congress Money Can Buy.* Washington, DC: Regnery Gateway, 1992. A highly critical appraisal of the influence of special interests on financing congressional campaigns.

SUE THOMAS, *How Women Legislate.* New York: Oxford University Press, 1994. A comparison of women's and men's legislative priorities and approach to the law making process.

MICHAEL USEEM, *The Inner Circle: Large Corporations and the Rise of Political Activity in the U.S. and U.K.* New York: Oxford University Press, 1983. This study emphasizes the links among corporate executives.

PART FOUR
Experiencing Social Stratification

Social stratification and inequality shape the way in which people experience their social and physical environment in direct and subtle ways, determining their access to the pleasures of life and influencing the way they perceive the world and organize their lives. Chapter 8 examines how experiences in the criminal justice and health care systems are linked to social class position, race, and gender. Chapter 9 explores the social organization of life at different class levels. Chapter 10 focuses on the way people think about the stratification system and their place in it.

CHAPTER 8

Class and Life Chances

THE CONCEPT OF LIFE CHANCES

Social classes are groups of individuals and families that occupy a common position in the economic system of production and distribution in industrial societies. Position in the class system has broad and significant implications. Striking income, status, and political differences separate bankers, bakers, beauticians, brokers, and bookkeepers, but the implications of class extend well beyond earnings to include the idea of life chances. Max Weber introduced the concept of **life chances,** which he described as "the typical chances for a supply of goods, external living conditions, and personal life experiences."[1] The concept of life chances focuses on the quality of life and the way that class position expands or limits access to desirable experiences such as good physical and mental health. Considerations of race and gender are, of course, also relevant.

The impact of class on life chances is often direct and conspicuous, as when limited financial resources impose some limits on the educational attainments of children or the quality of health care. The implications of class for life chances can also be less obvious and subtle. To illustrate, occupations locate people in a system

---

[1]The concept of life chances is introduced in Chapter 1.

CASE STUDY:
Class, Values, and Personality

Occupations locate individuals in a system of hierarchical authority, placing them under the jurisdiction of others and imposing some limits on their autonomy, initiative, and control over the pace and performance of their tasks. For example, work environments for members of the upper middle class tend to be intellectually challenging, offering the chance to exercise personal discretion and direct the activities of subordinates that contributes to an emphasis on self-direction and self-control. Alternatively, those occupying lower levels of the class system are typically faced with narrow repetitive tasks under close and punitive supervision that contributes to an emphasis on conformity and to instilling a more constrained and less optimistic view of the world.

Melvin L. Kohn and Carmi Schooler (1983) are among the sociologists who have explored the implications of authority relations at work on perspectives and attitudes away from the job. Their basic thesis, referred to as the **learning-generalization hypothesis,** argues that lessons learned in one sphere of life are carried over into other areas of life. Consequently, experiences encountered on the job may come to dominate not just perspectives toward work but also broader social values, social orientations, self-conceptions, and intellectual functioning. They focus on one of the most fundamental characteristics of work. Self-direction is granted, encouraged, and rewarded at the higher end of the system but discouraged at each lower level where conformity is demanded and rewarded.

This led Kohn and Schooler to explore the ways in which such lessons shape more general perspectives or values. They found a direct relationship between social class and positive self-evaluations such as having "good sense and good judgment," "self reliance," and "responsibility," all of which may be interpreted as consequences of having greater opportunities to wield responsibility on the job. There are also class differences in the characteristics people hope to instill in their children. Considerations of success, honesty, and happiness are widely defined as important, but others are apparently organized differently. There is an inverse relationship between class and an emphasis on conformity to external standards of behavior—obedience, personal neatness and cleanliness, having good manners. Thus, people at lower levels value in their children the kinds of traits that are demanded and rewarded by their class position. This pattern is replicated in other nations such as Australia, Italy, and Poland, suggesting that such value orientations may have their origins in industrial class systems (Kohn & Slomczynskai, 1990). It would seem that people's values are shaped by their work experiences, coming to value those traits that are attainable and subsequently attempting to inculcate them in the children.

of authority and power on the job that have implications for the way people perceive their world. In addition, jobs offer unequal promotion opportunities, with most upper-middle-class professional and managerial positions on career paths that present structured opportunities for people to improve their situation through individual effort. In contrast, other positions, especially unskilled and service work, offer few (if any) chances for upward movement regardless of the level of industriousness. Occupations also differ in the stability of work, offering relative security to some while confronting others with the unending threat of unemployment and financial devastation. Thus, it is evident that members of each higher class have much better chances of being promoted and much less chance of suffering unemployment.

Experiences encountered at work not only shape the way people respond to their specific jobs but also have the potential to extend beyond daily routines to the point of helping to shape their lifestyles and perceptions of the larger society and their place in it (see accompanying Case Study).

The implications of class position for life chances are highlighted by focusing on two of the most important areas of life, the criminal justice system and the health care system. Life chances within social classes are often modified by the impact of race, ethnicity, and gender.

. . . AND THE POOR GET JAIL: THE CRIMINAL JUSTICE SYSTEM

There is a widespread perception that delinquency and crime are the exclusive province of the poor, especially among young, urban, African-American males. This image is fueled by media coverage of criminal activity, and its force echoes in the words of Rev. Jesse Jackson, "There is nothing more painful to me at this stage of my life than to walk down the street and hear footsteps and start thinking about robbery—and then look around and see someone white and feel relieved" (Will, 1993). It is true that African Americans, who make up about 12 percent of the total population, comprise a disproportionate share of prison populations (32 percent of federal prisoners and 50 percent of state prisoners).[2] However, it must be remembered that ending up in jail is the end result of a long process and that the poor and minorities have different experiences at every stage of that process. Statistics show that the poor are more likely than the more affluent to be detained, arrested, charged, and convicted, and, if convicted, more likely to be sentenced to prison. In short, prison populations represent the end result of a series of decisions by people in the criminal justice system: police officers, prosecutors, juries, judges, and parole boards (Reiman, 1996).

Defining Crime.   Criminologists point out that the very act of defining crime is a social act, but the issue of the social construction of crime is beyond the scope of this volume. It can simply be noted that while certain acts are criminal by virtually

---

[2]There is some evidence that this is not a uniquely American situation. Minorities in Canada, Australia, England, and Wales are also overrepresented in prison populations (Tony, 1994).

any contemporary American definition of deviance—homicide, child abuse, arson—others are subject to different interpretations. The basic thesis is that the behavior of the poor is more likely to be defined as illegal by middle-class decision-makers (legislators, judges). Prostitution is one such case, largely illegal in the United States but lawful and licensed elsewhere. Prostitution remains illicit because the idea of sex for pay violates the values and beliefs of major segments of society. However, there are also many who favor decriminalizing prostitution because it is seen as a "victimless crime," a consensual act among adults. Prostitution is also frequently the province of poor and uneducated women, exploited by procurers and organized crime. Human rights groups claim that millions of poor women and children have fallen victim to global networks of sex traffickers since the 1970s (Pope, 1997). The women come from impoverished Asian nations and the former Soviet Union and eventually emerge in Los Angeles, New York, and Washington, DC.

The Incidence of Crime and Delinquency.   Criminologists continue to debate whether or not the men, the poor, and minorities initially commit a disproportionate share of crimes (Tittle & Meier, 1990). There is no definitive answer to that question because there are so many different kinds of crimes, ranging from vandalism to assault to embezzlement. The fact is, when asked, the majority of Americans at *all* social class levels admit that they have done things that could get them in trouble with the law. Petty theft, disorderly conduct, tax evasion, assault, auto theft, and concealed weapons are among the most common crimes. It is also clear that members of the middle classes commit many of the same crimes usually attributed to the urban poor—drugs, armed robbery, breaking and entering, and vandalism (Reiman, 1996). Most social scientists conclude that illegal behavior is relatively common at all levels in the stratification system, but that members of the criminal justice system respond differently to different groups at every point in the criminal justice process.

Detaining and Questioning.   In 1992, Robert Wilkins, an African-American Washington lawyer, was stopped and subjected to a drug search for no apparent reason other than his race. A subsequent investigation revealed that Maryland state police used race as a criterion in detaining and searching cars on Interstate 95, a major pipeline for traffickers moving drugs between Florida and the Northeast. A subsequent legal settlement prohibited the police from using race in making searches, but a 1996 review of police records revealed that an overwhelming majority (75 percent) of vehicle stops involved African Americans (Schneider, 1996). The state police note they have a clear policy prohibiting the use of race as a factor in stops and deny discrimination. Other research confirms that African Americans are more likely to be stopped by the police, although they do tend to be stopped for the same kinds of offenses (suspicion of drug possession, traffic violations, drunkenness) and are not always treated differently during the encounter (Norris, Fielding, Kemp, & Fielding, 1992).

Arrest and Charging.   It has long been known that for equally serious offenses, poor people are more likely to be arrested and, if arrested, more likely to be charged than those from higher social classes (Gold, 1966). The police are often singled out for censure on this point, with critics claiming that the police openly discriminate. Concentrating on individual biased police officers ignores the broader context in which crime occurs and the realities of policing. Police officers' actions are often determined by suspects' behavior or judgments of their character (Piliavin & Briar, 1964). To illustrate, the police (and most members of the public) are likely to respond differently to a belligerent drunk at an elegant country club or a campus fraternity house than to the same behavior at a saloon adjacent to an urban housing project. Moreover, contacts between police and civilians are more likely to end in arrest when the encounter becomes confrontational, and poor men are more likely to challenge police officers. Police also respond differently to different classes of people because they can anticipate different consequences. For example, when dealing with juvenile suspects, police officers can logically anticipate that the parents of wealthy youths are more likely to be aware of their Constitutional rights and will hire attorneys to defend themselves and consider lawsuits. The same kind of considerations influence the decisions of prosecutors who make the decision to bring formal charges. The race of suspects complicates matters for African-American males. Minority suspects are also exposed to more rigorous prosecution, including more severe charges, stiffer penalties, and full-scale prosecutions (Editors, 1988).

Conviction.   The most salient incident in the criminal justice process is conviction for a crime. Looking at all individuals accused of the same crime and having similar prior records shows that poor defendants are more frequently found guilty than the more well-to-do (Reiman, 1996). Two major factors combine to produce this result—the availability of bail and the quality of legal counsel—and both are influenced by finances.

Those released on bail are at an advantage because they are able to actively contribute to their own defense by collecting evidence and seeking out witnesses and supportive testimony. In contrast, the poor lacking the resources to meet bail are kept in prison, which is in and of itself a form of punishment. Moreover, those stranded in jail may also be more vulnerable to prosecutorial pressure and thus willing to accept plea bargains that will gain them shorter sentences or immediate release from custody.[3] The result is that they may be tempted to plead guilty to lesser charges (such as breaking and entering rather than burglary), which will set them free. Unfortunately, that freedom is bought at the cost of a criminal record that later makes it more difficult to find employment and contributes to their continued poverty.

Sentencing.   In the 1990s there is wide variation in sentences of whites and African Americans for similar offenses, showing that some jurisdictions deliver justice equally, while others do not (Crutchfield, Bridges, & Pitchford, 1994). Therefore, the overall overrepresentation of African Americans in prisons is influenced by that

---

[3]The vast majority of criminal convictions are the result of negotiated pleas, somewhere between 75 and 90 percent.

CASE STUDY:
Legal Defense for the Indigent

Court-appointed legal representation for indigent criminal defendants plays a crucial role in the criminal justice system. In 1992 about 80 percent of defendants charged with felonies in the nation's 75 largest counties relied upon a public defender or assigned counsel for legal representation (Smith & DeFrances, 1996). It is clear that government-supported counsel is not always as effective as that provided by private attorneys. In one study, public defenders won dismissals for their clients in only 11 percent of cases compared to 48 percent of the clients of private attorneys (Champion, 1989). A significant proportion of the fault must lie with the system rather than individual court-appointed lawyers or public defenders. They are often young and inexperienced in criminal work and frequently have very limited financial resources to devote to the collection of evidence and hiring expert witnesses. In addition, public defenders usually have heavy caseloads that preclude devoting enough time to each and every case. An American Bar Association study found that some public defenders have annual caseloads of more than 500 cases with up to 300 of them juveniles (Puritz, 1995).

The U.S. Supreme Court has repeatedly ruled that the threat of the death penalty puts a citizen at special risk, and consequently the legal system must be especially attentive in capital cases. Therefore, the states are obligated to provide legal aid for those too poor to afford an attorney. Unfortunately, it is often the case that, "indigent defendants on trial for their lives are frequently represented by ill-trained, unprepared, court-appointed lawyers so grossly underpaid they literally cannot afford to do the job" (Coyle, Strasser, & Lavelle, 1990: 30).

It is clear that the allocation of economic resources is a major part of the problem, either as a result of inattention or a disregard for the legal needs of the poor. For example, some states set unrealistically low limits on compensation for the lawyer's time, $1000 for the entire case in one state. For another, judges routinely deny requests for moneys for investigation and expert witnesses. Some states provide no pretrial training for lawyers preparing for capital cases, meaning that some embark upon cases with little or no experience with this special kind of case. The result is that the indigent are often represented by young and inexperienced lawyers with insufficient resources to mount an effective and credible defense.

---

consideration. Race appears to continue to play a role in certain situations, especially physical attacks (homicides and sexual assaults) against whites by African Americans (Paternoster, 1984; Spohn, 1994). In those situations African Americans consistently receive harsher sentences than whites. Between 1976 and 1994, 275 convicts were executed, and 84 percent of their victims were white, although less than one-half of all murder victims are white. Ours is still a society that reacts quickly to acts of interpersonal violence by minorities.

CASE STUDY:
Sentencing White-Collar Criminals

The very nature of some upper-middle-class occupations allows people to engage in illegal activity called white-collar crime. **White-collar crimes** are offenses committed by people acting in their legitimate occupational roles. The offenders are professionals, businesspersons, and government officials who are, by virtue of their jobs, in a position to engage in a variety of illegal or unethical acts. The crimes include accepting or paying bribes, fraud, tax evasion, and embezzlement. Billions of dollars are lost through white-collar crime. These crimes can only be committed by people in positions of authority and trust. Embezzlement(misappropriating funds that are entrusted to one's care) is a case in point. The people who have responsibility for clients' funds are lawyers, union officers, realtors, and stock brokers, not teachers, janitors, or plumbers. The proportion of all workers who embezzle or commit other white-collar crimes is small, but they are clearly treated differently than lower-class people who commit property crimes (Exhibit 8.1).

EXHIBIT 8.1 Sentencing Different Kinds of Crimes

	SENTENCED TO PRISON (PERCENTAGE)	AVERAGE SENTENCE (MONTHS)	AVERAGE TIME SERVED (MONTHS)
Crimes of the poor			
Robbery	99%	101.1 months	60.2 months
Burglary	82	62.8	26.0
Larceny/theft	39	17.9	15.2
White-collar crimes			
Fraud	48%	22.2	15.6
Tax law violation	43	25.2	11.6
Embezzlement	31	15.7	11.0

Data: *Sourcebook of Criminal Justice Statistics.* Compiled by Jeffrey Reiman, *The Rich Get Richer and the Poor Get Prison,* Boston, MA: Allyn & Bacon, 1995, Table 5, page 125.

Another consistent pattern of differential sentencing shows up in white-collar crimes. These are crimes of the upper middle class and are punished less severely than other crimes (see accompanying Case Study).

A STRATIFIED HEALTH CARE SYSTEM

The specter of ill health threatens everyone, but the risk of sickness, injury, and even death is not equally distributed across societies. One of the most consistent and disturbing findings in the health care field in the United States and elsewhere is that minorities and people lower in the stratification system suffer disproportionately from virtually every disease and have higher mortality rates than those above them in the system (Adler et al., 1993). To illustrate, a white female born in the United States has a life expectancy of 79.6 years, five years longer than a white male (73.3) or an African-American female (73.9), and almost fifteen years longer than an African-American male (64.9) (Singh, Kochanek & MacDorman, 1996). Perhaps the best single indicator of health status is the infant mortality rate, which varies dramatically among different groups in American society (Exhibit 8.2).

There is no single explanation for health risks; rather they reflect the interaction of many different factors, including poverty, health insurance coverage, unequal safety and health risks on the job, and lifestyles. Then too, for reasons that are not at all clear, there is some indication that rich and poor, African Americans and whites receive different kinds of treatments. For example, among people admitted to hospitals with heart problems, white patients were much more likely to undergo major life-saving procedures such as angioplasty, coronary bypass surgery, or cardiac catheterization (Wenneker & Epstein, 1989). This pattern prevailed regardless of age, overall health status, and insurance coverage.

Health Insurance

Living without health insurance is a constant worry, because there is apprehension that unexpected illness or injury will strike and medical bills accumulate. In 1994, about 40 million Americans (15 percent of the population) were without health insurance for the whole year, while many others were uninsured for shorter periods (Bennefield, 1995). The implications of being uninsured translate into constant worry and cause people to miss the kinds of treatments that would prevent more serious illness. For instance, one in twenty-five of the uninsured are unable to fill their prescriptions, and 30 percent report failing to get the care they needed (*The Economist,* 1997f).

Not surprisingly, the poor faced a much greater risk of being uninsured, 29 percent of the poor having no medical coverage. Minorities were also more likely to lack

---

EXHIBIT 8.2 **Infant Mortality Rates by Race and Ethnicity, 1988–1991**

Asian	6.6
White	7.4
Latina	7.6
All mothers	**9.0**
Native American	12.6
African American	17.1

Data: Deaths per thousand live births.

Source: National Center for Health Statistics, *Health, United States, 1995,* Hyattsville, MD: Public Health Service, 1996, page 99.

coverage, with about 20 percent of African Americans and one in three Latino/as without health insurance. Thanks to Medicare coverage for the elderly and Medicaid for the disadvantaged, only 13 percent of adults not in the labor force went without insurance. However, children fared badly, with one in three youngsters (18 and under) lacking health insurance for at least one month a year according to a health advocacy group (Bacon, 1997). Health insurance is an important consideration, especially for children, but universal coverage does not eliminate the link between class and health. There was, for example, no overall improvement in health indicators when Britain introduced its National Health Service (Adler et al., 1993). Moreover, Scandinavian countries that protect all citizens with universal health insurance have been able to weaken but not eliminate the link between class and illness.

Dumping Uninsured Patients.   In the 1980s the federal government mandated that hospitals that treat Medicare patients (virtually every hospital) must respond to every emergency room patient (insured or not). Hospitals must screen incoming patients, including pregnant women, and provide the minimum of care necessary to stabilize their condition before releasing them. The law was promoted by the common practice of **patient dumping,** in which hospitals turned away uninsured patients. However, a consumer group reports that the practice continues, claiming that although some 700 hospitals violated the law between 1986 and 1996, only sixty-seven hospitals were sanctioned (Associated Press, 1997). The Department of Health and Human Services admits that dumping occurs but claims that it lacks the staff to adequately enforce the law.

Occupational Safety and Health

Occupational safety and health is a major workplace issue because many people labor in environments that are dangerous in one way or another. A recent survey counted more than 6.8 million workplace injuries and illnesses, including 2.3 million that involved lost workdays (U.S. Bureau of Labor Statistics, 1995). In addition, 6000 workers were killed, an average of more than 16 workers per day in the United States (Toscano & Windau, 1994). These figures do not include long-term latent illnesses such as cancers that are difficult to link to specific workplace toxins and are consequently underreported.

Some lines of work are more hazardous than others; police work and fire-fighting are obvious examples. As a general rule, blue-collar work is more unsafe than white-collar work. Factories, mines, mills, shipyards, meat packing plants, auto assembly lines, and construction sites are dangerous places, teeming with moving machinery, power tools, electrical shocks, and toxic substances from which the effects may not appear for years. The number of occupational illnesses has been on the increase since the mid-1980s, and the bulk of that increase can be attributed to one cause, "repetitive trauma," which includes conditions due to repeated pressure, vibration, or motion. Workers facing this risk factor are clerical workers, truck drivers, meat packers, poultry processors, sewing machine operators, and assembly line workers of all kinds. In each case the job demands repeated movements or exposes people to frequent impact or shock that can cause disabling illness over time. The most well-known form of repetitive trauma is carpal tunnel syndrome, a painful wrist inflammation associated with working with computers (Kilborn, 1990).

Stress.   In addition, blue-collar work produces unexpected health risks. Despite the widespread emphasis on the dangers of the fast-paced, high-stress life of corporate executives, investment bankers, and neurosurgeons, the evidence suggests that lower-white-collar and blue-collar workers are the most likely to experience stress and be victims of heart disease (Rundel, 1987; Adler, 1989). In fact, when white-collar workers are compared to blue-collar workers, manual workers are 43 percent more likely to fall victim to coronary disease. A combination of work-related stress factors contributes to this situation, including repetitive and boring tasks (garment workers), unremitting pace (assembly lines), continual deadlines (bus drivers, waiters). All are factors over which the individual has little or no control.

Workplace Violence.   It is estimated that in 1992–93 at least 2.2 million people (3 percent of all workers) were physically attacked on the job, leading to over 1000 deaths, and another 6 million were threatened with violence (Anfusco, 1994). In fact, homicide became the second leading cause of fatalities in the workplace in the 1990s. Working-class and lower-middle-class women and men are most vulnerable to this danger because their work routines expose them to crime, usually robberies. Taxi drivers, gas station attendants, convenience store clerks, and fast-food restaurant workers all have relatively high-risk jobs. Mehrle Reeker, a sixty-year-old convenience store clerk in Florida, is a classic case, murdered during a robbery that yielded the bandit a mere $52. The overrepresentation of women in many of these sales or service jobs helps to explain why homicide is the leading cause of death for women on the job and the third leading cause for men (Anfusco, 1994).

Lifestyles

Social class differences in lifestyles that have health implications are another factor. Upper-middle-class persons appear to have been quicker to reject unhealthy lifestyles. These include behaviors such as cigarette smoking, lack of exercise, and poor nutrition, all of which are more common at lower levels in the stratification system and are associated with heart disease and some forms of cancer. Lower-class people are also less likely to engage in preventive care. To illustrate, women at each higher social class level are more likely to have Pap tests and mammograms. It appears that the poor are unlikely to develop a self-management approach to health care; rather they seek help for specific illnesses but tend not to assume a proactive approach to the behaviors that help to prevent illness (Cockerham, Lueschen, Kunz, & Spaeth, 1986).

Outreach and patient education programs can weaken but not eliminate the class–lifestyle link. However, it is important to note that lifestyles are not always simply a matter of individual choice but also a matter of opportunities. For example, there are class differences in the way health programs are offered and organized. While employees are increasingly encouraged or forced into managed-care plans, some executives continue to enjoy no-cost coverage and unlimited access to physicians and specialists (Myerson, 1996). Corporate-supported wellness and health programs are also much more likely to be aimed at members of the executive and managerial levels than the production workers on the factory floor (Rundel, 1987). In some businesses, health facilities remain an executive prerogative, a status symbol. Moreover, even where programs and facilities are available to all workers, blue-collar workers will find it more difficult to gain access to the facilities. It is, for example, difficult for large numbers to use company fitness facilities during the same fixed lunch break, and they do not have the flexibility of scheduling that executives do.

CONCLUSION: ENVIRONMENTAL JUSTICE

Most poor people face a continuing struggle. They struggle to find work, to feed their families, to maintain their homes, to educate their children, to survive on a daily basis in substandard housing and in poor neighborhoods where crime rates are high (Federman et al., 1996). The rigors of poverty thus introduce a level of everyday stress that the more advantaged do not face, and research shows that exposure to stressful life events can increase the susceptibility to illnesses such as heart disease. A new hazard was recognized in the 1980s when it was found that toxic waste sites were disproportionately located in poor and minority areas. One recent study estimates that 30 percent of minorities live in communities with commercial hazardous waste sites, up from 25 percent in 1980. One example is to be found in the Manchester area of Houston, Texas (Potok, 1994). The community surrounding a sulfuric acid regeneration plant has a per capita income of $6031, and one-third of the residents live in poverty. Ninety-eight percent of the residents are minorities, largely Latino/a.

Not all analyses confirm the link between pollution, race, and poverty, sometimes floundering on the definition of "near." Moreover, the rationale for locating chemical plants and other pollutants in these areas is multifaceted, motivated by economic considerations, the lack of political influence among the poor, and ideological racism. Proximity to toxic wastes and emissions is linked to birth defects, cancer, lupus, and a whole host of other health problems.

The implications were significant enough to prompt President Clinton to issue an executive order in 1994 requiring that federal agencies include considerations of **environmental justice** in their work, meaning that they must identify and address the potentially adverse human health effects of their actions on minority and low-income populations. Environmental justice is a complex problem that must consider the impact of construction and land use on both the physical environment and the socioeconomic environment and that includes factors such as literacy, lifestyles, occupations, property values, and community values (Millan, 1997). Therefore, a number of different projects have been challenged. In Kansas, a federal highway project was stalled because of potential damage to wetlands and the cultural life of the Haskell Indian Nations University (Lavelle, 1996). In another case, licensing for a uranium plant was denied because it was adjacent to two small African-American communities (Millan, 1997).

KEY CONCEPTS

environmental justice	**life chances**	**white-collar crime**
learning-generalization	**patient dumping**	
hypothesis		

SUGGESTED READING

JOHN IRWIN AND JAMES AUSTIN, *It's About Time: America's Imprisonment Binge,* 2nd ed. Belmont, CA: Wadsworth. The authors offer a critical analysis of the way the American criminal justice system responds to criminal behavior.

DEBORAH PROTHROW-STITH, *Deadly Consequences.* New York: Harper, 1991. A disturbing look at the epidemic of violence that puts young black males at serious risk of premature death.

JEFFREY REIMAN, . . . *and the Poor Get Prison: Economic Bias in American Criminal Justice.* Boston, MA: Allyn & Bacon, 1996. This analysis demonstrates that the poor are at a disadvantage at every stage of the criminal justice process from arrest to incarceration.

SAMUEL WALKER, CASSIA SPOHN, AND MIRIAM DELONE, *The Color of Justice.* Belmont, CA: Wadsworth, 1996. An indictment of racial and ethnic discrimination in the criminal justice system.

CHAPTER 9

Class and Lifestyles

THE CONCEPT OF LIFESTYLES

Members of social classes often display distinctive lifestyles that separate them from members of other classes. **Lifestyles** are class-based values, attitudes, and forms of behavior. There are, for example, class differences in spending patterns that extend beyond those determined by earnings, family patterns, gender roles, and relationships that are to some extent influenced by location in the stratification system.

Lifestyles are conditioned by the distinctive social and physical environments that members of different classes face. Among the most salient considerations in understanding class-linked styles of life are work situation and economic, financial, and political inequalities. Members of the elite, for example, occupy a position of financial security, high social status, and considerable political influence. This situation molds their approach to the world and the future. In contrast, the poor face constant financial insecurity, degraded social status, and limited political influence. Their world view and perceptions of the future are likewise molded by their situation.

THE CAPITALIST ELITE

Members of the capitalist elite are the individuals and families who possess vast economic assets in the form of money, property, stock, and bonds. Their wealth has typically passed through several generations and they are shaped by a tradition of wealth and power. The lifestyles of the economic elite are heavily dominated by concerns for the maintenance and perpetuation of accumulated wealth and power.

The Family and the Transmission of Privilege

The most enduring segment of the elite is born to wealth and power and dedicated to the maintenance of their advantaged social position through the preservation of the family, the upper class, and the economic and political system that supports it. Families play a central role in this process because the family line is both the source of position and the mechanism for transmitting social position to future generations. Consequently, they are socialized to think of themselves not so much as individuals, but as "a stage in the development of a historical family" (Caven, 1969: 85) Moreover, since the fortunes of specific families are linked to the survival of the elite class, they forge powerful allegiances with other members of the same class.

The socialization of each new generation is organized around the perpetuation of family and class. Primary responsibility for teaching appropriate behavior and instilling proper attitudes falls to mothers (Domhoff, 1970). Children are, from the start, taught to believe that they are different from the children of other classes, and a clear element of moral superiority is instilled (Ostrander, 1984). Socialization means immersion in the elegant lifestyle that wealth offers and a strong emphasis on appropriate upper-class behavior. This includes the need for sons to follow parents in careers as business and governmental leaders. For daughters it includes responsibility for participation in community affairs (Daniels, 1987). For both there is great stress on the importance of "good marriages," which means a union with a member of another elite family. Good marriages are facilitated by limiting children's circle of acquaintances to other members of the elite. This is accomplished through an intricate system of informal social activities, private schools, exclusive clubs, and debutante activities.

Children are expected to assume positions of influence and work to maintain family fortunes, but they also face some unique problems, one of the most troublesome being that their privilege denies them the opportunity to prove their own self-worth through individual accomplishment (Ostrander, 1984). Many Americans seek to validate themselves in the occupational world, often measuring success by income. The children of wealth are denied that opportunity, because not only are they born to wealth, their route to future positions of influence is virtually guaranteed. Consequently, some are destined to forever wonder how well they might have fared on their own merits.

A different challenge emerges in social relationships because there is always the underlying suspicion that people around them are attracted to their wealth and position, not to them as individuals. Thus, in every generation a few renounce their wealth or change their names to disassociate themselves from their wealth, and a few are driven to seek psychiatric help to cope with the need to create a meaningful life.

It has long been noted that upper-class families tend to be conservative and emphasize traditional values (Warner & Lunt, 1941; Blood & Wolf, 1960). Families tend toward patriarchy with husbands and fathers controlling major decisions within the context of the family—decisions about jobs, housing, major expenditures. Patriarchy prevails despite the fact that most wives possess substantial wealth inherited from their families. This pattern is inconsistent with the experience in families in other classes where the relative income of spouses influences the distribution of authority. Although this is an apparent source of marital dissatisfaction among elite wives, it seldom produces open challenges to husbands' authority.

It is believed that several factors contribute to the survival of the upper-class tradition of patriarchy. One factor is that upper-class women derive their social identities from their class position and their community work, not their family roles. But perhaps the most salient reason is the economic and political position of upper-class men outside the family, where they dominate their communities and the society. They are men accustomed to control and unlikely to voluntarily relinquish power in any area.

Noblesse Oblige

A recurrent theme running through both the socialization of children and the activities of capitalist class families is an emphasis on responsibility for the less advantaged members of society, the concept of *noblesse oblige*. A member of the Rockefeller family recalls, "My mother and father's greatest fear was that their children might take their wealth for granted and grow up spoiled and arrogant. They wanted us to learn that with wealth comes responsibility" (New York Times, 1988 :4F). This pattern was set by the business leaders of the nineteenth century. It is estimated that oil man John D. Rockefeller, Sr., donated over $500 million to charity in his lifetime, an amount equivalent to $5.4 billion in current dollars (Tanaka, Branscum, & Borsook, 1996). Paul Mellon, heir to a banking fortune, has donated at least a billion dollars over his lifetime.

Members of the elite are also active in countless national and local benevolent activities that range from fund-raising for charitable causes to acting as caretakers for vast international philanthropic organizations. The Rockefeller Foundation alone has assets of $2 billion, used to support higher education, the arts, and environmental causes. Heirs to some of the major fortunes in America such as Pillsbury and Oscar Mayer work through a group called the Funding Exchange to funnel money into social reform efforts such as nuclear disarmament and voter registration (Neuborne, 1990).

Noblesse oblige activities serve different motives. Some members of the upper class sincerely accept this idea as a moral obligation that accompanies inherited wealth. Critics point out that philanthropy also serves a less noble purpose. It is a matter of control, a means of moving into positions of authority where they can direct organizations' resources in ways they see as most appropriate. For example, members of urban elites often control fund-raising for metropolitan orchestras and opera houses, and although these organizations give public performances, it is largely elites who fill the audience (Arian, 1971). There is also the matter of justifying and legitimizing privileged position. The devotion of time, money, and effort to public service helps to deflect potential criticism and as such is a way of perpetuating the position of their family and class.

The financial contributions of the very rich are often quite large, involving millions of dollars. However, on the whole, the rich tend to contribute a smaller proportion of their wealth than ordinary upper-middle-class Americans. It is estimated that the "very rich" (with assets over $1.3 million) donate about one half of one percent (0.5 percent) of their fortunes to charity annually, but those with assets of $40,000 to $1.3 million give between 0.8 and 1.5 percent (Fabrikant & White, 1995). Moreover, charitable gifts are often contingent upon public display of family names on buildings or monuments.

THE INSTITUTIONAL ELITE

Members of the institutional elite are newcomers to wealth, power, and status. They are the new millionaires created by the entertainment industry (where film actors such as Jim Carey can command more than $20 million for a single movie), professional sports (Michael Jordan regularly earns over $50 million per year in salary and endorsements), independent entrepreneurs, or corporate leaders (such as Michael Eisner of Disney with a multimillion dollar salary). The institutional elite display two different lifestyles, the highly visible, conspicuous consumption of the rich and famous and the much more private and sedate world of the majority.

Conspicuous Consumption

One segment of the institutional elite deliberately participates in an extravagant lifestyle, sometimes actually encouraging television and the tabloids to peek into their homes, their lavish parties, and personal lives (Taylor, 1989). Thorstein Veblen's (1899) insight into the behavior of the newly rich at the end of the nineteenth century continues to have contemporary relevance. He interpreted their ostentatious and extravagant expenditures as **conspicuous consumption,** the open and public display of luxury for the express purpose of flaunting their vast wealth.

The contemporary geographic capital of conspicuous consumption is California, especially places like Hollywood and Beverly Hills, where many of the newly rich congregate. The lifestyles of Beverly Hills spawned a popular television series. It boasts the wealthiest ZIP code in the nation, with an average household income of $154,776 (compared to a national average of about $35,000). Modest homes start at $500,000, and the most expensive can cost $30 million (Ferrell, 1990). Originally the home of stars of the movie industry, it has since become the locale for those whose wealth originated in popular music, the television industry, professional athletics, real estate, or finance.

Beverly Hills is a relatively small city of 33,000 permanent residents (and 45,000 cars), yet each year $2 million is spent to decorate the streets for Christmas (Stewart & Dunn, 1989). The influx of city workers, shopkeepers, bankers, gardeners, real estate brokers, and tourists inflates that number to 150,000 during the day. The community houses 170 beauty salons, 122 jewelry stores, 65 banks (with deposits of $9 billion), 24 furriers, 14 limo services, 22 auto dealers, and at least one department store requiring an appointment for the privilege of spending money. Stores on the famed Rodeo Drive feature items such as $25,000 leather jackets.

Some children of the newly rich live in pampered elegance. Alison, 13, for example, calculates the number of her personal staff:

> I have a personal trainer, I have a counselor, I have a nutritionist, I have a singing coach. And I think that's it. Oh, yeah, I have a driver, too (Greenfield, 1997).

Wendy, 23, laments her graduation gift:

> When I graduated from college, my dad wanted to buy me a new car. . . . Because he has two Mercedes he has a very good relationship with the Mercedes people. I had wanted a BMW really badly, and I was really uncomfortable about getting a Mercedes, but I didn't have a choice. . . . I just didn't think it was an appropriate car for a 21-year-old. It's the stigma attached to a Mercedes (Greenfield, 1997).

The Millionaires Next Door

Not all of the newly rich choose extravagant lives. The largest segment of the institutional elite is made up of self-employed businesspersons who built their fortunes in conventional businesses such as fast-food franchises, auto dealerships, or software. They, along with some entertainers and business leaders, prefer more private, relatively frugal lives (Stanley & Danko, 1996). A look at the lives of America's millionaires shows that more drive Fords than any type of car, and few have ever spent more than $600 for a suit of clothes or paid more than $250 for a wristwatch. Warren Buffet, worth over $12 billion dollars, still lives in the same home he bought for $31,500 in 1958 (Lewis, 1995).

Their working lives are consistent with their spending habits. Most continue to work long hours at their businesses and place a major share of their earnings into savings and investments rather than conspicuous consumption. In a very real sense they continue to pursue the American Dream of hard work and thrift. Microsoft's Bill Gates, the richest American, still puts in seventy-hour work weeks and doesn't worry about financial failure. "I would," he claims, "still eat the same hamburgers" if his fortune collapsed.

Members of the newly wealthy institutional elite are not particularly well known for their philanthropic contributions. There are several exceptions to this, Bill Gates (Microsoft) and Ted Turner (CNN) among them. Gates donated about $70 million to charity in the 1990s, and Turner pledged $1 billion to the United Nations.

THE UPPER MIDDLE CLASS

The upper middle class of experts occupies an advantaged position in the occupational sphere. It is not uncommon for the upper middle class to have responsibility for organizing and directing the activities of large numbers of subordinates. In fact, some occupations (*e.g.,* paralegals, hygienists) have evolved as structurally subordinate to established professions, and the parameters of their work are set by these professions. In a larger sense the upper middle classes organize and direct both the work and the *nonwork* lives of those below them in the class structure—the lower middle class, the working class, and the poor. Relations between the upper middle class and the bulk of society are a one-way dialogue, with managers and supervisors, journalists and teachers, social workers and judges, physicians and lawyers controlling the flow of information, making judgments, and issuing commands and instructions to lower classes (Ehrenreich, 1989).

Their work also offers both autonomy and opportunity. Their authority is focused on specific areas and usually subject to limitations by the highest levels of authority. Yet, most are likely to be free from routine and direct supervision, granted wide latitude in the conduct of their work and allowed to establish their own schedules within broad limits. Most occupy career paths that offer opportunities for upward mobility, and a small number may realistically look forward to movement into the institutional elite.

Members of the upper middle class enjoy economic security, social status, and political influence at the state and local levels, but they also hold a structurally ambiguous position. Although they possess some significant authority, they lack final decision-making responsibility for the goals of their organizations. Managers and most professionals are organizational employees, lacking ownership of significant productive resources beyond their own expertise and ultimately expected to carry out decisions enacted by the institutional elite at the highest organizational levels. Consequently, they have something in common with all employees in the lower middle and working classes, although they are granted much greater discretion.

There is also economic insecurity in the upper middle class. Once free from the worry of unemployment that constantly threatens the lives of the poor and the working class, the upper middle class now face the consequences of the globalization of the economic system that has led to downsizing and corporate restructuring. Workers at all levels are vulnerable, but broad levels of middle management are now also at risk.

Most members of this class have succeeded on the basis of educational attainments. However, claims to upper-middle-class position—skill and knowledge—cannot, unlike real capital, be hoarded or preserved or bequeathed to their children (Ehrenreich, 1989). Consequently, their legacy to their children must be in the form of accessibility to the best possible educational credentials. In extreme cases, parents endure high taxes so that their children have access to quality public schools and expend large amounts of money on private tutors and test-preparation courses. Teachers in the greater New York City area can easily earn an extra $50,000 tutoring students on nights and weekends (Gross, 1997). Unfortunately this exposes children to high expectations of success and intense stress.

THE LOWER MIDDLE CLASS

The lower middle class includes people in a variety of work settings and situations. There are clerical or administrative workers (secretaries, bookkeepers, shipping clerks, insurance policy processors, bank tellers, data entry operators, timekeepers, postal service workers, dispatchers, stock clerks), retail sales and service workers (cashiers, clerks), some salaried professionals (paralegals, nurses, physical therapists, teachers, social workers) and technicians (drafters, dental hygienists). Despite the diversity, several common themes define their situation.

Most members of the lower middle class tend to have a high school education and some university credits or community college degrees. Salaried professionals are the exception, filling jobs that require college degrees. Earnings are moderate when judged against the standards of the upper middle class, and in many instances fall below that of blue-collar crafts workers and operatives. Moreover, although some proportion of lower-middle-class workers can look forward to rising to first-line supervisory positions, careers are largely blocked beyond that level because of the increasing demand for advanced education for middle-management positions. There are thus some real limits on the potential for advancement and making major gains in earnings, meaning that lower-middle-class workers can anticipate performing the same routines over the course of their careers.

The work of the lower middle class neither allows room for personal discretion nor grants much in the way of authority; rather their work is more likely to be defined for them by strict job descriptions or administered by upper-middle-class professionals or managers. They are people who have large segments of their work lives directed by others. Even professionals such as nurses and teachers, who have college degrees, occupy clearly subordinate positions in the organizational hierarchy. Subordination is most pronounced among office workers. Supervisors oversee them and in extreme cases their activities are monitored by electronic surveillance devices that observe and record virtually every aspect of workers' behavior. Electronic surveillance includes videocameras overseeing workspaces and rest areas, audiotapes of the length and content of telephone conversations, and software programs embedded in computers that record the interval between keystrokes and measure the length of rest periods. Consequently, there is the risk of a reprimand if coffee breaks extend beyond the norm or if there are unexplained breaks in the rhythm of typing. It is even alleged that one company used special chairs with sensors in the seats to measure movements, using the rationale that wigglers are not working efficiently (Rothfeder & Galen, 1990). Employees may not even be aware of the surveillance. Workers complain that electronic surveillance is an invasion of their privacy and that constant monitoring is extremely stressful. Comparisons of monitored and unmonitored workers often reveal stronger feelings of anxiety, tension, fatigue, and anger among those under surveillance (Smith et al., 1992). One of the major sources of stress is that workers constantly being monitored feel pressure to work harder and worry they risk punishment for tiny deviations in productivity. In short, electronic surveillance contributes to feelings of powerlessness and loss of control over their own work.

Thus, although the work of the lower middle class is important and essential to the functioning of society, it is not work that yields major rewards or supports claims to social status at work or in the larger society. In fact, the gap between the rewards of the upper middle class and the lower middle class is sizable and seems to be increasing as the rewards of high-tech jobs increase. Moreover, adhering to the work habits of effort and dedication endorsed by the ideology of individualism does not offer much chance for major advancement.

Class and Status in the Lower Middle Class

Most analysis of the lower middle class suggests that they are sensitive to the fact that their accomplishments seem modest compared to those of the upper middle class (Mills, 1951; Gans, 1967; Hamilton, 1972). There is often dissatisfaction with their standard of living, but they are not poor and take pride in their ability to acquire con-

---

CASE STUDY:
Two-Tier Marketing

Americans at all class levels are tempted by consumer goods. Clothing, cars, and electronic gadgets make life more amenable but are also a claim to social status. Not everyone can afford to shop in Beverly Hills, but virtually anyone can display a Rodeo Drive credit card. Retailers respond to the lure of prestige-enhancing impulses with a two-tier marketing strategy that offers similar products or name brands to two quite different income groups. Marketing people call it the "Tiffany/Wal-Mart" strategy (Leonhardt, 1997).

Two-tier marketing is readily evident in cars and designer jeans. At the top end of the automotive market are luxury cars and lavish sport-utility vehicles, and Lexus offers both with price tags over $50,000, but an ES300 series sedan costs about half that. People who are satisfied with a new car that does not have the status of the Lexus name can turn to General Motors and buy a basic Saturn for under $11,000. Gap Inc. sells jeans for $58 at its Banana Republic stores or for about $22 at Old Navy stores. Those content with generic jeans find even better bargains at Wal-Mart.

Another aspect of two-tier marketing is found in the resale of used products. There has always been a market for pre-owned cars and homes, but the sale of used clothing, furniture, and electronics doubled between 1987 and 1997. Name-brand merchandise is cleaned and refurbished and sold at a fraction of the original cost. One clothing store even repackages its items in shrink-wrap to convey the image of newness.

sumer goods that are the visible announcements of purchasing power—consumer goods, homes, and cars—and validate a measure of economic success. Obviously, the consumer goods they purchase cannot approach the quantity and quality of the more affluent (see accompanying Case Study).

Despite relatively modest accomplishments, there is a strong emphasis in the lower middle class on standards of behavior that exemplify the ideology of the American Dream—hard work and individual effort. Lower middle class families tend to be strongly family-oriented and child-oriented, especially in the field of education where they encourage strong aspirations in their children, reflecting the recognition of the importance of education in the success of their children (Gans, 1967).

Religion also plays a central role in their life, and there is some indication that lower-middle-class families are more likely to adhere to more conservative standards of morality in areas such as personal honesty and modesty in sexual behavior. One interpretation that has gained some attention is that concern with traditional standards of respectability is also a claim to social status. Consequently, their ambiguous accomplishments in the economic sphere are translated into concern with social status and social respectability in their personal and social lives (Mills, 1951).

THE WORKING CLASS

The working class has two sides. On the one side are the skilled crafts workers such as automotive technicians, machinists, and electricians, and on the other are factory workers who operate machines or work the assembly lines. All employees face the threat of joblessness, but unemployment rates for the working class consistently stand above those of white-collar workers. Jobs are continuously being lost to globalization and technology. The globalization of the economic system has resulted in the displacement of large numbers of manufacturing jobs in the United States and other advanced industrial nations to developing nations. Technological developments, especially automation, have also taken a toll by using machines to replace people in some job categories. The working class has been especially hard hit in autos, textiles, and steel production. Consequently, very few see themselves free of economic worries, which is one of the factors that contributes to the large number of two-career families.

The Segregation of Work and Social Roles

Much manual work is intellectually uninteresting, offers few opportunities for innovation or creativity, and holds little chance of winning meaningful promotions. In addition, blue-collar workers face strong pressure for productivity. Assembly line workers must struggle to keep pace with the unremitting tempo of the line while others work under piece-rate systems that link wages to output. Supervisors regularly and continuously monitor their levels of effort. Consequently, it is not uncommon for blue-collar workers to segregate their work from their social lives and seek fulfillment in leisure activities (Shostak, 1969; Halle, 1984). Large blocks of free time are devoted to active participation in softball, bowling, hunting and fishing, and attendance at spectator sports such as football and baseball games. Neighborhood bars, taverns, and clubs are the locale for watching games on television as well as for social drinking.

Blue-collar men tend to express a preference for male companions, and there is a tendency for leisure activities such as hunting to be segregated along gender lines. This is not a firm line, and many activities involve both spouses, with some wives involved in sports; and visiting among family and friends is a shared activity. The origins of segregated activities probably have their roots in the gender segregation of jobs that prevailed for most of the twentieth century. Whole categories of skilled crafts and factory jobs were men's work, and lower-white-collar jobs were women's jobs, meaning that people spent their work day in the company of people of the same sex. It is logical that friendships forged at work would be extended to leisure activities. Many marital disputes apparently have their origins in a conflict over the division of time between male friendships and marital and family activities (Halle, 1984: 55).

Working-Class Husbands and Wives

The division of labor and power within blue-collar families has long been divided along gender lines. Husbands filled the role of provider in the paid labor force while wives assumed responsibility for the home, although many also held jobs outside the home. Accompanying this was the location of authority in the family with male superiority legitimized on the grounds that the husband provided the major economic support for the family unit. At least some blue-collar husbands, especially poorer ones, became quite authoritarian, imposing severe restrictions on the lives of their wives, attempting to dictate how they could spend their time and money and even who they could visit (Rubin, 1976).

As more and more women in blue-collar families become critical financial contributors and as traditional gender roles weaken in the larger society, there is some significant renegotiating of authority and roles within the family (Rosen, 1987; Earle & Harris, 1989). Their financial contribution to families plagued by economic insecurity allows them to resist their husbands' preference for a nonworking spouse. Major decisions are more likely to be joint endeavors, and husbands assume a somewhat larger (albeit not large) role in domestic chores once delegated almost exclusively to wives. Thus, although there is still a tendency for working-class males to hold to the idea of husband-centered decision-making, there is also support for women's careers and shared household tasks.

Blue-collar women are sensitive to the fact that the role of "provider" is still a powerful aspect of defining and validating the male role at work and in the larger society. Hence, while negotiating a larger role in decision-making and shared domestic tasks they continue to publicly define their husbands as the major provider or "breadwinner" and devote their paychecks to "extras" such as consumer goods that enrich their lifestyles and verify their status in society. This is a social fiction that helps them avoid marital conflict.

It should be noted that blue-collar women, like wives at all class levels, assume a disproportionate share of domestic tasks. This exacts a heavy toll in time and effort, but working-class women value both paid employment and unpaid home and family activities (Ferree, 1985). Paid work offers economic rewards that grant a degree of financial security and an enhanced standard of living, but work relationships are often seen as impersonal and exploitative. The family may be hierarchical but simultaneously offers support, intimacy, and love. Thus, each role offers what the other cannot. Domestic life permits a partial escape from the inhumane demands of factory work while paid work allows temporary escape from patriarchal domination (Rosen, 1987).

Gender distinctions between provider and homemaker roles are generally not as rigid in African-American families as in white families (Taylor, Chatters, Tucker, & Lewis, 1990). A key factor underlying this pattern is the fact that African-American women have historically been more likely to be in the paid labor force because of the depressed earnings of African-American men. Despite this, married African-American women also perform a majority of domestic tasks in the home.

THE POOR

The poor occupy the lowest levels of the stratification system. The poor includes several different groups. There are, first, the working poor who work on a regular or periodic basis, but in jobs that are part-time or offer marginal wages. People in this category are unskilled workers, domestics, factory workers, and some service workers. Racial and ethnic minorities have been concentrated in these forms of work at every stage of the industrialization process in the United States. The poor also includes those not currently working—the unemployed, the unemployable, and the discouraged. At one extreme are the short-term jobless who are displaced but are subsequently reemployed and are able to survive with the aid of unemployment insurance and welfare payments. At the other extreme are the long-term unemployed who lack the skills or training to be permanently attached to the labor force.

Life at the bottom of the stratification system is often overshadowed by financial deprivation and economic insecurity. Many work, but the pay is low and the threat of unemployment is a common and constant reality. To illustrate, in any given year less than 10 percent of the unemployed voluntarily leave jobs; the majority (about 60 percent) are displaced due to plant closings and industrial transformations that eliminate jobs (textiles are a prime example) and temporary or seasonal layoffs (agricultural and construction workers). Thus a large part of unemployment can be traced to the vagaries of the economic system. The remainder are young people entering the workforce for the first time or older workers attempting to reenter the workforce. Adult women are overrepresented, attempting to rejoin the paid labor force because of a change in family status or at the conclusion of child-care responsibilities.

The marginal economic situation of the poor is reflected in their lifestyles and life chances (Exhibit 9.1). Fewer than half enjoy home ownership, and in addition, while things such as cars and telephones are taken for granted by most middle-class Americans, sizable proportions of the poor lack them. The lack of a phone or car is

EXHIBIT 9.1 Living Poor in the United States

	NONPOOR FAMILIES	POOR FAMILIES	POOR SINGLE-PARENT FAMILIES	WELFARE FAMILIES
Total income	$55,394	$8,501	$6,794	$12,678
Own a home	77.6%	40.8%	24.3%	24.9%
Own a car	97.2	76.8	64.1	66.3
Have a phone	97.2	76.7	69.9	67.5
No health insurance	12.1	26.8	18.0	n/a
Infant mortality (per 1000 births)	8.3	13.5	14.6	14.3
Violent crimes (per 1000 people)	26.2	53.7	87.5	n/a
Two or more persons per room	4.2	19.2	16.7	24.9
Deprivations:				
at least one	13.0	55.1	56.8	65.4
three or more	1.0	11.8	12.9	14.6

Definitions: *Poor* are people in families with incomes below the poverty threshold. *Poor single-parent families* have an unmarried head of household and at least one child under age 18. *Welfare families* include families with children under 18 receiving some welfare assistance. *Deprivations* include the following: eviction, discontinuation of gas or electric service, lacking food, crowded living conditions, and no refrigerator, stove, or phone.

Source: Mary Federman et al. "What does it mean to be poor in America?" *Monthly Labor Review* 119 (May, 1996), pp. 3–17.

more than an inconvenience; it is also a barrier to finding work. Employers have more difficulty reaching potential employees without phones, and the lack of a vehicle makes it more difficult for city dwellers to take jobs across town or in the suburbs.

Certain health risks among the poor are also evident. Fewer have health insurance, which contributes to inadequate prenatal care, which, in turn, shows up in significantly higher infant mortality rates. The poor are also more susceptible to violence. Residents of poorer neighborhoods with concentrations of substance abuse problems show a much greater likelihood of being the victim of a violent crime. The stresses of life on the underside are summarized in the number of deprivations they face. Deprivations include burdens such as eviction; discontinuation of telephone, gas, or electricity; lacking sufficient food within the last four months; crowded living conditions; and no refrigerator, stove, or phone that families experience in the course of a year.

The problems of economic insecurity are compounded by the social and political position of the poor in American society. The work they do carries little prestige, and the individualistic themes that dominate society mean that some segments of their society hold them in disrepute, believing that they are largely responsible for their own plight. One consequence is that social welfare programs designed to buffer the effects of economic deprivation—unemployment insurance, minimum wage laws, social welfare programs—typically encounter opposition in the political arena, meaning that benefits often fail to achieve their goals. For example, Congress raised the minimum wage to $5.15 per hour in 1997, but a full-time, year-round worker with a family of three earns less than the official poverty level even at that rate.

Considering the social and economic handicaps encountered by the poor it might be anticipated that they would have lost faith in the dominant ideology of hard work and open opportunity. In fact, it has long been known that this is generally not the case (Goodwin, 1972). Some do express less optimism about the system and their chances in it than do the more affluent, but a majority believe in an open opportunity structure and are optimistic about their own chances for success. For example, despite the obvious limits on opportunities for those without a high school degree, surveys show only about one-fifth feel they have a less-than-average chance for success (Kluegel & Smith, 1986: 68–72). Women generally see the system as less open, perhaps reflecting an awareness of the more limited occupational chances for females. African Americans at all levels have a less favorable assessment of the opportunity structure, and among the poor a large majority feel they have not had a fair chance to succeed.

Growing Up Poor

One of the largest segments of the poor is infants and children. In fact, the risk of a child living in poverty in America was greater in the 1990s than in the 1970s (O'Hare, 1996). About one in every five children in the United States (over 15 million children under age 18) is growing up poor, including nearly 6 million under the age of six. This includes over 45 percent of all African-American children and 39 percent of Latino/a children. It is a situation that ranks the United States at the bottom of international comparisons of child poverty in industrial nations (Smeeding, O'Higgins & Rainwater 1991). To illustrate, child poverty is 22 percent in the United States, 13 percent in Canada, 12 percent in Ireland, 10 percent in Italy, and below 5 percent in the Scandinavian countries.

The long-term educational prospects for poor children seem dismal by all standards. Their living conditions are more precarious, their neighborhoods less safe, they have fewer educational resources (books or computers) at home. Despite the handicaps imposed by poverty, most parents try to sustain positive aspirations for their children. As a result, the children of the poor are likely to be imbued with aspirations and hopes not unlike more advantaged youngsters. Nine out of ten school children living in poverty plan on continuing past high school, and four out of five believe they will graduate from college (Federman et al., 1996). Admittedly, their goals are different, because their aspirations often center on stable blue-collar work, manufacturing, construction, the military—certainly not the lofty professional and business careers held by the children of the middle class, but a secure and constructive place in the class system. For example, a poor urban teenager rehearses a future that is not unlike the aspirations of children of the more advantaged, "I'll have a regular house, y'know, with a yard and everything. I'll have a steady job, a good job. I'll be living the good life, the easy life" (MacLeod, 1987: 5).

CONCLUSION: HUNGER IN THE WORLD, HUNGER IN AMERICA

In 1974 Secretary of State Henry Kissinger vowed that world hunger would be eradicated "within ten years" (Owen, 1996). Two and a half decades later the proportion of chronically undernourished has been reduced by only one-fifth, leaving 840 million people worldwide facing hunger on a continuing basis. Hunger has been alleviated largely by improvements in food production that have tripled the output of rice, grains, and other staple crops. The most dramatic progress has been made in East Asia, but the problem has actually worsened in sub-Saharan Africa, where the number of undernourished has doubled to over 200 million. Nations such as Zaire are the most dramatic examples of mass starvation.

A lack of nutrition endangers everyone, but children and pregnant women face the greatest risks. Undernourished expectant mothers risk anemia and expose the child to a whole range of deficiencies, not the least of which is low birth weight. Frail infants have a much higher infant mortality rate, and those who survive are more likely to have growth and development problems later. Hunger causes weakness and lethargy; thus, hungry children in the schools have more difficulty concentrating and seem to fall behind their peers. Chronic nutritional problems also have physiological consequences. Iron deficiency, for example, causes cognitive disabilities.

The problem of hunger has not even been solved in the United States, one of the richest nations in the world, and it touches many more people than is generally understood. There are two ways of thinking about inadequate nutrition. The medical community defines **hunger** as a "chronic shortage of nutrients necessary for growth and good health" (Physician Task Force, 1985). Reliable data on hunger are scarce, but one study estimates that 5.5 million children are hungry and face the risk of health problems (Shapiro, 1994). An alternative way of focusing on the problem of hunger is the concept of food security. **Food security** means having a "culturally acceptable, nutritionally adequate diet, through *non-emergency* food sources at all times" (U.S. House of Representatives, 1990). The key point is that an adequate supply of food is available on a regular basis. Second Harvest, a nationwide network of food banks, reports that more than 25 million Americans occasionally visit soup kitchens, food pantries, or other food distribution centers each year (Shapiro, 1994). About one-third of the people depending on these emergency food sources are working for at least part of the year. They turn to these sources because of unemployment or family crisis or simply because their regular diet is inadequate. In short, one in ten Americans, about half of them children under age seventeen, must worry about having a decent diet.

KEY CONCEPTS

conspicuous consumption	food security hunger	lifestyles noblesse oblige

SUGGESTED READING

MAYA ANGELOU, *I Know Why the Caged Bird Sings.* New York: Bantam, 1970. A poignant remembrance of rural poverty in Arkansas by this world-famous African-American author and poet.

RICK BRAGG, *All Over but the Shoutin'.* New York: Pantheon, 1997. A young man's rise from "white trash" poverty in rural Alabama to celebrated correspondent for *The New York Times.*

DAVID HALLE, *America's Working Man.* Chicago: University of Chicago Press, 1984. A rich and detailed account of the lives of members of the working class.

LEALAN JONES AND LLOYD NEWMAN WITH DAVID ISAY. *Our America: Life and Death on the South Side of Chicago.* New York: Scribner, 1997. Two inner-city Chicago teenagers confront a world of poverty, drugs, and crime, but their deep humanity survives in this chronicle told in their own words.

FRANK MCCOURT. *Angela's Ashes.* New York: Scribner, 1996. This account of the world of a poor Irish family in Limerick in the 1930s and 1940s earned the 1997 Pulitzer Prize.

C. WRIGHT MILLS, *White Collar.* New York: Oxford University Press, 1951. The pioneering analysis of class and status among lower-middle-class workers.

SUSAN A. OSTRANDER, *Women of the Upper Class.* Philadelphia: Temple University Press, 1984. A detailed account of the world of elite women whose lives center on the transmission of privilege.

LILLIAN RUBIN, *Worlds of Pain: Life in the Working Class Family.* New York: Basic Books, 1976. An in-depth analysis of the struggles of women and men in low-paying and unstable blue-collar jobs.

CHAPTER 10

Class Consciousness

SUBJECTIVE PERCEPTIONS OF INEQUALITY AND STRATIFICATION

Americans are very sensitive to the magnitude of economic, social, and political inequality in their society. In fact, when asked if there is anything they are not particularly proud of about the United States, a full one-third volunteer the words "inequality" or "poverty" (Robinson, 1983). Such responses are not unexpected, because it is difficult to discount the homeless or ignore the cars, clothing, and jewelry of the wealthy. Even the more comfortable suburban middle classes, often socially insulated from direct contact with other classes, cannot escape the magazines and television that glorify the lifestyles of the rich and famous or the graphic images of the plight of the poor and homeless.

The presence of hierarchies of income and wealth, social status, and political power raises the question of how people view the stratification system and their place in it. As Marx observed in making the distinction between *klasse an sich* and *klasse fur sich,* classes are no more than aggregates of people in the same market position unless those distinctions shape their awareness, attitudes, and behavior. He saw conflicts between classes as the driving force in historical change, and at some places in his writings he argued for the inevitability of class conflict because members of the emerging urban industrial proletariat would develop a collective consciousness and take action to overthrow the ruling bourgeois. The United States is certainly not on the verge of armed class conflict, nor do Americans exhibit the same level of allegiance to trade unions or class-based political parties found in European nations, but that does not mean that Americans do not visualize a society divided into classes and express some feelings of rapport with others at the same level.

The larger issue of perceptions of the class structure and identification with others in it is much more complex than sensitivity to gross economic inequalities. **Class consciousness** is used here as a generic term to describe subjective perceptions of the division of society into relatively distinct classes and self-placement in that structure. It is important to note that this is not the way in which Marx used the term. There are obviously several different forms or degrees of class consciousness, ranging from the most basic (acknowledgment of a hierarchy of classes) to participating in overt action to enhance class-based interests. For analytic purposes it is possible to identify, as shown in Exhibit 10.1, four different forms of class consciousness. **Class awareness** is the weakest level of class consciousness and involves recognition of the partition of society into two or more classes. Because people may be aware of class divisions but unwilling to locate themselves in that system, the term **class identification** is used for taking the step of self-placement in a specific class. Class identification also presupposes recognition of other classes. **Class solidarity** implies a sense of unity and sharing values and interests with other members of the same class. Class solidarity includes the idea of other classes with divergent values and interests. **Class action** means taking, or being willing to take, some overt action to further the perceived interests of one's class. This level of consciousness implies a degree of confrontation or conflict with other classes.

Conceptualizing Class

A key issue in the examination of class consciousness is the question of the criteria people use to define social class membership. It is easy to believe that class is strictly an economic concept, because Americans tend to rely on words such as

---

EXHIBIT 10.1 Types of Subjective Awareness of Social Stratification

Concept	AWARENESS	IDENTIFICATION	SOLIDARITY	ACTION
Dimensions	Cognitive	Cognitive Attitudinal	Cognitive Attitudinal	Cognitive Attitudinal Behavioral
Measurement	Verbalization	Verbalization Self-placement	Verbalization Self-placement Reference group Differential association	Verbalization Self-placement Reference group Differential association Behavior

"rich," "millionaires," "poor," and "average" to describe members of different classes. Moreover, when forced to mention one single factor Americans will usually choose income. However, more detailed analysis shows that class has a much more complex meaning. Class encompasses a number of specific factors, with lifestyles (73 percent), beliefs and attitudes (69 percent), occupation (68 percent), income (60 percent), education (59 percent), and family background (49 percent) all being rated as either "very important" and "somewhat important" in defining class position (Jackman & Jackman, 1983: 37). There is a tendency to believe these factors are interrelated, suggesting that people have multidimensional concepts of class, not a single unidimensional one. In contrast, occupation seems to play a much greater role in defining classes in countries such as Canada and Britain (Pammett, 1987; Johnston & Baer, 1993).

CLASS AWARENESS

The idea of a classless society is consistent with the ideology of individualism in the United States that emphasizes individual performance rather than social structure. Moreover, denying class also deflects attention away from the advantages of inherited wealth and privilege or the handicaps of poverty. The idea of a classless society is encouraged by politicians, the media, and the popular culture (DeMott, 1990). In the 1990s, for example, broad media attention focused on the issues that television personalities such as Joan Lunden and Connie Chung faced as working mothers, somehow implying that these multimillionaire celebrities faced the same dilemmas in finding quality child care as poor or working-class women. The message was that although class differences in wealth and social status do exist, all people have the same problems and rewards. Hollywood is famous for its use of love stories to perpetuate the myth that no social barriers separate the rich, the poor, and the middle classes (see accompanying Case Study).

Systematic studies of sensitivity to class divisions date back to the 1940s (Centers, 1949). All attempts to measure class awareness raise complex methodological problems. The major problem is that the very process of posing questions about classes can alert people to the issue and cause them to think about matters not previously considered relevant. Or, they may feel pressure to give a particular response because they believe that it is appropriate or socially acceptable. Some researchers have attempted to deal with this problem by determining if people will spontaneously raise the issue of classes when discussing inequality. The paradox is that the failure to volunteer class-based answers does not guarantee that people are unaware of them, merely that they did not volunteer them.

With these limitations in mind there is consistent evidence that most Americans visualize a society divided into social classes. More than nine out of ten people acknowledge classes. Only a very tiny proportion—usually less than 2 or 3 percent—assert that the United States is a classless society. Some manual workers tend to emphasize the basic cleavage between blue-collar work and white-collar work, but most people spontaneously visualize a minimum of at least three classes, the wealthy,

---

CASE STUDY:
Class and Love in Hollywood

American filmmakers like to craft love stories that have happy endings. It is a simple and effective story line: True love between partners prevails over all obstacles. One of the more popular and enduring versions of the Hollywood romance begins with encounters between young men and women from dissimilar class backgrounds, but any social class differences have faded into insignificance by the end of the film (McDonald, 1997).

The classic love story that announced class did not matter is *Love Story* (a 1970 release), where a baker's daughter and an aristocrat's son learn that love means you never have to say you're sorry. More recently, in *Pretty Woman,* a wealthy and ruthless businessman and a warm-hearted street prostitute ultimately find happiness, and in the process he is transformed into a compassionate and caring person. In *Titanic,* Hollywood turns a tragedy at sea into a love story between a penniless artist and a young society woman. And, in *Fools Rush In,* the issue of class is compounded by ethnicity, because he is a rich, white junior executive and she is the daughter of a working-class Mexican-American family who works in a gambling casino. In one revealing scene the man's elitist parents mistake her for his housekeeper.

To some this is harmless fantasy, pure entertainment that no one believes or takes seriously. Other observers argue that Hollywood is guilty of trivializing the implications of differences in background. Social class differences in attitudes and perspectives developed during infancy and childhood demand accommodations if meaningful long-term relationships are to survive. "In the movies you get the feeling that . . . it doesn't matter that you went to Utica State and your wife went to Wellesley," when it fact it makes a great deal of difference (McDonald, 1997). At a more abstract level, it may be argued that Hollywood plays a major role in perpetuating a myth of an open and classless society without barriers to advancement. That is an idea that can be traced to Karl Marx, who suggested that the major cultural images of society are perpetuated by those who benefit the most from them.

---

the poor, and a broad middle class (MacKenzie, 1973). However, people are more likely to also identify a separate working class and to make a distinction between upper and lower levels within the middle class.

CLASS IDENTIFICATION

The vast majority of Americans identify themselves as members of a particular social class (Exhibit 10.2).[1] Well over 95 percent are willing to locate themselves in the

---

[1]The number of options that are presented to people influences the distribution of responses. Most working-class and upper-middle-class people will choose "middle class" if they have only three options.

EXHIBIT 10.2 Occupation and Class Identification

CLASS IDENTIFICATION

	Poor	Working	Middle	Upper middle	Upper
Professional	<1%	17%	62%	20%	<1%
Managerial	<1	20	59	18	2
Sales	3	22	61	12	1
Clerical	7	43	41	9	0
Craft workers	5	53	39	3	<1
Operatives	10	53	35	<1	1
Service	22	46	30	2	<1
Unskilled	17	51	30	1	0
Totals	8	37	43	8	1

Note: Class identification is reported for those who responded to the following question: "People talk about social classes such as the poor, the working class, the middle class, the upper middle class, and the upper class. Which of these classes would you say you belong in?"

Source: Mary R. Jackman and Robert W. Jackman. *Class Awareness in the United States.* Berkeley, CA: University of California Press, 1983, Table 4.1, p. 73. Copyright © 1983 by the University of California Press.

stratification system, and most people report strong attachment to their class. When asked about the intensity of their feelings, a full one-half reported feeling "very strongly" about their membership in that class. Another 28 percent reported "some-what strong" feelings, and only one in five defined their attachment as "not too strong" (Jackman, 1979).

The most obvious feature of class identification in the United States is the pow-erful tendency of Americans to think of themselves as middle class, regardless of their income. The majority of people, except for those in households with income close to the poverty level (below $15,000), identify themselves as middle class. Many factors contribute to this pattern. Language is an obvious one, for common class terms have disagreeable connotations that people prefer to avoid; "poor" and "rich," "upper class" and "lower class" are not neutral terms. More important than semantics is recognition of the fact that most people are neither very rich nor exceedingly poor.

Therefore, when prompted, Americans are willing and able to locate them-selves within a more complex class system. The data on class identification reported in Exhibit 10.2 are organized by occupation and show a pronounced correspondence between structural position and subjective evaluation, emphasizing the importance of work in shaping the broad outlines of the stratification system. Most professionals and managers think of themselves at the upper end of the stratification system, favor-ing the middle-class or upper-middle-class label. Sales workers tend to make the same distinctions, while clerical workers typically divide themselves between middle class or working class. A much clearer pattern is found in blue-collar occupations where a majority of manual workers place themselves in the working class, although about one-third do favor the middle-class designation, and some see themselves among the poor. Service workers and the unskilled are the most likely to identify themselves as the poor.

As would be expected, education and income modify class identification. People with less formal education and lower incomes place themselves at lower levels. This is apparent among that segment of blue-collar and service workers who identify with the poor and among the better-educated and better-paid clerical workers who identify with the middle class. Thus, the link between occupation and class is well established in people's minds, but gains in income and education can cause people to place themselves in a higher class, just as lower pay can cause reduced self-placement.

CLASS SOLIDARITY

The idea of class solidarity involves a step beyond self-identification and focuses on the extent to which people feel they share values and interests with other members of the same class and feel a sense of unity with them. Although there is some sense of compatibility with members of the same social class, who are perceived as sharing similar values and lifestyles, this perspective does not widely extend to feelings that classes have *conflicting* economic and political interests. Rather, people are more likely to feel that classes have divergent but not incompatible interests. Thus, blue-collar workers might agree that manual workers have different interests than managers but simultaneously feel that all classes are members of a "team" in which each makes an essential contribution (MacKenzie, 1973). It is very uncommon for Americans to see different classes as "enemies." This holds true despite the fact that there are strong feelings among the middle and lower levels of society that the political and economic system is tilted in favor of the wealthy. For example, surveys show that a majority of Americans believe owners and corporate executives have disproportionate influence on the government (Kluegel & Smith, 1986: 120).

It is believed that one of the major reasons that individuals do not develop a sense of solidarity with other members of their class is that potential class loyalties are overwhelmed by internal divisions based on income, race, ethnicity, gender, and other factors, which serve to divide rather than unite. Race appears to be among one of the most salient sources of diversity. One survey revealed only 19 percent of whites and 26 percent of African Americans thought they shared "a lot" of common interests with members of the other race in the same social class (Colasanto & Williams, 1987).

Race in America also has implications for class consciousness in another way. Lower-middle-class African Americans emphasize race more than class as a form of self-identification (Durant & Sparrow, 1997). This suggests that less advantaged African Americans see race as a more decisive factor in their social and economic lives than social class. In contrast, although upper-middle-class African Americans are not insensitive to racial prejudice, they are more likely to identify with their class position.

CLASS ACTION

This form of class consciousness exists when overt action is contemplated or under-taken in an attempt to further the interests of one's own class or inhibit the interests of some other class. This form of behavior is rare in the contemporary United States, which is not surprising considering that few people see classes separated by vastly divergent interests. Only small numbers of workers, for example, express much inter-est in joining with others in picketing or other actions (Leggett, 1968). Labor unions and political parties are two of the organizations that articulate the interests of the social classes, especially the working class, and they have different histories in the United States and Europe.

The Role of Labor Unions

Nineteenth-century workers responded to industrialization in different ways. Some, such as printers, formed unions that sought to protect the wages and working condi-tions of members of their own occupation. Others attempted to develop broadly based labor unions that united *all* workers. The Knights of Labor recruited at the class level, seeking to unite all working people—skilled and unskilled, women and men, white and African American—except for liquor dealers, professional gamblers, bankers, and stockbrokers, under the slogan that "an injury to one is the concern of all" (Bailey, 1956: 538). At its peak in the 1880s, the Knights claimed a membership of one million workers out of an urban labor force of 10 million. Still others chal-lenged the very foundations of capitalism. In the United States the Western Federa-tion of Miners was one of the groups that sought to "abolish the wage system" (Dubofsky, 1969).

Most employers staunchly resisted the labor union movement, and the govern-ment often came to the aid of employers, with, for example, federal troops used to quell railroad strikes in 1877 and again in 1894. Over the course of the first two decades of the twentieth century the Knights, along with other more radical unions such as the Western Federation of Miners, were superseded by the American Feder-ation of Labor, representing only the skilled trades. The AFL took a more moderate and less confrontational stance and was able to win important concessions on wages, hours, and working conditions for members of crafts occupations.

Unskilled and semiskilled factory workers were largely ignored by the AFL, in part because such jobs tended to be filled by racial and ethnic minorities that sepa-rated them from crafts workers who were typically native-born (Mink, 1986). The devastating economic dislocation of the 1930s stimulated successful attempts to unionize whole industries—auto workers, steel workers—represented by the rival Congress of Industrial Organization. The unionization of these industries was not accomplished without strikes and violence, and it did finally establish the right of unions to exist and collectively bargain for their members. They won significant wage concessions for members of some industries, such as the auto industry, but in the process increased the economic discrepancy between the top and bottom of the working class (Form, 1985).

Union membership began to decline soon after, and stands at less than 15 percent of the workforce at the end of the 1990s. In contrast, membership approaches 30 percent in Germany, 40 percent in Ireland, and 90 percent in Sweden. Contracting membership reflects a number of factors, including the erosion of traditional blue-collar industries such as steel and automobiles combined with limited success in unionizing white collar and service workers. The declining strength of labor unions in the United States is also measured by the shrinking number of large scale work stoppages. There are often small strikes involving a few dozen or even a few hundred workers, but major strikes involving at least a thousand workers have dropped from 187 in 1980 to only 35 in 1995 and 37 in 1996 (Swoboda, 1997). This suggests labor unions are less likely to be able to close down major companies or industries. Organized labor today acts as an interest group in Washington (and the state capitals) lobbying for workers' interests in areas such as occupational health and safety, worker privacy, minimum wage legislation, and supporting pro-labor candidates for political office, but it has not been as successful as union movements in other nations. Moreover, although unions are able to exert some influence on the voting choices of their members, it is very modest (Juravich & Shergold, 1988), meaning that they cannot deliver blocks of votes for candidates.

Political Parties

Political parties in some industrial democracies have come to be explicitly aligned with the interests of different classes. This is most evident in Western European nations that have parties such as Labour (Britain) or Social Democratic (Germany or Sweden) that expressly pursue working-class interests. In contrast, political parties in the United States have typically been loose coalitions of voting blocks rather than ideological groups. The Republican party is divided into a more liberal Northeastern wing and a more conservative Midwestern wing and is more typically identified with the interests of the more affluent segments of society on economic issues and the more conservative on social issues. The Democratic party as we know it was created in the 1930s as a coalition of workers, immigrants, and racial and religious minorities and has traditionally favored governmental action to buffer the worst effects of capitalism; it has won the allegiance of minorities through its support for civil rights.

The links among social class, labor unions, and political parties are less pronounced in the United States than in Europe, but there is a strong tie between unions and the Democrats. Almost all (over 90 percent) of unions' political contributions go to Democrats, and the Democratic party is favored by blue-collar workers, union members, and the poor, but it has never been an exclusively partisan working-class party, nor has it ever held a monopoly of working-class votes. About one in three union members vote Republican in most years, and support for Republicans is even more pronounced at the Presidential level, where more than 40 percent of union members voted for Nixon, Reagan, and Bush during the 1970s and 1980s (Greenhouse, 1997b). Consequently, both major parties are better understood as coalitions rather than rigidly ideological groups.

Despite its orientation toward workers, the Democratic party was formed by a representative of the capitalist elite (Franklin Roosevelt), later chose another member of the elite as its national standard-bearer (John F. Kennedy), and long depended upon the financial support of wealthy contributors, even before the proliferation of "soft money" contributions in the 1990s (Ferguson & Rogers, 1986). Therefore, American political parties do not offer voters a clear choice along economic or class lines. Some ascribe the notoriously low voter turnout rates in the United States to this: Voters choose not to vote rather than support a party that fails to articulate their interests (Vanneman & Cannon, 1987).

The Interplay of Unions, Parties, and Class Solidarity

The links among class consciousness, union membership, and political strength are more pronounced in European nations (Kautsky, 1996). Those nations had aristocratic traditions that highlighted social differences between nobles and the rest of society and excluded workers from participation in major social and political institutions. Working-class solidarity emerged from their vulnerability and fostered the creation of unions and political parties pursuing workers' interests. Large and powerful unions are able to exert influence on the political process and win legislation benefiting workers, and political success in turn reinforces the sense of class solidarity. Four out of five voters in Britain believe that there is a "class struggle" going on in their nation (*The Economist,* 1997f). Sweden is probably the best example of a nation with a large and powerful union movement (90 percent of salary and wage workers are union members), political dominance by a working-class–oriented Social Democrat party, and an extensive social welfare program that includes generous health care and retirement benefits (Johnston & Baer, 1993).

CLASS CONSCIOUSNESS AND THE WORKING CLASS

Much attention has been devoted to the analysis of class consciousness among blue-collar workers, in large part because of the major historical role assigned to this group by Karl Marx. It is clear that a certain configuration of characteristics that are consistent with Marx's reasoning tends to increase working-class identification among manual workers. Union members and the youngest, least-educated, lowest-paid, most dissatisfied manual workers, with the least autonomy on the job, are the most likely to locate themselves in the working class (Zingraff & Schulman, 1984). Thus, as a general rule, it is the most disadvantaged blue-collar workers who identify with the working class, while the more advantaged are more likely to see themselves as middle class.

Sociologists have long sought to understand why blue-collar manual workers in the United States fail to develop a broader sense of working-class solidarity with lower-middle-class white-collar workers and the working poor, who typically encounter the same experiences on the job (low pay, a lack of autonomy and responsibility, sometimes harsh supervision), and why members of the working class seldom press for dramatic changes in the political economy, despite the belief that the economic and political system is biased in favor of a wealthy minority.

Studies of male blue-collar workers in stable, well-paying jobs suggest that part of the answer may be found in the fact they perceive more than one stratification criterion and simultaneously locate themselves on two quite different hierarchies (MacKenzie, 1973; Halle, 1984). One identity is based on the characteristics of their work and leads them to divide the world into four classes—the rich; the poor; a broad middle class of professionals, managers, and clerical workers; and the working class. Blue-collar workers perceive a definite and fundamental distinction between those who are working people and those who are not. One important feature is the characteristics of the work—productive, manual, strenuous, difficult, and dangerous (Halle, 1984). The other feature is control and authority, or more accurately, the lack of it (Vanneman and Pampel, 1977). Thus their work and their class position are determined by the type of work they do and their subordination to the orders of organizational superiors. Managers certainly do not work, merely hiring others to work. Other white-collar work is often characterized as little that is productive and meaningful— "shuffling papers," "working with their mouths," even literally doing nothing ("They just sit on their butts all day"). Thus, there is a clear sense of working-class identification limited to those who engage in certain kinds of productive manual labor.

The concept of "working man" also includes considerations of class, race, and gender (Halle, 1984). The poor are not working people because they are unable or unwilling to work. An emphasis on working class tasks as strenuous, dirty, and dangerous has traditionally also made them *men's* tasks in the minds of many, just as clerical work is defined as women's work. The recent movement of increasing numbers of women into blue-collar work is contributing to a reevaluation of the concepts of both class and gender. A person's race and ethnicity are also important, apparently more important than any definition of social class. Therefore, African Americans or Latino/as may do the same kind of work or have similar lifestyles but tend not to be accepted as members of the same class. Peoples' race or ethnicity is powerful enough to divide them from other blue-collar workers.

A second blue-collar perspective on the class system is based on education, income, and material possessions. Working-class families tend to have education comparable to that of lower-middle-class workers, and their income allows them to enjoy consumer goods and live in pleasant neighborhoods with lower-middle-class and some upper-middle-class families. Hence they also identify themselves as "middle class," a very broad and amorphous group based largely on similar lifestyles. There is such diversity in this group that it is difficult to draw a line between middle class and the rich at the top of the system and the poor at the bottom.

Halle's study also offers another insight. He suggests that confrontational class action does not develop because there is a strong commitment to the American system of government as superior to all others. Although there is widespread belief in corruption among politicians and control of the government by economic interests, this rarely translates into attraction for radical restructuring of society. For one thing, the basic system is believed to be sound but to have been subverted by the actions of people. Moreover, the lure of alternative political systems is dampened by the belief that reform could only be accomplished at the expense of individual liberty and freedom.

FAMILY, GENDER, AND CLASS CONSCIOUSNESS

The question of the formation of class consciousness is made more complex by the fact that many families include spouses occupying different class levels. Using occupation as the measure of social class reveals that somewhere between one-half and two-thirds of all employed husbands and wives are in occupations that would place them in different classes (Exhibit 10.3). This fact has its origin in the gender segregation of occupations: the concentration of women in clerical jobs, retail sales work, and service occupations compared to the overrepresentation of men in blue-collar jobs. Moreover, even spouses in the same occupational category can be separated by a number of gender-based forms of inequality; women earn less (the earnings gap), are less likely to exercise workplace authority, and have limited mobility opportunities because of the glass ceiling. In short, spouses at the same class level may very well have very different experiences at work.

Class consciousness is also influenced by some gender variation in thinking about class. There is some indication that men and women have different conceptions of class, at least in making the distinction between working class and middle class (Robinson & Kelley, 1979; Vanneman & Cannon, 1987; Simpson, Stark & Jackman, 1988). The most important factors contributing to women's identification with the working class are employee status (as opposed to self-employed), full-time rather than part-time employment, being in a female-dominated job, and being a member of a union; the lack of authority that is so important in fostering working-class identification among men is somewhat less important for women. One interpretation is that blue-collar women are not insensitive to their subordination, merely that they are more willing to accommodate to it than to focus on it as a major source of potential conflict (Rosen, 1987: 72).

The question of how members of families define their class standing is an intriguing one. One of the most common responses to disparate class positions is the **status maximization strategy** of claiming the highest class level possible to optimize social status (Davis & Robinson, 1988). This is the tendency of people to "borrow" the best attributes of their spouse in locating themselves in the system. Blue-collar husbands might, for instance, emphasize the white-collar occupation of their school-teacher wives in defining their social class position (Baxter, 1994). Borrowing thus allows people to elevate their class level beyond their own accomplishments. This

EXHIBIT 10.3 Class Location of Husbands and Wives

OCCUPATION OF WIFE

OCCUPATION OF HUSBAND	Managerial	Professional	Technical	Sales	Clerical	Crafts	Operative/ Unskilled	Service	Not Employed
Managerial	14%	16%	3%	8%	25%	1%	2%	6%	27%
Professional	9	28	2	7	18	1	2	6	27
Technical	10	15	7	6	24	1	3	9	26
Sales	10	11	3	14	23	1	3	7	27
Clerical	8	9	4	7	28	1	6	10	26
Crafts	6	7	2	9	22	3	9	12	30
Operative/ unskilled	4	4	2	8	20	2	13	14	31
Service	7	7	2	8	20	2	5	19	31
Not Employed	8	11	2	12	25	3	12	25	<1

Data are limited to married couples with earnings, excluding members of the armed forces. Rows do not add to 100 due to rounding.

Source: U.S. Bureau of the Census. Current Population Reports, P-60, No. 165. *Earnings of Married Couple Families, 1987.* Table 2, p. 10. Washington, DC: Government Printing Office.

process happens among both women and men but is most common among married women, not in the paid work force, who must almost out of necessity rely on their husband's class in defining their class placement, because the role of unpaid homemaker occupies an ambiguous place in the class system. Moreover, this way of thinking about class is also grounded in the tradition of a male head of household and implies that they use the family as the unit of analysis in locating themselves in the stratification system.[2]

However, the situation is more complicated for married women in the paid work force because they possess their own claims to class standing. In such situations it appears that both spouses consider the others' class in defining their own class, but the husband's class has a greater impact (Baxter, 1994; Zipp & Plutzer, 1996). Women are more likely to elevate or depress their own class identification on the basis of their spouses' occupation than are men. This pattern holds generally in Australia, Norway, and Sweden as well as the United States.

Dependence upon husbands' occupation in wives' class placement is reduced in some situations, but the magnitude of the change is unclear (Davis & Robinson, 1988; Zipp & Plutzer, 1996). Wives' class identification is now, compared to the 1970s and earlier, somewhat more likely to be based on their own occupational and educational accomplishments. Full-time employment, higher levels of education and pay, and contributing a greater share of the family's income have all been shown to increase reliance upon their personal situation in subjective definitions of class. Therefore, it can be predicted that as women move into jobs that offer greater rewards and contribute ever-greater proportions of family income, they will develop more individualized conceptions of their class position.

CONCLUSION: FACTORS MITIGATING AGAINST CLASS CONSCIOUSNESS

Americans recognize significant social, political, and economic inequalities and a hierarchy of classes and their position in the larger system. Social class is definitely a conscious factor in social relationships and lifestyles, but class consciousness does not extend to strong feelings of common identity, a belief that social classes are at odds with each other, or a belief that major structural change or a massive redistribution of resources is necessary. Marx was, during his own lifetime, acutely aware of the failure of Americans to develop a sense of *klasse fur sich*. A number of factors combine to explain the absence of clearly articulated feelings of class consciousness

---

[2]The issue of the social class of family units also surfaces in studies that must depend upon objective class placement, such as research on intergenerational social mobility (Chapter 10). Erikson and Goldthorpe (1993) argue that all members of a family occupy the same class position (because members share resources) and that a family's class position is best defined by the position of the person with the highest commitment to the labor market. That is almost always the husband, because women's participation is limited by family responsibilities.

in American society, even among the less-advantaged segments of society who do not enjoy major benefits.

History.   It is important to recognize that the history of the United States is, in some important ways, unique. Formed as a new nation in the eighteenth century, it lacked the feudal tradition of a hereditary aristocracy so common to many European nations. In addition, it was founded on abstract principles of democracy and equality before the law and voting rights. These were not rights that extended to all people at the outset—slaves, women, and the propertyless were not included—but the legal guarantees incorporated in the Bill of Rights were eventually extended to ever-greater segments of the population, albeit slowly and only under political pressure. The United States is a nation that flourished under capitalism and produced widespread prosperity that made it possible for large numbers of blue-collar workers to enjoy a relatively high standard of living. Thus, it is argued that American society did not produce the widespread deprivation likely to foster broadly based discontent and anger.

Immigration.   America, being a nation of immigrants, continually accommodates waves of immigrants. Immigrants are often relegated to the lowest levels of the stratification system, but differences hinder the development of class solidarity with other disadvantaged members of society. Their religious, cultural, and linguistic diversity impedes communication and often generates hostility and antagonism. Such antagonisms often have an economic as well as a cultural basis, because minorities often compete for the same jobs. Employers have been known to actively exploit ethnic and gender divisions in battles against unions, using women and members of minority groups as strikebreakers (Foner, 1964). Consequently, the potential for solidarity based on common economic position is subverted by the disintegrating factors of race and ethnicity.

Gender.   Gender has often operated in the same way as race and ethnicity in driving a wedge between workers in the same class by objective criteria. Print shop owners in the nineteenth century recruited unskilled women workers from the clothing and textile industries to undermine the strength of the trade union by training them to perform some of the tasks that master printers controlled. The women were attracted to the opportunities in printing because of the notoriously poor pay and working conditions in the textile factories (Baron, 1982). In other cases women were employed as strikebreakers at newspapers in Boston, New York, and Chicago.

The other aspect of gender that serves to divide members of the working class is the fact of occupational segregation. Large numbers of women and men labor in different jobs, work different hours, and have different experiences. All of these factors serve to separate rather than integrate workers.

Social Mobility.   Another factor inhibiting the development of group consciousness is the characteristic belief in an open opportunity structure and the chance for individual mobility that permeates all levels of the society. Polls indicate that a majority of Americans believe there is plenty of opportunity for those with ambition and who are willing to work hard. These beliefs are, to some extent, supported by their own experiences, because many are the children or grandchildren of immigrants who have been able to significantly improve their relative position in society. The consequence is that less-advantaged Americans are able to think of their position as temporary rather than as permanent membership in a particular class.

Multiple Hierarchies.   A number of factors are used to define subjective class position—type of work, authority or lack of it, income and wealth, manual or mental work, and a behavioral dimension (lifestyles). Consequently, class location on one dimension need not coincide with position on other dimensions. Occupationally defined classes may, for example, include families with very different incomes. Work in factories, for example, is "working class" by any standard, but it encompasses women and men who are skilled crafts workers, first-line supervisors, janitors, machine operators, and laborers who earn very different incomes and have very different lifestyles. In fact, many better-paid blue-collar workers see themselves as having a middle-class lifestyle.

The Ethos of Individualism.   The dominant ideology of individualism leads most Americans to believe they are just about where they belong in the system considering their talents and efforts. Blue-collar workers typically explain their position in personal terms, rather than their modest origins or the workings of the system (Halle, 1984: 169). They are likely to cite their intellectual limitations, their lack of effort in school, or that they lacked the boldness to set up their own business. Thus, Americans are constrained to think in personal terms rather than structural terms.

KEY CONCEPTS

class action	class identification	status maximization
class awareness	class solidarity	strategy
class consciousness		

SUGGESTED READING

MARY R. JACKMAN AND ROBERT W. JACKMAN, *Class Awareness in the United States.* Berkeley, CA: University of California Press, 1983. This somewhat dated analysis of class consciousness in America remains one of the most thorough analyses of the subject.

REEVE VANNEMAN AND LYNN WEBER CANNON, *The American Perception of Class.* Philadelphia, PA: Temple University Press, 1987. This approach to class consciousness emphasizes the way that class is experienced.

PART FIVE

Inheritance and Mobility

A key feature of the ideology of individualism affirms that upward social mobility is based on individual effort and ability, unfettered by gender, race, or modest social class origins. This perspective has attracted and sustained generations of immigrants. Yet parental location in the stratification system is not irrelevant, influencing the educational and occupational attainments of their children. This chapter explores the direct and subtle ways that class, race, ethnicity, and gender can facilitate or hinder movement across class lines.

CHAPTER 11

Patterns of Social Mobility

SOCIAL MOBILITY: OPEN AND CLOSED SYSTEMS

Children invariably inherit their place in the stratification system from their parents. Each infant begins life with economic resources, social rank, and a lifestyle shaped by the class position of his or her parents. In some kinds of stratification systems parental position has fixed and permanent consequences for subsequent generations, confining them to the class level of their birth. Feudal societies were, for example, rigidly divided between peasants and aristocracy. In the Hindu caste system, caste membership was hereditary, and it was virtually impossible for individuals to hope to succeed by their own efforts. Consequently, social class is an inherited position and such arrangements are described as **closed** stratification systems.

Closed systems are organized to perpetuate privilege and inequality. Structural barriers are erected in law or custom to assure that access to the higher classes is closed to all except the children of the advantaged. Educational systems may be segregated along caste lines, denying lower-level children access to the skills and credentials that might allow them to aspire to more advantageous positions. Such practical barriers are legitimized by prevailing sociocultural ideas and beliefs. A common feature of closed system ideologies posits some intrinsic divisions along class lines. Theories of genetic inferiority (*e.g.,* ideological racism) claim the existence of inherent biological differences among the classes that predispose members of those groups for certain levels at birth. Aristocracies usually claim the right to rule on the basis of a combination of breeding (biological) and training (social) disparities. Rulers in medieval estate systems sometimes declared divine support for their power. Each of these ideologies supports the continuation of stable patterns of inequality through time and generations. There is always some social mobility, even in the most inflexible situations. Closed systems are much more likely to be found in stable agricultural societies and tend to be threatened by the process of industrialization.

In a completely **open** stratification system—admittedly an ideal type—there are no formal or ideological barriers to mobility and people rise or fall (relative to their parents) on the basis of their own abilities, efforts, and accomplishments. In short, there is no necessary link between the class levels occupied by parents and the ultimate class position of their children. All democratic industrial class systems tend toward more openness than is found in agricultural societies, because urbanization and the industrial transformation increase opportunities for social mobility. In the early stages of industrialization, for example, the most profound transformation is the shift from agriculture to manufacturing, and rural workers and small farm owners are able to move into the urban working class. The switch to factory work represents a dramatic improvement in earnings and working conditions for many propertyless rural farm workers. However, for others, the pay and working conditions in urban sweatshops must be considered downward mobility because they suffer intolerable working conditions.

Thus, stratification systems differ in the extent to which one generation's accomplishments and opportunities are determined by the class level of their parents, and it is useful to visualize societies falling along a continuum from open to closed, although no society is at either extreme.

Intergenerational and Intragenerational Mobility

Social mobility is formally defined as the movement of individuals and families from one level in the stratification system to another, either upward or downward. The study of social mobility focuses on experiences of individuals and is tracked in two different ways. **Intergenerational mobility** compares the social position of parents and their children and is considered the most basic measure of the openness of a society.[1] **Intragenerational mobility** traces changes occurring during the life cycle

---

[1]There are a number of complex methodological and conceptual problems inherent in the study of intergenerational social mobility. The single most difficult issue is that of specifying the point in the life cycle of both generations (children and parents) at which to measure social class position, because people experience changes in their situation over the course of their careers. A common way of handling this is to focus in on parental class at the time the child is in the fourteen- to eighteen-year-old range, assuming that this is the age at which parents have established their careers and the most consequential educational and occupational paths are taken by children.

Another issue is the question of determining the class position of the parental generation. Much older (pre-1980s) research focused on specific pairs of individuals, *i.e.,* fathers to sons. This narrow approach ignored daughters and the role of mothers in the socialization process, typically based on the assumption that the husband was the "head of the household" or that his occupation determined the class

of individuals, from their first job to the end of their careers. Intragenerational mobility involves movement among jobs or careers at different class levels. (Individuals also often make many lateral moves among jobs that do not alter their class position.) Intragenerational mobility is studied as a separate topic and is also treated as a stage in the process of intergenerational mobility.

The Status Attainment Model of Social Mobility

Studies of intergenerational social mobility divide the process into three stages or steps. The first stage is the connection between social class origins and educational attainments. The second stage is the link between social origins and educational attainments and first job in the adult labor market. The third stage focuses on the ties among social origins, education, and first job with employment later in the career. Research in this tradition, known as the **status attainment model,** began in the 1960s and clearly established the continuing impact of parental class location on their children's accomplishments (Blau & Duncan, 1967). The original research established empirical relationships among the basic variables in the process. Subsequent work added cognitive (ability measures) and social psychological factors (mobility aspirations) to the process (Sewell, Haller, & Ohlendorf, 1970).[2] Contemporary research focuses on the institutional arrangements that influence progress through educational systems and careers (Kerckoff, 1976, 1995). The status attainment model is clearly an oversimplification, but it remains a useful starting point for understanding intergenerational continuity and mobility (Exhibit 11.1).

The basic model has a clear logic to it, confirmed by a substantial body of empirical research.[3] In the first stage of the process, social class origins are directly correlated with academic ability and levels of educational attainment and with each other. In the second stage, social origins, academic ability, and years of education are directly correlated with the level of the first job. The third stage focuses on the second generation's later jobs, which are correlated with social origins, ability, levels of education, and the level of the earlier job. Perhaps the key finding is that parental class has some impact on every factor in the process. In short, social class origins are never irrelevant.

---

position of the family. More recent studies are exploring four different combinations of individuals—fathers to sons and daughters, mothers to sons and daughters—and the interaction among the different combinations.

[2]This research project followed the careers of people in Wisconsin and is sometimes referred to as the Wisconsin status attainment model.

[3]The status attainment model has been widely criticized because it has a number of shortcomings. The links in the model are statistical correlations and do not necessarily explain how the links are articulated. Moreover, the statistical correlations explain less than one-half of the variance, meaning that important considerations beyond the variables contained in the model impinge upon the process. In addition, it must be emphasized that these relationships are more complex than suggested by this graphic representation. Most importantly, relationships are interactive. For example, while higher educational aspirations can inspire higher attainments, rising scholastic attainments can likewise encourage ever-higher aspirations. Thus, continued academic success can stimulate a subsequent rise in aspirations, and likewise, repeated failure has the potential to dampen aspirations.

EXHIBIT 11.1 A Status Attainment Model

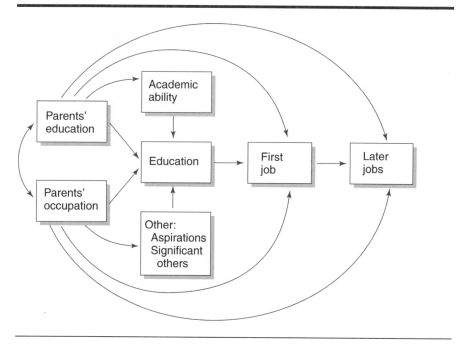

Structural Mobility. Structural changes in the economic system of production and distribution have a forceful impact on the opportunities for individual mobility and the total amount of mobility that occurs within societies. Shifts in the economy close out opportunities for some while opening them for others. A substantial number of people experience intragenerational downward mobility precipitated by the loss of a job followed by reentry into the labor market at a lower level in the system. Advanced stages of industrialization in some nations bring the decline of the manufacturing sector, shrinking opportunities for stable working-class positions. The losses of working-class jobs in the steel and garment industries are the most common examples. At the same time the burgeoning of technologically based upper-middle-class occupations creates new channels of mobility for the better-educated children of lower-middle-class or working-class parents. These patterns are referred to as **structural mobility,** movement due to expansion and contraction of the underlying economic system.

INTERGENERATIONAL MOBILITY

America is justly celebrated as the epitome of an open system, a society in which individual effort and ability rather than family background determine location in the stratification system. This is, of course, the basic tenet of the "ideology of individu-alism," and it is relatively easy to find cases that validate the American Dream. For example, *Time* magazine's 1997 Person of the Year was a penniless immigrant to the United States who eventually rose to become CEO of a major international corpora-tion. However, moving beyond such anecdotal evidence suggests a more complex picture. A broader, more comprehensive view of the total society suggests that the United States is simultaneously a fluid system with people circulating among levels but also a stable system with a sizable share of children inheriting the same class level as their parents.

The mobility experiences of a sample of white and African-American males is reported in Exhibit 11.2 and illustrates some basic patterns of inheritance and mobil-ity. There is inheritance at every level, but it is most pronounced among children of upper-white-collar and manual-worker fathers. White-collar parents are more afflu-ent and are thus able to provide their children with educational and social resources that enable them to earn similar jobs. In contrast, the children of lower manual work-ers, many of whom are the working poor, are less likely to be able to facilitate the mobility of their children. The inheritance found in the upper reaches of blue-collar

---

EXHIBIT 11.2 Patterns of Intergenerational Mobility, Fathers to Sons, United States

FATHER'S POSITION	SON'S CLASS POSITION				
	Upper white collar	Lower white collar	Upper manual	Lower manual	Farm
Upper white collar					
White	**59.3%**	7.0%	14.2%	18.0%	1.5%
African American	**37.0**	9.3	16.7	37.0	0
Lower white collar					
White	48.1	**10.8**	15.2	25.3	.6
African American	42.1	**15.8**	21.1	21.1	0
Upper manual					
White	36.0	5.5	**33.7**	23.5	1.2
African American	18.2	8.0	**33.0**	40.7	0
Lower manual					
White	28.8	6.7	26.7	**36.9**	1.1
African American	17.9	12.1	19.6	**50.4**	0
Farm					
White	24.9	4.6	22.1	25.8	**17.1**
African American	9.6	2.6	22.4	55.8	**9.6**
Totals					
White	40.4	6.3	23.3	25.4	**4.9**
African American	18.3	8.5	22.4	48.1	**2.8**

Source: Theodore J. Davis, "Social mobility of African Americans in the 1980s: A controversy revisited." Unpublished paper, Department of Political Science, University of Delaware, 1991.

work reflects the fact that such occupations are perceived as desirable and thus children often choose to follow their parents. The handicaps for people at the bottom of the stratification system are more pronounced for African Americans and the advantages for people at the top are more pronounced for whites.

The major path of upward mobility is from lower- to upper-white-collar jobs. Four in ten children, both African American and white, move into higher-level white-collar positions from other white-collar jobs. Significant numbers of children from other levels also succeed in reaching the better white-collar jobs. Clearly, formal education is the key to making this move, because the boundary between managerial and professional jobs is expertise. To put it another way, the boundary separating the upper middle class from other class levels is "permeable," open to the combination of effort, achievement, and good fortune. There are differences in patterns of upward mobility in industrial nations, but education is always a primary route (Western & Wright, 1994). There is also a significant amount of downward mobility, with, for example, 40 percent of white upper-white-collar children and 60 percent of African-American upper-white-collar children failing to achieve that level in their own careers.

The class destinations of daughters suggest both differences and similarities between male and female patterns (Erikson & Goldthorpe, 1992). Comparing sons to daughters tends to show higher overall levels of mobility because downward mobility exceeds upward mobility. Larger numbers of white-collar daughters than sons end up in the low-skill working class (downward mobility). In part this is a function of sex-segregated occupational opportunities, which means that a disproportionate number of women are likely to end up in lower-middle-class forms of work. Moreover, women experience more downward mobility resulting from the breakdown of families through death, divorce, or abandonment. Downward mobility rates are higher in the United States than Europe because those nations tend to have broader social welfare programs.

A Vicious Cycle of Poverty?

One of the most pressing issues facing industrial nations is the potential for a **vicious cycle of poverty**, the intergenerational transmission of poverty from parents to children. If the children of poor parents are themselves doomed to poverty, there is the risk of creating a permanent underclass of citizens mired in poverty. It is a situation that limits the opportunities of children because of the social origins of their parents and violates the ideal of equal opportunity.

There is considerable upward mobility, but children of poor parents do face a much greater likelihood of being poor as adults than do children of parents above the poverty threshold. When those in poor and nonpoor backgrounds are compared, children in poverty achieve less formal education, earn less, and are more likely to be poor as adults. To illustrate, white children raised in poverty average $22,141 in annual wages compared to $33,655 for the nonpoor. African-American children raised in poor families are 2.5 times more likely to be poor as adults than African-American children raised in nonpoor families. The risk is even greater among white families, where poor children are 7.5 times more likely to be poor as adults than non-poor children (Corcoran, 1995). Explaining the factors that contribute to the inheritance of poverty is difficult, and it appears that it is the result of the interaction of a number of different factors.

The Structure of Neighborhoods and Labor Markets.   The immediate physical and social environment in which poor children mature limits their opportunities and imposes burdens upon them not usually faced by the nonpoor. The poor are typically segregated in distressed neighborhoods that are isolated from the larger society. This is a greater problem for minority youths because of the added burden of racial discrimination. Entry-level jobs there are disappearing. The broad pattern of deindustrialization is constantly reducing the number of blue-collar manufacturing jobs available to youths with limited educational and occupational credentials (Wilson, 1987; 1996). These jobs are being replaced by jobs in service and retail sales, most of which offer low pay and limited career opportunities.

Families that are successful typically desert the inner cities for the more comfortable neighborhoods of the suburbs. The out-migration of better-educated middle-class families deprives poor urban youths of role models that could foster hope and optimism. They are also deprived of links to the social networks that provide leads on jobs. Instead, ghetto residents are "surrounded by failure and come to expect the same" (Ellwood, 1987). The loss of the middle class also has the potential to weaken important institutions—political machines, social clubs, and churches—that could offer links to the larger community.

Family Resources and Family Structure.   The modest financial resources of poverty parents means they must allocate more of their income to current survival and less to investments in their children's education and schooling in the form of books and magazines, computers, visits to museums, and other educational experiences. Poverty parents also have more limited residential options and are thus more likely to raise their children in areas with poorer schools.

Growing up in single-parent or nonintact families is an additional risk factor for children and a significant one. It doubles the danger that such youths will be high school dropouts, doubles their chances of being teenage parents, and almost doubles the probability that they will enter adulthood without a job and not in school (McLanahan & Sandefur, 1994). This situation holds true, regardless of race, ethnicity, or gender, although there are some differences among these groups.

The risks are produced by a combination of limited economic, social, and community resources. Nonintact families are poorer, and thus have fewer financial resources to share with children for educational goals. Children growing up in married-couple families also have access to greater social resources in the form of time parents spend with their children, help with school work, parental supervision, and parental aspirations. Community resources are also entwined with family status in the sense that nonintact families reside in communities with poorer schools and fewer educational resources.

CLASS, RACE, ETHNICITY, GENDER, AND HIGHER EDUCATION

The fundamental importance of educational attainments in advanced industrial nations cannot be questioned. Each major benchmark (*e.g.,* high school diploma, associate's degree) in the educational process is important, but the baccalaureate may be the most significant educational credential. It is readily apparent that access to virtually all positions in the institutional elite and upper middle class demands a minimum of a bachelor's degree. Those lacking credentials are effectively barred from access to these classes. Moreover, the introduction of computer technology is imposing the same requirements on upper-level working-class jobs. Auto mechanics in the 1960s were able to repair most problems with hand tools. Today, they must be able to monitor and service the miniature computers that control most automotive functions. Advanced education is no guarantee of social mobility, because many college graduates are "underemployed," working in jobs below their skill level. One estimate claims that 20 percent of college graduates are either unemployed or in "high school jobs" (Hecker, 1992). However, the college degree remains a *prerequisite* to most of the better jobs.

The importance of formal education is shown in Exhibit 11.3, which compares the median earnings of full-time workers with different levels of education. Each increment of formal education pays financial dividends, although the earnings gap means that women earn only about 70 or 75 percent of men. Workers—men and women—with only an elementary school education are stalled at or near the poverty level and have little chance of ever improving their status. A high school diploma is worth $8000 a year to a male, $4000 to a female. A bachelor's degree pays significant benefits, about $15,000 for men and $12,000 for women. Advanced degrees show additional gains.

The basic relationship between class and education is unequivocal: the higher the social class of parents the greater the educational attainments of children. This is

EXHIBIT 11.3   Education and Median Earnings

EDUCATION	WOMEN	MEN
Nine years or less	$ 7096	$11,723
One to three years of high school	$ 8057	$15,791
High school graduate	$12,046	$23,365
Some college, no degree	$15,552	$28,004
Associate degree	$19,450	$31,027
Bachelor's degree	$24,065	$39,040
Master's degree	$33,509	$49,076
Professional degree	$38,588	$66,257
Doctorate	$39,821	$57,356

Source: U. S. Bureau of the Census, Current Population Report P60-193, *Money Income in the United States, 1995.* Washington, DC: U.S. Government Printing Office, 1996. Table 7.

a connection that shows up in the United States and in many other industrial societies including Great Britain, France, Israel, and the Netherlands (Shavit & Blossfeld, 1993). The most pronounced class bias occurs at the lower educational levels and is less for advanced levels of education. Thus, lower-class children who survive into post-secondary level face fewer obstacles. There are two major factors that combine to explain this link between class and education. Children from higher-class backgrounds have greater access to educational resources that help them in school, and the social organization of schools favors high-status youths.

Class and Educational Resources

Parents at higher levels in the stratification system are able to furnish their children with several different advantages that facilitate progress through the educational system. The basic economics of class cannot be ignored, but there are also more subtle social advantages that combine to help to reproduce class levels through the generations.

Public Schools: The Funding Gap.   The impact of social class emerges early in the education process in the form of inequality of resources in the schools they attend. American public education systems have traditionally relied on property taxes to support a large proportion—about 40 percent—of their school budgets. Deteriorating property values in poorer areas, especially inner cities and depressed rural areas, have contracted the tax base in many areas. The consequence is that poorer districts have less money to devote to the schools, and less money translates into lower teacher salaries, larger class size, and fewer enrichment activities. In some cases the discrepancies in expenditures are dramatic, resulting in court intervention in many states. The Texas courts, for example, demanded a reexamination of funding procedures when it was shown that the 100 wealthiest districts in Texas spent an average of $7233 per student compared to $2978 among the poorest 100 (Suro, 1990: 28). Thus it is evident that children of the poor are more likely to attend schools with fewer advantages than the children of the upper middle classes. Clearly, money isn't everything, because research shows that increasing financial outlays produce only mixed results in the quality of education as measured by test scores.

Cultural Capital.   Wealthier parents can also offer their children a different kind of advantage, something referred to as **cultural capital** (Bourdieu, 1977). Cultural capital is the configuration of knowledge and social skills that place their children at a distinct advantage in the school setting. It is the result of exposure to a wide range of cultural ideas and experiences over the course of the socialization process. It begins in infancy when parents speak to their babies (Hart & Risley, 1996). Children of professional parents hear, on average, 2100 words per hour during their first year of life, compared to 1200 words per hour in working-class families and 600 words per hour in poor families. The number of words infants hear increases their ability to reason, think conceptually, and solve problems later in life. As they grow older, elite and upper-middle-class parents buy their children more books, visit more museums and galleries, and attend more concerts than parents at lower levels and engage in other activities that make their offspring conversant with the ideas and values that are rewarded in most school systems. Consequently, their superior cultural literacy results in better grades and more schooling (DiMaggio, 1982; Aschaffenburg & Maas, 1997).[4] In contrast, children of the working class and the poor are more likely to lack this cultural capital contributing to lower subsequent academic and occupational success.

The concept of cultural capital has also been extended beyond academic literacy to a configuration of social skills, work habits, and styles (Lamont & Lareau, 1988). The reasoning is that educational attainments—and grades more specifically—reflect *both* cognitive mastery of subject matter and the manner in which students behave in the context of the classroom; appearance, cooperation, class participation, and effort are all aspects of this form of cultural capital rewarded in the schools. Research in this area is not consistent, although there is some evidence that poor children, Latino/as, and African Americans are *perceived* as having poorer work habits, and that such observations are associated with lower grades when controlling for performance on tests (Farkas, Grobe, Sheehan, & Yuan, 1990).

Class and the Organization of Schools: Tracking

Despite the tradition of free and open public education, it is evident that not all school systems are created equal and that class, race, and gender are relevant throughout the educational process. Increasingly, sociologists are focusing on structural arrangements and social dynamics occurring within classrooms to help to explain unequal educational outcomes. The interaction of class and school attainments is nowhere better illustrated than in the dynamics of tracking. **Tracking** sorts students into different curriculum programs, ostensibly on the basis of abilities and aspirations. Tracking was invented as a form of educational specialization to provide appropriate preparation for students heading for advanced education, while at the same time retaining potential dropouts by directing them toward viable vocational training. There are typically three routes or tracks, "college prep," "general," and "vocational" or "career." Although theoretically equal, track placements have the potential to produce differential educational experiences that recreate inequality and privilege.

Children of color and those from poor and blue-collar origins are more likely to end up on the "general" or "career" tracks, and it is very likely they will stay on those tracks (Oakes, 1985). One class-based factor in track assignment is that higher-class students score better on the standardized tests where their background gives them an advantage. Another is that teachers sometimes have lower academic expectations for children of the poor (Baron, Tom, & Cooper, 1985). Social origins also make a difference here, for higher-status parents have more contacts with schools and are more effective in influencing student placement and progress in the school system (Lareau, 1989).

---

[4]Empirical research on cultural capital has produced mixed results. Research in France (Robinson & Garnier, 1985) and Greece (Katsillis & Rubinson, 1990) did not support Bourdieu's formulation.

Experiences on different tracks are often organized to virtually guarantee inequality of outcome. College prep tracks attract better teachers and enjoy an enriched curriculum where students are encouraged to grow and develop individual abilities. Vocational tracks tend to fill instructional time with experiences that are likely to depress ambition and attainment. For instance, honors English classes may be organized around discussions of Romeo and Juliet while lower tracks fill in blanks on preprepared work sheets. At one school, vocational preparation in "food service" meant mopping floors in the cafeteria (Lightfoot, 1983). As a result, the size of the gap in academic performance between upper and lower tracks increases. In some cases test scores on the vocational track decline (Rosenbaum, 1975). The same pattern is repeated in Britain, where schools are more openly organized to sponsor and encourage the success of different ability groups (Kerkhoff, 1993). Perhaps the most disturbing consequence is the enduring stigma that accompanies tracking. A lower-track student reveals her feelings: "I felt good when I was with my class, but when they separated us, that changed . . . the way we thought about each other and turned us into enemies toward each other—because they said I was dumb and they were smart" (Rachin, 1989: 52).

Class and Academic Test Scores

Cultural capital and economic resources combine with natural talent to shape something called "intelligence" or "academic ability." The idea of academic ability is an elusive concept, but for a variety of reasons educators depend on batteries of standardized tests to measure it. For example, public schools administer 100 million tests each year, an average of 2.5 tests per student per year (Leslie & Wingert, 1990). These numbers are one indication of the major role that standardized testing plays in the educational system in the United States. Standardized tests are employed to decide admissions, allocate children among curricula within schools, and advise students, and they are a factor in college (SATs), graduate school (GREs), and professional school admissions (LSATs). Perhaps the most decisive standardized tests are the Scholastic Aptitude Test (SAT) and the American College Test (ACT) taken each year by hundreds of thousands of high school seniors hoping to gain admission to the college of their choice. It is estimated that 95 percent of entering freshmen at four-year colleges take the SAT tests (Marklein, 1997). To many observers standardized tests stand as symbols of the structural barriers to educational opportunity that exist in the society. There are now, and have been for decades, pronounced differences in scores associated with class, race, and gender (Carmody, 1989).

Using either parental income or parental education as a measure of social class standing shows dramatic 250 point differences in SAT scores! To illustrate, the average combined math and verbal score of students with family incomes of less than $10,000—families living in poverty—is 873, compared to scores of 1015 for children of middle-income parents ($50,000 to $60,000) and 1130 for the wealthiest group ($100,000 and over) of youths (Marklien, 1997). Considerations of gender and color are also associated with variations in average test scores. There is a small gender gap in math, with males outscoring females by an average of 50 points, and although members of minority groups have made relatively large gains in recent years, all except Asian Americans continue to lag behind the white majority.

Such tests at best measure only certain types of abilities—verbal and mathematical skills—and ignore skills and abilities such as creativity, inventiveness, and imagination. In addition, critics have argued that these tests are biased against the lower classes and minority groups who have acquired less cultural capital. Despite the widespread belief, such tests do not measure "innate intelligence" so much as they reflect the backgrounds, preparation, and training of students. An executive of one testing agency openly acknowledges that college entrance examination scores "reflect the inequities that continue to exist in our society (and) disparities in academic preparation" (Ordovensky, 1989). This point is best illustrated by the experiences of Asian Americans.

Asian Americans: Culture and Test Scores.   Asian Americans' college entrance test scores rival all other groups on standardized test scores, and they consistently outrank other students on the math section of the SATs, leading to their being labeled the "model minority." Asian-American success has been traced to cultural traditions that stress academic effort. In a survey of San Francisco–area high school students, it was found that female Asian Americans spent an average of 12.3 hours per week doing homework, compared to 9.2 for African Americans, and 8.6 for whites (Butterfield, 1986). Comparable figures for males were 11.7 for Asian Americans, 6.3 for African Americans and 8.0 for whites. Moreover, Asian-American students had consistently better attendance records and cut classes less frequently.

Asian-American parents at all economic and social class levels seek to instill a high level of dedication to educational attainment in their children. At a general level this reflects the influence of Asian culture, specifically Confucian philosophy, which emphasizes self-discipline, hard work, and humility. For example, in a comparison of Chinese American, Japanese American, and Anglo parents, Asian Americans place the strongest emphasis on the importance of hard work in school (Stevenson, 1982). They are likely to subscribe to the idea that anyone can do well if they study hard. In contrast, Americans are more likely to attribute school success to natural talent, thus de-emphasizing the importance of effort in the form of attendance and homework. Moreover, Asian culture emphasizes the importance of bringing honor to the family, and one way in which this can be done is through educational accomplishments. Still another aspect of this philosophy is that it encourages personal humility. When ratings of intellectual ability are compared, Anglo-American parents give their children the highest ratings, and the children typically rate themselves as above average. It may be that this creates a sense of complacency that reduces the levels of effort. In contrast, Japanese Americans and Chinese Americans are more likely to rate themselves average or below, thus instilling greater effort to achieve.

Class and College

The chances of a youth attending college are directly related to social class. As shown in Exhibit 11.4, an increasingly larger proportion of children in each higher income

EXHIBIT 11.4 Family Social Class and Higher Education

FAMILY INCOME	PERCENTAGE WITH CHILDREN IN COLLEGE	FAMILY INCOME	PERCENTAGE WITH CHILDREN IN COLLEGE
Under $10,000	16%	$40,000–$49,999	47%
$10,000–$19,999	25	$50,000–$74,999	53
$20,000–$29,999	32	$75,000 and over	64
$30,000–$39,999	39		

Note: Only families with college-age children are included. Data include all forms of post-secondary education, including community colleges and four-year institutions.

Source: U.S. Bureau of the Census, Current Population Report P20-487, *School Enrollment—Social and Economic Characteristics of Students: 1994.* Washington, DC: U.S. Government Printing Office, 1996. Table 19.

bracket are currently enrolled in some form of higher education. Children of African-American and Latino/a parents are less likely to be attending college, but among those that do the same overall association between class and education is repeated. Even if there were no other factors at work, the sheer financial burden of higher education is prohibitive for some segments of society. One year of higher education in 1995–96 cost $9600 at a public institution, $20,361 at a private school. Clearly, such costs will put education beyond the reach of many parents at the lower end of the class system.

Children of the more affluent also have the resources to enlist the aid of private college counselors, private consultants who work with individual students, offering lists of possible colleges, counseling—beginning as early as eighth grade—on course selection, tutoring on improving admission test scores, and coaching and role playing on how to conduct campus visitations. The total cost of this help can be thousands of dollars.

Various forms of financial aid are designed to lessen the impact of class but cannot eliminate it. Moreover, during the 1980s federal aid for students declined in absolute dollars, although the number of students increased, meaning more students were competing for fewer dollars of financial aid. There has also been a shift in the pattern of financial aid from grants to loans that must be repaid. Many low-income students are reluctant to accumulate large debts to attend college. It should also be noted that the decline in the availability of student aid has a greater impact on minorities because average family income is below that of whites.

Gender and the Science Pipeline.   Increasing numbers of upper-middle-class occupations depend on a firm grounding in science and mathematics. Engineering, medicine, academic science, and system analysis are among the most obvious examples. Preparation for these careers can be visualized as forming a **science pipeline** of training beginning with elementary school training in the basics and continuing through advanced university education to employment in these fields (Berryman,

---

CASE STUDY:
Educational Networks among the Elite

Breaking into the institutional elite of leadership positions in business, education, and government is the epitome of successful upward mobility. A review of the class origins of these men and women suggests that although the stratification system is open to people of modest social origins, it is heavily weighted in favor of those from more advantaged class backgrounds. A significant proportion of the elite are children of elite parents, and most who originate outside this class are recruited from the ranks of the upper middle class. The number of persons who started life in the lower middle or working class is small, and it is extremely rare for children of the poor to achieve such success.

Many of the advantages of the elite are articulated through a network of high-prestige schools that simultaneously prepare these children for future positions of leadership and virtually guarantee that they will achieve these positions by introducing them to a network of other children of the institutional and capitalist elites. For many children the first step is enrollment at one of a narrow circle of exclusive boarding schools (Cookson & Persell, 1985). Prep schools such as Choate and St. Andrews provide a rigorous and sound academic preparation for future educational accomplishments and polish the social skills and values—the cultural capital of the elite—necessary for access to subsequent positions of power and influence. In addition, the students begin to associate with a network of other individuals who will also occupy such positions. The process continues with enrollment at a relatively small core of select undergraduate colleges—places such as Columbia, Harvard, Pennsylvania, Princeton, Stanford, and Yale (Useem & Karabel, 1986; Kingston & Lewis, 1990).

Such schools are among the most exclusive and expensive, which narrows the pool of candidates, although they are increasingly open to the general population. Moreover, many of these colleges grant preferential admission to the children of alumni, thus giving them an additional advantage. Alumni children typically comprise 12 percent of Harvard's entering class, and Notre Dame reserves 25 percent of its openings for alumni (Leslie, 1991). This is a practice not likely to change, because all colleges and universities depend upon their wealthy alumni for donations, and it will continue to give the children of the elite another advantage.

Nonelite students who are capable and fortunate enough to gain access to such schools dramatically increase their chances of upward mobility. One study of corporate executives showed that one-half had earned a B.A. from one of just eleven elite colleges (Useem & Karabel, 1986). It is at these schools that children of parents at lower levels in the stratification system can acquire the combination of skills, cultural capital, and social contacts that will help them later. The major organizations recruit from these schools, and research shows that the least able graduates (measured by standardized tests) of select colleges have a higher chance of economic success than the most able students from low-status schools (Kingston & Smart, 1990: 162).

1983). The number of students in the pipeline narrows over time because science is cumulative and a lack of preparation at any one point excludes people from subsequent training. Following the experience of students in the pipeline reveals that women's participation declines more rapidly than men's beginning in the high school years. This holds true in the United States, Canada, Japan, and Sweden (Hanson, Schaub & Baker, 1996).

This is a puzzling development because girls, as a rule, tend to get better grades in all subjects (science and math included) from the earliest school years into high school (Stockard & Wood, 1984). Younger girls (under age 14) also outperform boys on both verbal and math standardized test scores, but male scores in math begin to outpace those of females in junior and senior high school (Wentzel, 1988). This manifests itself in an advantage of about 50 points on SAT tests at the completion of high school. Moreover, beginning in high school, girls express less interest and less confidence about their computer skills than boys (Krendl, Broihier, & Fleetwood, 1989). Thus, women and men have different experiences in the pipeline, suggesting the impact of sociocultural factors.

Boys are very early subtly and directly encouraged in the direction of scholastic performance in computer science and mathematics, often because math skills are presumed to be more consistent with conventional sex-typed masculine traits such as "analytic ability." This shows up in the fact that parents and counselors tend to be more supportive of males following math-based careers. Parents also subtly encourage boys more than girls by the amusement they choose for them. Video games are most children's first exposure to computers, and 75 percent of all video games are bought for boys (O'Neal, 1998). Interestingly, only one game in ten has any female roles.

There are also differential experiences in the context of the classroom. Girls with high math aptitude are less likely to be assigned to "high ability" groups than boys (Hallinan & Sorensen, 1987). Teachers tend to initiate more academic contact with boys and give more attention to male students than female students. In addition, males who give incorrect answers are usually exhorted to greater effort while females are praised simply for trying. The experiences of African-American children in the area of math are not as well researched but parallel those based on gender in other contexts. Teachers tend to devote more attention to white children, sometimes giving more praise, and are likely to grant African-American children only conditional praise for academic effort (*e.g.,* "A good paper, for a change"), thus subtly suggesting a fundamental intellectual inferiority (Grant, 1984).

However, the inconsistency between grades and standardized test scores is perplexing (Kimball, 1989). It has been suggested that the higher grades earned by females may reflect the fact that social competencies as well as cognitive skills enter into the grading process. Females, on average, have an advantage in social competencies, being more cooperative and attentive and having more positive attitudes toward teachers. This leaves the decline in females' test scores to be explained. One interpretation is that it is due to the increasing salience of conventional gender roles that surfaces in later adolescence. This is the age at which conforming to culturally defined gender roles looms large and subtly encourages females to underemphasize competence at cross-gender skills such as math, which is still accepted as an area of male competence. The interaction between gender and math achievement is not fully understood, but the implications remain, especially among America's 2 million working engineers, of whom only about 8 percent are women.

Educational Attainments of Minorities.   African Americans and Latino/as have lower educational attainments than white students; they are less likely to finish high school and fewer of those with diplomas subsequently pursue higher education (Exhibit 11.5). A number of factors converge to produce this situation. The financial resources of parents are one factor, because minority children are more likely to be working class or lower middle class. Those from inner cities often attend underfunded and understaffed schools that are unable to meet student needs. In addition, there are language barriers for Latino/a students who are the children of recent immigrants. Although minority enrollments in higher education continue to lag behind those of whites, the numbers show an upward trend. For example, minorities posted significant increases in higher education between 1994 and 1995, with a 9.8 percent increase in associate degrees, 8.5 percent in bachelor's degrees, and 9.7 percent in professional degrees (ACE, 1997).

EXHIBIT 11.5 High School Graduation and College Enrollments

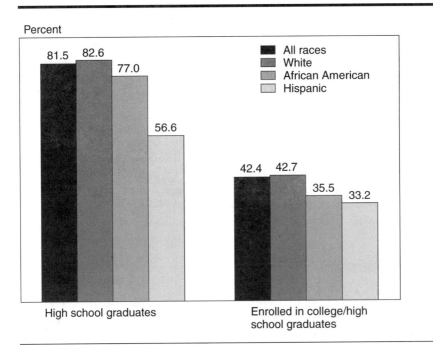

Source: U.S. Bureau of the Census, Current Population Report P20-487, *School Enrollment—Social and Economic Characteristics of Students: 1994.* Washington, DC: U.S. Government Printing Office, 1996. Figure 2.

DISCRIMINATION IN HIRING

Educational attainments do not translate directly into occupational attainments because so many social factors influence the transition from school to jobs. One consistent pattern is that women and minorities do not earn the same benefits from additional education that white males do. This suggests that discrimination still haunts the marketplace. Law and custom have long combined to restrict employment opportunities for older applicants, women, and people of color, and the survival of outright discrimination cannot be ignored in the United States, even in the 1990s. New York City, for example, sued several employment agencies for discriminating against African Americans and older people in making placements (Buder, 1990). They are accused of referring African Americans and older citizens to fewer jobs, less desirable jobs, and lower-paying work. Lawsuits in New York and elsewhere are typically based on the experiences of pairs of "testers," simulated candidates with similar qualifications who apply for the same jobs, a Latino/a and a white for example, or a man and a women. Because their qualifications are matched, they should have roughly the same degree of success in finding jobs. Testers in Philadelphia found that men were twice as likely to get job interviews and five times as likely to be offered servers' jobs in expensive restaurants (Koretz, 1995).

One of the most systematic studies using testers was conducted in Chicago and San Diego and showed dramatic differences in treatment (Cross, Kenny, Mell, & Zimmerman, 1990). Teams of "job applicants" were created by matching Anglo and Latino men on physical characteristics (age, height, weight) and subjective attributes (demeanor, appearance, communication skills), and then sending them through a two-and-one-half-day training session to prepare them to exhibit constant behavior during the application interview. Upon completing the training and armed with similar resumes, they answered newspaper advertisements for entry-level jobs requiring a high school education.

They approached 360 firms, and Anglo applicants were more successful at every stage in the process. In about one-third of the 360 situations where both candidates answered an ad, Latino/as were treated less favorably than Anglos. Anglos received 33 percent more interviews and 52 percent more job offers than Latino/as. In addition, there were a number of more subtle aspects of unequal treatment. For example, interviewers devoted less time to Latino/a applicants than to Anglos, averaging about one-third more time with candidates who were eventually offered jobs.

DOWNWARD MOBILITY

Social origins and other factors combine to influence the place where people begin their careers. Obviously, not all people remain at their original class level over the course of their entire careers. There is continual movement among organizations and jobs, and people take time out from their careers for additional education and retraining. Most movement is horizontal within the same occupational level, meaning that the majority of people remain at their original class level (Winfield, Campbell, Kerckhoff, Everett, & Trott, 1989).

Beginning in the 1980s workers at all levels in the stratification system became acutely aware of the potential for a loss of status due to the restructuring of the economy. The problems are often symbolized by a single word—**downsizing.** It means to reduce the work force of a company through plant closings and large-scale layoffs, layoffs prompted by economic considerations—rising costs, declining sales, global competition, cyclical business, languishing stock prices, or some combination of these factors. Layoffs have taken a heavy toll on jobs during the 1990s, with 500,000 jobs eliminated each year (Lohr, 1996).

The risk of unemployment is inherent in the structure of market economies, and workers are regularly displaced even in periods of prosperity. Displaced workers are thrown into the labor market where they must compete for jobs, and some lose their place in the class system. Prolonged joblessness can cause people to fall into poverty. The very threat of unemployment produced by widespread instability in employment creates a threatening environment. Very few people are free from the worry that future rounds of layoffs will cost their jobs and their future. Add to that the fact that remaining workers are expected to increase their levels of effort in order to compensate for departed coworkers. Human resources professionals worry that their firms are understaffed (Olsten Corporation, 1996), and large proportions of corporate survivors felt overworked (Light & Tilser, 1994).

Those who survive corporate layoffs may also experience both short-term and long-term attitudinal changes. Some survivors suffer survivor guilt, an uncomfortable feeling of remorse because they have jobs while friends and coworkers have lost theirs (Kirk, 1995). Not unexpectedly, there is a heightened sense of anxiety and insecurity, even among survivors who do not face imminent job loss (Roskies & Louis-Guerin, 1990). Insecurity can erode the quality of work performance and contribute to negative attitudes toward management and a general decline in morale. These problems highlight the ultimate irony of downsizing, that layoffs inspired by the need to improve the economic position of firms may simultaneously set in motion changes that can weaken productivity and dilute loyalty to the firm.

Joblessness and Downward Mobility

The one obvious event with the potential to have an impact on the direction of careers is involuntary unemployment. Each year hundreds of thousands of people are displaced from their jobs, usually for structural reasons such as plant closings, technological change, or corporate downsizing. Losing a job is a painful experience, in and of itself, but it also compels people to seek to reestablish their careers, often at a lower class level.

The experiences of American workers displaced during the early 1990s reveal the scope of downward mobility (Gardner, 1995). Between January of 1991 and December of 1992 about 5.5 million workers permanently lost their jobs to various forms of structural unemployment—plant closings, company failures, jobs abolished, or layoffs due to a lack of work. More than one-half had been in their jobs for at least three years. Members of the working class faced the greatest risk of unemployment, while professionals and service workers had the lowest rates of displacement.

Those workers were surveyed again 1994, and it was found that about three-quarters had found new jobs; but many settled for jobs that were inferior to those lost (Exhibit 11.6). About one-third (31.8 percent) were reemployed in full-time positions that paid the same or more than the jobs they lost. All the rest had not survived as well. About one-quarter were employed on a full-time basis but had taken a pay cut. (About one-third of this group took a pay cut of 20 percent or more.) Another 15 percent were earning less because they were in part-time work, were self-employed, or were unpaid family business workers. In a few cases involuntary unemployment actually proved beneficial, although the trauma of unemployment is typically very painful. Some workers were freed from dead-end jobs and benefited from retraining programs that allowed them to secure better positions.

The remainder were less fortunate. More than one in ten were unemployed in 1994, meaning that some had been without regular work for two or three years. The unemployment rate for Latino/a and African-American workers was much higher (18 percent) than for white workers (10 percent). Another 12.4 percent had left the labor force, some joining the ranks of "discouraged" workers and others accepting the role of "retired." Thus, not only did these 5.5 million people have to endure the shock of losing their livelihood, most were worse off financially than before.

Earlier studies of displaced workers show that the risk of downward mobility is greater for women, minorities, and people at the bottom of the stratification system

---

EXHIBIT 11.6 Displaced Workers: Old Jobs and New

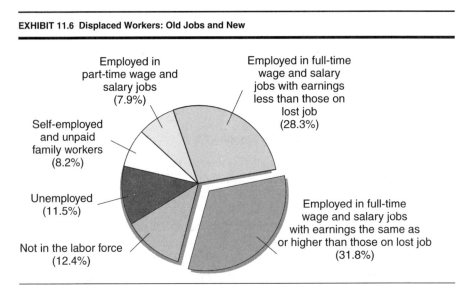

Source: Jennifer M. Gardner, "Worker displacement: A decade of change," *Monthly Labor Review* 118 (April, 1995), Chart 1, page 50.

(Flaim & Sehal, 1985). The threat of unemployment is greater in the jobs of the poor and the working class, and thus also increases the risks for minorities who hold a higher proportion of such jobs. Displaced African-American and Latino/a workers and women all experience longer periods of unemployment.

The Implications of Downward Mobility

Downward mobility carries with it the potential for personal stress as well as demanding significant readjustments in social relations and self-image. It may require a reorientation of lifestyles, especially when it is accompanied by financial loss. Moreover, it is not solely an individual experience because it has an impact on whole families, requiring spouses and children to reexamine lifestyles and long-term goals (Newman, 1988). Individuals socialized into the standards and values of one class during childhood can experience feelings of anxiety and isolation as they adjust to the situation of a different class. Some studies suggest a link between downward mobility and more serious forms of personal adjustment problems, mental illness, and even suicide (Lopreato & Chafetz, 1970; Kessin, 1971). Such problems prevail despite the fact that the sources of downward mobility can often be traced to structural sources beyond the control of the individual.

CONCLUSION: INDEPENDENT BUSINESSES AND THE AMERICAN DREAM

Countless people aspire to begin their own business, and many risk it each year although the failure rate is high. Included in this category are grocery stores and restaurants, liquor stores and bars, consulting firms, small factories, fishing boats and taxicabs, service stations and dry cleaners. In many ways, the independent businessperson epitomizes the American Dream. These businesses are begun by people who believe in the idea and are willing to risk their savings, go into debt, and work the long hours necessary to make a success of it.

The lure of owning a small business has many sources, both structural and personal. Many believe they have a new idea or product and are sustained by stories of the financial success of others. Jerry Yang and David Filo, for example, who perfected Yahoo!, were multimillionaires by age 30. Their celebrated successes hold out the possibility that anyone with talent and initiative can prosper. Monetary rewards are only one enticement, and other factors may well outweigh the potential for making money. Some are attracted by the challenge of independent effort, seeing it as a chance to test their abilities.

People are also propelled in the direction of independent businesses because of the lack of meaningful employment opportunities elsewhere. One important factor is independence, the opportunity to be free from supervision and the opportunity to exercise some initiative. One group in this situation is people in jobs without realistic opportunities for career advancement. Members of the lower middle class and working class are often in this situation because their jobs offer limited promotion opportunities and are subject to strict authority on the job. Their own business offers them independence. Limited mobility opportunities are also a salient factor. Women at all levels in the class system face limited mobility horizons because of glass ceilings, and in the 1990s women began to form small businesses at a rate twice that of men. A major motive is the limitations they experience in the workplace.

Racial and ethnic minorities also typically confront structural barriers. They face discrimination in the search for work and experience disadvantages in the labor market (Light, 1972). It is, for example, often difficult for professional and managerially trained immigrants to find employment in upper-middle-class jobs when they reach a new nation. Recent immigrants may also lack the communication skills necessary to compete for jobs. Therefore, minority groups show a penchant for small businesses in societies around the world, Greeks and Koreans in the United States, Indians and Turkish Cypriots in Britain, the Chinese in Southeast Asia (Cobas, 1986).

In addition, racial and ethnic minorities may be able to take advantage of opportunities not available to others (Cobas, 1986; Aldrich & Waldinger, 1990). New immigrants typically settle in older, inner city neighborhoods. The concentration of minorities in urban enclaves creates "protected markets," markets for goods and services that can best be met by minority business owners who have special insight into community tastes and preferences. In addition, urban immigrants are often concentrated in geographic areas that large national firms such as supermarkets and banks abandon. Founding and operating small businesses within ethnic communities are in some instances enhanced by communal ties and networks. Some Asian immigrants, for example, bring with them the practice of informal community savings and loan arrangements that allow aspiring businesspersons to borrow money at low rates. This emphasizes that the success of immigrant entrepreneurs is often a group phenomenon that depends upon the resources of the community for employees, financing, and customers (Aldrich & Waldinger, 1990).

Small businesses do not necessarily bring great economic rewards, and the failure rate is daunting. However, small businesses are an attractive alternative to organizational employment, especially for workers at the lower ends of the stratification system, women, and people of color. They offer opportunities for independence, autonomy, and a route for overcoming the social barriers that societies erect. Despite the risk and the heavy investment of effort, small businesses continue to have a powerful symbolic attraction.

KEY CONCEPTS

closed systems	intragenerational mobility	status attainment model
cultural capital	open systems	structural mobility
downsizing	science pipeline	tracking
intergenerational mobility	social mobility	vicious cycle of poverty

SUGGESTED READING

PETER M. BLAU AND OTIS D. DUNCAN, *The American Occupational Structure.* New York: Wiley, 1967. The original formulation of the status attainment model.

PETER W. COOKSON, JR., AND CAROLINE HODGES PERSELL, *Preparing for Power: America's Elite Boarding Schools.* New York: Basic Books, 1985. A firsthand account of the schools where future members of the elite are socialized.

GREG DUNCAN, *The Consequences of Growing Up Poor.* New York: Russell Sage, 1997. The implications of poverty follow children into their adult lives.

ROBERT ERIKSON AND JOHN H. GOLDTHORPE, *The Constant Flux: A Study of Class Mobility in Industrial Societies.* New York: Oxford University Press, 1992. A broad-based analysis of patterns of mobility among families in nine European nations.

KATHERINE S. NEWMAN, *Falling from Grace: The Experience of Downward Mobility in the American Middle Class.* New York: Free Press, 1988. A chronicle of the experiences of skilled blue-collar and white-collar workers coping with unemployment.

JEANNIE OAKES, *Keeping Track: How Schools Structure Inequality.* Santa Monica, CA: Rand Corporation, 1985. A detailed discussion of the organization of tracking systems and the consequences for youths on different tracks.

FREDERICK R. STROBEL, *Upward Dreams, Downward Mobility.* Lanham, MD: Rowman & Littlefield, 1993. A discussion of the economic and political factors that have contributed to the deterioration in earnings of the middle class. Suitable for advanced students.

WILLIAM JULIUS WILSON, *When Work Disappears.* New York: Knopf, 1996. An eminent sociologist explores the causes of inner-city poverty and offers some suggestions for dealing with it.

Bibliography

ACE (AMERICAN COUNCIL ON EDUCATION). 1997. *Status Report on Minorities in Higher Education.* New York.

ADAMS, THOMAS S., AND HELEN L. SUMNER. 1985. *Labor Problems.* London: Macmillan.

ADLER, NANCY E.; W. THOMAS BOYCE; MARGARET A. CHESNEY; SUSAN FOLKMAN; AND LEONARD SYME. 1993. "Socioeconomic inequalities in health." *JAMA* 269: 3140–3145.

ADLER, VALERIE. 1989. "Little control=lots of stress." *Psychology Today* April: 18–19.

ALDRICH, HOWARD E., AND ROGER WALDINGER. 1990. "Ethnicity and entrepreneurship." *Annual Review of Sociology* 16: 111–135.

ALEXANDER, JEFFREY C. 1990. *Structure and Meaning: Rethinking Classical Sociology.* New York: Columbia University Press.

ALEXANDER, KEITH. 1997. "American Airlines apologizes for manual." *USA Today* (August 21): 2B.

ALLEN, THEODORE. 1994. *The Invention of the White Race.* New York: Verso.

ALLPORT, GORDON. 1954. *The Nature of Prejudice.* Cambridge, MA: Addison-Wesley.

ANDERSEN, MARGARET L. 1997. *Thinking about Women.* 4th ed. Needham Heights, MA: Allyn & Bacon.

ANDERSEN, MARGARET L., AND PATRICIA HILL COLLINS (eds). 1992. *Race, Class and Gender.* Belmont, CA: Wadsworth.

ANDERSON, KAREN. 1988. "A history of women's work in the United States." Pp. 25–41 in Ann Helton Stromberg and Shirley Harkness (eds.), *Women Working.* Mountain View, CA: Mayfield.

ANFUSCO, DAWN. 1994. "Deflecting workplace violence." *Personnel Journal* (October): 26–33.

ANGELOU, MAYA. 1970. *I Know Why the Caged Bird Sings.* New York: Bantam.

APPLE, R. W. 1995. "Poll shows disenchantment with politicians and politics." *The New York Times* (August 12): 1–8.

211

ARIAN, EDWARD. 1971. *Bach, Beethoven, Bureaucracy: The Case of the Philadelphia Orchestra.* Tuscaloosa, AL: University of Alabama Press.

ASCHAFFENBURG, KAREN, AND INEKE MAAS. 1997. "Cultural and educational careers." *American Sociological Review* 62: 573–588.

AUERBACH, JERALD S. 1976. *Unequal Justice.* New York: Oxford University Press.

BACON, JOHN. 1997. "Uninsured kids." *USA Today* (March 28): 3A.

BAILEY, THOMAS A. 1956. *The American Pageant.* Boston, MA: D. C. Heath.

BALTZELL, E. DIGBY. 1958. *Philadelphia Gentlemen: The Making of a National Upper Class.* New York: Free Press.

BALTZELL, E. DIGBY. 1964. *The Protestant Establishment: Aristocracy and Caste in America.* New York: Random House.

BANFIELD, EDWARD. 1970. *The Unheavenly City.* Boston, MA: Little, Brown.

BARBANEL, JOSH. 1987. "Societies and their homeless." *The New York Times* (November 29): 8E.

BARON, AVA. 1980. "Women and the making of the American working class: A study in the proletarianization of printers." *Review of Radical Political Economics* 14: 23–42.

BARON, REUBEN M.; DAVID Y. H. TOM; AND HARRIS M. COOPER. 1985. "Social class, race and teacher expectations." Pp. 251–269 in Jerome B. Dusek (ed.), *Teacher Expectancies.* Hillsdale, NJ: Lawrence Erlbaum Associates.

BARRERA, MARIO. 1979. *Race and Class in the Southwest.* Notre Dame, IN: University of Notre Dame Press.

BARRETT, EDITH J. 1995. "The political priorities of African-American women in state legislatures." *Legislative Studies Quarterly* 20: 223–247.

BARRY, SKIP. 1996. "Rents out of reach." *Dollars & Sense* 208: 42–43.

BATES, TIMOTHY, AND DARRELL L. WILLIAMS. 1993. "Racial politics: Does it pay?" *Social Science Quarterly* 74: 507–522.

BAUERS, BOB, AND MERRITT WALLICK. 1989. "Chemical industry wrote laws we live by." *Wilmington, DE News Journal* (June 11): 1–19A.

BAXTER, JANEEN. 1994. "Is husband's class enough? Class location and class identity in the United States, Sweden, Norway and Australia." *American Sociological Review* 59: 220–235.

BECK, ULRICH. 1995. *Ecological Politics in an Age of Risk.* Cambridge, MA: Polity Press.

BELTON, BETH. 1997. "New Chamber chief targets lawyers, unions." *USA Today* (June 12): 4B.

BENDIX, RINEHARD. 1962. *Max Weber: An Intellectual Portrait.* Garden City, NY: Doubleday.

BENNEFIELD, ROBERT L. 1995. *Health Insurance Coverage: 1994.* Current Population Reports pp. 60–190. U.S. Government Printing Office.

BENNET, JAMES. 1997. "Lumps, ghosts and chips. It's the Lincoln bedroom." *The New York Times* (March 2): 1–20.

BENNETT, CLAUDETTE. 1995. *The Black Population in the United States.* Current Population Reports, Series pp. 20–480. Washington, DC: U.S. Government Printing Office.

BERGER, JOSEPH M.; HAMIT FISEK; ROBERT Z. NORMAN; AND MORRIS ZELDITCH, JR. 1977. *Status Characteristics and Social Interaction.* New York: Elsevier.

BERRIMAN, GERALD. 1973. *Caste in the Modern World.* Morristown, NJ: General Learning Press.

BERRYMAN, S. E. 1983. *Who Will Do Science?* New York: Rockfeller Foundation.

BERUBE, ALLAN, AND FLORENCE BERUBE. 1997. "Sunset Trailer Park." Pp. 16–39 in Matt Wray and Annalee Newitz (eds.), *White Trash: Race and Class in America.* New York: Routledge.

BETEILLE, ANDRE. 1992. *The Backward Classes in Contemporary India.* New York: Oxford University Press.

BIANCHI, SUZANNE M., AND DAPHNE SPAIN. 1996. *Women, Work, and Family in America.* Washington, DC: Population Reference Bureau.

BIANCHI, SUZANNE M., AND DAPHNE SPAIN. 1997. "U.S. women make workplace progress." *Population Today* 25 (January): 1–2.

BLAU, PETER M., AND OTIS DUDLEY DUNCAN. 1967. *The American Occupational Structure.* New York: Wiley.

BLAUNER, ROBERT. 1972. *Racial Oppression in America.* New York: Harper & Row.

BLOCK, FRED L. 1992. "Capitalism without class power." *Politics and Society* 20: 277–302.

BLOOD, ROBERT O., AND D. M. WOLFE. 1960. *Husbands and Wives: The Dynamics of Married Life*. New York: Free Press.

BOBO, LAWRENCE, AND FRANKLIN D. GILLIAM, JR. 1990. "Race, sociopolitical participation, and black empowerment." *American Political Science Review* 84: 377–393.

BOECK, GREG. 1991. "Baseball, NFL struggle to match NBA model." *USA Today* (December 18): 5C.

BORDEWICH, FERGUS M. 1996. *Killing the White Man's Indian*. New York: Doubleday.

BORRUS, AMY. 1997. "The end of corporate welfare as we know it?" *Business Week* (February 10): 36–37.

BOSE, CHRISTINE E. 1987. "Dual spheres." Pp. 267–285 in Beth B. Hess and Myra Marx Ferree (eds.), *Analyzing Gender: A Handbook of Social Science Research*. Newbury Park, CA: Sage.

BOSE, CHRISTINE E., AND PETER H. ROSSI. 1983. "Gender and jobs: Prestige standings of occupations as affected by gender." *American Sociological Review* 48: 316–330.

BOTTOMORE, TOM, AND ROBERT J. BRYM, eds., 1989. *The Capitalist Class*. New York: New York University Press.

BOURDIEU, PIERRE. 1977. "Cultural reproduction and social reproduction." Pp. 487–511 in J. Karabel and A. H. Halsey (eds.), *Power and Ideology in Education*. New York: Oxford University Press.

Bradwell v. Illinois. 1873. (83 U.S. 16 Wall 141).

BRAGG, RICK. 1996. "Just a grave for a baby, but anguish for a town." *The New York Times* (March 31): 14.

BRAGG, RICK. 1997. *All Over but the Shoutin'*, New York: Pantheon.

BRAUN, DENNY. 1997. *The Rich Get Richer: The Rise of Income Inequality in the United States and the World*. 2nd edition. Chicago: Nelson-Hall.

BRAVERMAN, HARRY. 1974. *Labor and Monopoly Capitalism*. New York: Monthly Review Press.

BRENNER, O. C.; JOSEPH TOMKIEWICZ; AND VIRGINIA ELLEN SCHEIN. 1989. "The relationship between sex role stereotypes and requisite management characteristics revisited." *Academy of Management Journal* 32: 662–669.

BRINK, WILLIAM, AND LOUIS HARRIS. 1967. *Black and White*. New York: Simon & Schuster.

BROOKS, THOMAS R. 1971. *Toil and Trouble*. New York: Delacourt.

BROWN, PHIL, AND FAITH I. T. FERGUSON. 1995. "Making a big stink: Women's work, women's relationships, and toxic waste activism." *Gender & Society* 9: 145–172.

BUDER, LEONARD. 1990. "Employment agency accused of bias." *The New York Times* (February 21): 3B.

BULLARD, ROBERT D.; J. EUGENE GRIGSBY III, AND CHARLES LEE, eds. 1994. *Residential Apartheid*. Los Angeles, CA: CAAS Publications.

BURKETT, ELINOR. 1997. "God created me to be a slave." *The New York Times* (October 12): 56–60.

BURRIS, VAL. 1986. "The discovery of the new middle class." *Theory and Society* 15: 317–349.

BUTTERFIELD, FOX. 1986. "Why Asians are going to the head of the class." *The New York Times* (August 3): 18–22.

BYRNE, JOHN A. 1996. "How high can CEO pay go?" *Business Week* (April 22): 100–106.

CARMODY, DEIRDRE. 1989. "Minority students gain on college entrance tests." *The New York Times* (September 12): 16A.

CASPER, LYNNE, SARA S. MCLANAHAN AND IRWIN GARFINKLE. 1994. "The gender–poverty gap: What we can learn from other countries." *American Sociological Review* 59: 594–605.

CAVEN, RUTH. 1969. *The American Family*. New York: Crowell.

CENTERS, RICHARD. 1949. *The Psychology of Social Classes*. Princeton, NJ: Princeton University Press.

CHAMPION, DEAN J. 1989. "Private counsels and public defenders: A look at weak cases, prior record, and leniency in plea bargaining." *Journal of Criminal Justice* 17: 253–263.

CHANDLER, SUSAN. 1995. "Look who's sweating now." *Business Week* (October 16): 96–98.

CLANCY, PAUL. 1988. "Camel companions." *USA Today* (December 28): 2A.

CLAWSON, DAN; ALAN NEUSTADTL; AND DENISE SCOTT. 1992. *Money Talks: Corporate PACs and Political Influence*. New York: Basic Books.

COBAS, JOSE A. 1986. "Paths to self-employment among immigrants: An analysis of four interpretations." *Sociological Perspectives* 29: 101–120.

COCKERHAM, WILLIAM; GUENTHER LUESCHEN; GERHARD KUNZ; AND JOE L. SPAETH. 1986. "Social stratification and self-management of health." *Journal of Health and Social Behavior* 17: 1–13.

COLASANTO, DIANE, AND LINDA WILLIAMS. 1987. "The changing dynamics of race and class." *Public Opinion* 9:50–53.

COLEMAN, RICHARD P., AND LEE RAINWATER. 1978. *Social Standing in America: New Dimensions of Class*. New York: Basic Books.

COLLINS, RANDALL. 1986. *Weberian Sociological Theory*. New York: Cambridge University Press.

COLLINS, RANDALL. 1994. *Four Sociological Traditions*. New York: Oxford University Press.

COLLINS, RANDALL, AND MICHAEL MAKOWSKY. 1984. *The Discovery of Society*, 3rd ed. New York: Random House.

COLLINS, SARA. 1994. "The new migrant workers." *U.S. News & World Report* (July 4): 53–55.

COOKSON, PETER W., JR., AND CAROLINE HODGES PERSELL. 1985. *Preparing for Power: America's Elite Boarding Schools*. New York: Basic Books.

CORCORAN, M. "Rags to rags: Poverty and mobility in the United States." *Annual Review of Sociology* 21: 237–268.

COSE, ELLIS. *The Rage of the Privileged Class*. New York: HarperCollins.

COUGHLIN, ELLEN K. 1995. "America's dilemma." *The Chronicle of Higher Education*. (September 8): 10–23.

COUNTS, GEORGE S. 1925. "The social status of occupations: A problem in vocational guidance." *School Review* 33: 16–27.

COYLE, MARCIA; FRED STRASSER; AND MARIANNE LAVELLE. 1990. "Fatal defense." *The National Law Journal* 13 (June 11): 30–44.

CRARY, DAVID. 1996. "Remark leaves Toronto cold." *The Wilmington News Journal* (April 6): 7A.

CROOK, CLIVE. 1997. "The future of the state." *The Economist* 344 (September 20): 1–48S.

CROSS, HARRY; GENEVIEVE KENNY; JANE MELL; AND WENDY ZIMMERMAN. 1990. *Employment Hiring Practices: Differential Treatment of Hispanic and Anglo Job Seekers*. Washington, DC: Urban Institute.

CROSSETTE, BARBARA. 1996. "U.N. survey finds world rich–poor gap widening." *The New York Times* (July 15): 3a.

CRULL, SUE R., AND BRENT T. BRUTON. 1985. "Possible decline in tolerance toward minorities: Social distance on a Midwest campus." *Sociology and Social Research* 70: 57–61.

CRUTCHFIELD, R.D.; G.S. BRIDGES; AND S. R. PITCHFORD. 1994. "Analytical and aggregation biases in analyses of imprisonment: Reconciling discrepancies in studies of racial disparity." *Journal of Research in Crime and Delinquency* 31: 166–182.

CULLEN, JOHN B., AND SHELLY M. NOVICK. 1979. "The Davis-Moore theory of stratification: A further examination and extension." *American Journal of Sociology* 84: 1424–1437.

DAHL, ROBERT A. 1958. "A critique of the ruling elite model." *American Political Science Review* 52: 463–469.

DAHRENDORF, RALF. 1959. *Class and Class Conflict in Industrial Society*. Stanford, CA: Stanford University Press.

DANIELS, ARLENE KAPLAN. 1987. *Invisible Careers: Women Civic Leaders in the Volunteer World*. Chicago, IL: University of Chicago Press.

DANIELS, ROGER. 1990. *Coming to America*. New York: HarperCollins.

DAVIES, CHRISTIE. 1982. "Ethnic jokes, moral values and social boundaries." *British Journal of Sociology* 33: 383–403.

DAVIS, DAVID B. 1966. *The Problem of Slavery in Western Culture*. Ithaca, NY: Cornell University Press.

DAVIS, KINGSLEY. 1953. "Reply to Tumin." *American Sociological Review* 18: 394–397.

DAVIS, KINGSLEY, AND WILBERT E. MOORE. 1945. "Some principles of stratification." *American Sociological Review* 10: 242–249.

DAVIS, NANCY, AND ROBERT V. ROBINSON. 1988. "Class identification of men and women in the 1970s and 1980s." *American Sociological Review* 53: 103–112.

DAVIS, THEODORE J. 1991. "Social mobility of African Americans in the 1980s: A controversy revisited." Unpublished paper. Department of Political Science, University of Delaware.

DEAR, MICHAEL J., AND JENNIFER R. WOLCH. 1987. *Landscapes of Despair: From Deinstitutionalization to Homelessness*. Princeton, NJ: Princeton University Press.

DEAUX, KAY, AND MARY E. KITE. 1987. "Thinking about gender." Pp. 92–116 in Beth B. Hess and Myra Marx Ferree (eds.), *Analyzing Gender: A Handbook of Social Science Research*. Newbury Park, CA: Sage.

DEAUX, KAY, AND LIONEL L. LEWIS. 1984. "Structure of gender stereotypes: Interrelationships among components and gender label." *Journal of Personality and Social Psychology* 46: 991–1004.

DEL PINAL, JORGE, AND AUDREY SINGER. 1997. *Generations of Diversity*. Washington, DC: Population Reference Bureau.

DEMOTT, BENJAMIN. 1990. *The Imperial Middle: Why Americans Can't Think Straight about Class*. New York: Morrow.

DEPARLE, JASON. 1991. "New rows to hoe in the 'Harvest of Shame.'" *The New York Times* (July 28): 3E.

DESIPIO, LOUIS. 1996. *Counting the Latino Vote*. Charlottesville, VA: University of Virginia Press.

DIMAGGIO, PAUL. 1982. "Cultural capital and school success: The impact of status culture participation on the grades of U.S. high school students." *American Sociological Review* 47: 189–201.

DOMHOFF, G. WILLIAM. 1970. *The Higher Circles*. New York: Vintage.

DOMHOFF, G. WILLIAM. 1974. *The Bohemian Grove and Other Retreats: A Study in Ruling Class Cohesiveness*. New York: Harper & Row.

DOMHOFF, G. WILLIAM. 1990. *The Power Elite and the State: How Policy Is Made in America*. New York: Aldine De Gruyter.

DREW, ELIZABETH. 1997. *Whatever It Takes: The Real Struggle for Political Power in America*. New York: Viking, 1997.

DUBOFSKY, MELVYN. 1969. *We Shall Be All: A History of Industrial Workers of the World*. Chicago: Quadrangle.

DUGAS, CHRISTINE. 1997. "Nationwide settles relining charges." *USA Today* (March 11): 1B.

DUNCAN, CYNTHIA M., ed. 1992. *Rural Poverty in America*. Westport, CN: Praeger.

DUNCAN, GREG J. 1984. *Years of Poverty, Years of Plenty*. Ann Arbor, MI: University of Michigan Institute for Social Research.

DUNCAN, GREG. 1997. *The Consequences of Growing Up Poor*. New York: Russell Sage.

DUNCAN, GREG J.; J. BROOKES-GUNN; AND P. K. KLEBANOV. 1994. "Economic deprivation and early-childhood development." *Child Development* 6: 296–318.

DURANT, THOMAS J., JR., AND KATHLEEN H. SPARROW. 1997. "Race and class consciousness among lower- and middle-class blacks." *Journal of Black Studies* 27: 334–346.

DUSTER, TROY. 1990. *Backdoor to Eugenics*. New York: Routledge.

DYE, THOMAS. 1986. *Who's Running America?* Englewood Cliffs, NJ: Prentice Hall.

DYE, THOMAS R. 1995. *Who's Running America: The Clinton Years*. Upper Saddle River, NJ: Prentice Hall.

EARLE, JOHN R., AND CATHERINE T. HARRIS. 1989. "College students and blue-collar workers: A comparative analysis of sex-role attitudes." *Sociological Spectrum* 9: 455–466.

The Economist. 1997a. "The coming car crash." *The Economist* (May 10): 21–23.

The Economist. 1997b. "It's wise to deindustrialize." *The Economist* (April 26): 78.

The Economist. 1997c. "Homelessness and race: Black hole." *The Economist* 342: (January 18): 30–31.

The Economist. 1997d. "Integrated but unequal." *The Economist* 242 (February 8): 58–59.

The Economist. 1997e. "Politicians for rent." *The Economist* (February 8): 23–25.

The Economist. 1997f. "Fighting the class war." *The Economist* (September 27): 63.

The Economist. 1997g. "Still too scarce." *The Economist* (December 23): 27.

The Economist. 1997h. "Women in Work." *The Economist* (November 29): 110.

EDITORS. 1988. "Developments in the law—Race in the criminal process." *Harvard Law Review* 101: 1520–1532.

EDMONDS, PATRICIA. 1991. "By the numbers, tracking segregation in 219 metro areas." *USA Today* (November 11): 3A.

EDMONDS, PATRICIA. 1994. "Have schools really changed?" *USA Today* (May 12): 2A.

EHRENREICH, BARBARA. 1989. *Fear of Falling*. New York: Pantheon.

EHRENREICH, BARBARA, AND DEIRDRE ENGLISH. 1979. *For Her Own Good*. Garden City, NY: Anchor Press.

ELLER, T. J. 1996. "Who stays poor? Who doesn't?" U.S. Bureau of the Census. *Current Population Report* pp. 70–155. Washington, DC: U.S. Government Printing Office.

ELLIS, ROBERT A., AND W. CLAYTON LANE. 1967. "Social mobility and social isolation." *American Sociological Review* 32: 237–253.

ELLWOOD, D. 1987. *Understanding Dependency: Choices, Confidence, or Culture?* U.S. Department of Health and Human Services. Washington, DC: U.S. Government Printing Office.

Employment and Earnings. 1996a. "Employed civilians by detailed occupation, sex, race, and Hispanic origin." *Employment and Earnings* 43 (January): 168–174.

Employment and Earnings. 1996b. "Weekly earnings in 1995." *Employment and Earnings* 43 (January): 163–164.

Employment and Earnings. 1997. "Employed civilians by detailed occupation." *Employment and Earnings* 44 (January): 177–184.

ENGELS, FRIEDRICH. 1972. *The Origin of the Family, Private Property, and the State*. New York: International Publishers.

ERIKSON, ROBERT, AND JOHN H. GOLDTHORPE. 1992. *The Constant Flux: A Study of Class Mobility in Industrial Societies*. New York: Oxford University Press.

ERIKSON, ROBERT, AND JOHN H. GOLDTHORPE. 1993. *The Constant Flux: A Study of Social Mobility in Industrial Societies*. New York: Oxford University Press.

ETAUGH, CLAIRE, AND PATRICIA POERTNER. 1991. "Effects of occupational prestige, employment status and marital status on perceptions of mothers." *Sex Roles* 24: 345–353.

FABRIKANT, GERALDINE, AND SHELBY WHITE. 1995. "Noblesse oblige . . . with strings." *The New York Times* (April 30): 3F.

FARKAS, GEORGE; ROBERT P. GROBE; DANIEL SHEEHAN; AND YUAN SHUAN. 1990. "Cultural resources and school success: Gender, ethnicity, and poverty groups within an urban school district." *American Sociological Review* 55: 127–142.

FARLEY, REYNOLDS, AND WILLIAM H. FRY. 1994. "Changes in segregation of whites from blacks: Small steps toward a more integrated society." *American Sociological Review* 59: 23–45.

FARLEY, REYNOLDS; CHARLOTTE STEEH; AND MARIA KRYSAN. 1994. "Stereotypes and segregation: Neighborhoods in the Detroit area." *American Journal of Sociology* 100: 750–780.

FAUNCE, WILLIAM A. 1989. "Occupational status-assignment systems: The effect of status on self esteem." *American Journal of Sociology* 95: 378–400.

FEAGIN, JOE R. 1972. "Poverty: We still believe that God helps those who help themselves." *Psychology Today* (November): 101–129.

FEAGIN, JOE R. 1984. *Racial and Ethnic Relations*, 2nd ed. Englewood Cliffs, NJ: Prentice Hall.

FEAGIN, JOE R., AND CLAIRECE BOOHER FEAGIN. 1996. *Racial and Ethnic Relations*, 5th ed. Upper Saddle River, NJ: Prentice Hall.

FEDERAL ELECTION COMMISSION. 1996. *PAC Summary, 1996*. http://www.tray.com/cgi-win/pacsum.exe

FEDERMAN, MARY; THESIA I. GARNER; KATHLEEN SHORT; W. BORMAN CUTTER IV; JOHN KIELY; DAVID LEVINE; DUANE MCGOUGH; AND MARILYN MCMILLEN. 1996. "What does it mean to be poor in America?" *Monthly Labor Review* 119 (May): 3–17.

FERGUSON, THOMAS, AND JOEL ROGERS. 1986. *Right Turn: The Decline of the Democrats and the Future of American Politics*. New York: Hill and Wang.

FERREE, MYRA MARX. 1985. "Between two worlds: German feminist approaches to working class women and work." *Signs* 10: 517–536.

FERRELL, DAVID. 1990. "Too much still isn't enough." *Wilmington (DE) News Journal* (March 11): 1–6J.

FEUER, LEWIS S. 1959. *Marx and Engels: Basic Writings on Politics and Philosophy*. Garden City, NY: Doubleday.

FINDER, ALAN. 1995. "Despite tough laws, sweatshops flourish." *The New York Times* (February 6): 1A–4B.

FISCHER, CLAUDE. 1982. *To Dwell among Friends: Personal Networks in Town and City.* Chicago, IL: University of Chicago Press.

FISHER, GORDON M. 1992. "The development and history of the poverty thresholds." *Social Security Bulletin* 55: 3–14.

FITZGERALD, MARK. 1997. "Media perpetuate a myth." *Editor & Publisher* 130 (August 16): 13.

FLAIM, PAUL O., AND ELLEN SEHAL. 1985. "Displaced workers of 1979–1982: How well have they fared?" *Monthly Labor Review* 108 (June): 3–15.

FONER, PHILIP S. 1964. *History of the Labor Movement in the United States.* New York: International Publishers.

FORM, WILLIAM. 1985. *Divided We Stand: Working Class Stratification in America.* Urbana, IL: University of Illinois Press.

FRANKLIN, BENJAMIN. 1961. *Autobiography and Other Writings.* New York: New American Library.

FREDRICKSON, RONALD H.; JUN-CHIH GISELA LIN; AND SHAOMIN XING. 1992. "Social status ranking of occupations in the People's Republic of China, Taiwan and the United States." *The Career Development Quarterly* 40: 351–360.

FRIEDSON, ELIOT. 1986. *Professional Powers: A Study of the Institutionalization of Professional Power.* Chicago: University of Chicago Press.

GABLE, DONNA. 1993. "Series shortchange working-class and minority Americans." *USA Today* (August 30): 3D.

GALLUP POLL. 1985. "Blame for poverty." *The Gallup Poll Monthly* 234 (March): 24.

GALLUP POLL. 1990. "Americans disagree widely on what constitutes 'rich.' " *The Gallup Poll Monthly* 298 (July): 28–36.

GALLUP POLL. 1991. "Americans say police brutality common." *The Gallup Poll Monthly* 306 (March): 53–55.

GALLUP POLL. 1995. "Satisfaction with personal life, U.S." *The Gallup Poll Monthly* 357: 7.

GALLUP POLL. 1996. "Wealth distributed fairly?" *The Gallup Poll Monthly* 368 (May): 34.

GALLUP POLL. 1997. "Fund-raising ethics doubted." *USA Today* (October 8): 6A.

GANS, HERBERT. 1967. *The Levittowners.* New York: Random House.

GANS, HERBERT. 1995. *The War against the Poor: The Underclass and Antipoverty Policy.* New York: Basic Books.

GARCIA, JOHN A. 1997. "Latino national political survey." *ICPSR Bulletin* 18 (September): 1–5.

GARDNER, JENNIFER M. 1995. "Worker displacement: A decade of change." *Monthly Labor Review* 118 (April): 45–57.

GILBERT, DENNIS, AND JOSEPH A. KAHL. 1993. *The American Class Structure.* 4th ed. Belmont, CA: Wadsworth.

GLASTER, GEORGE. 1990. "Racial steering by real estate agents: Mechanisms and motives." *The Review of Black Political Economy* 19: 39–62.

GLASTRIS, PAUL; JULIAN E. BARNES; KENT JENKINS; AND NANCY SHUTE. 1997. "Hang on to your wallet." *U.S. News & World Report* (April 14): 26–31.

GOLD, MARTIN. 1966. "Undetected delinquent behavior." *Journal of Research in Crime and Delinquency* 3: 27–46.

GOLDBERG, CAREY. 1996. "Asian immigrants help bolster U.S. economy, new report says." *The New York Times* (March 31): 32.

GONZALEZ, DAVID. 1992. "What's the problem with 'Hispanic'? Just ask a 'Latino.' " *The New York Times* (November 15): 6E.

GOODE, WILLIAM J. 1978. *The Celebration of Heroes: Prestige as a Social Control System.* Berkeley, CA: University of California Press.

GOODWIN, LEONARD. 1972. *Do the Poor Want to Work?* Washington, DC: The Brookings Institute.

GORDON, MILTON. 1964. *Assimilation in American Life.* New York: Oxford University Press.

GOTTSCHALK, PETER; SARA MCLANAHAN; AND GARY SANDEFUR. 1994. "The dynamics and intergenerational transmission of poverty and welfare participation." Pp. 89–102 in S. Danziger,

G. Sandefur, and D. Weinberg (eds.), *Confronting Poverty: Prescriptions for Change*. Cambridge, MA: Harvard University Press.

GRABB, EDWARD G. 1997. *Theories of Social Inequality: Classical and Contemporary Perspectives*, 3rd ed. New York: Harcourt Brace.

GRANT, LINDA. 1984. "Black females' place in the desegregated classroom." *Sociology of Education* 57: 98–110.

GREENBERGER, ELLEN; WENDY A. GOLDBERG; THOMAS J. CRAWFORD; AND JEAN GRANGER. 1988. "Beliefs about the consequences of maternal employment for children." *Psychology of Women Quarterly* 12: 35–59.

GREENFIELD, LAUREN. 1997. *Fast Forward: Growing Up in the Shadow of Hollywood*. New York: Knopf/Melcher Media.

GREENHOUSE, STEVEN. 1997a. "Accord to combat sweatshop labor faces obstacles." *The New York Times* (April 13): 1–20.

GREENHOUSE, STEVEN. 1997b. "Debating union dues and political don'ts." *The New York Times* (October 12): 3WK.

GROSS, JANE. 1997. "Stress on Wall Street? Try the eighth grade." *The New York Times* (October 5): 37–38.

GROVER, CHRIS, AND KEITH SOOTHILL. 1996. "'A murderous underclass?' The press reporting of a sexually motivated murder." *The Sociological Review* 44: 398–416.

GRUSKY, DAVID B., ed. 1994. *Social Stratification: Class, Race & Gender*. Boulder, CO: Westview Press.

HALL, RICHARD. 1994. *Sociology of Work*. Thousand Oaks, CA: Pine Forge Press.

HALLE, DAVID. 1984. *America's Working Man*. Chicago: University of Chicago Press.

HALLINAN, MAUREEN T., AND AAGE B. SORENSEN. 1987. "Ability grouping and sex differences in mathematics achievement." *Sociology of Education* 60: 63–72.

HAMILTON, RICHARD. 1972. *Class and Politics in the United States*. New York: Wiley.

HANSON, SANDRA L.; MARYELLEN SCHAUB; AND DAVID P. BAKER. 1996. "Gender stratification in the science pipeline: A comparative analysis of seven countries." *Gender & Society* 10: 271–290.

HARRINGTON, MICHAEL. 1962. *The Other America: Poverty in the United States*. New York: Macmillan.

HART, BETTY, AND TODD R. RISLEY. 1995. *Meaningful Differences in the Everyday Experiences of Young American Children*. Baltimore, MD: Paul H. Brookes.

HAUG, MARIE R., AND HAROLD A. WIDDISON. 1975. "Dimensions of occupational prestige." *Sociology of Work and Occupations* 2: 3–27.

HECKER, DANIEL E. 1992. "Reconciling conflicting data on jobs for college graduates." *Monthly Labor Review* 115 (July): 3–12.

HEDDEN, SUSAN. 1993. "Made in the U.S.A." *U.S. News & World Report* (November 22): 48–55.

HENSON, KEVIN. *The Temp*. Philadelphia, PA: Temple University Press.

HERRING, CEDRIC. 1989. *Splitting the Middle: Political Alienation, Acquiescence, and Activism among America's Middle Layers*. New York: Praeger.

HILL, ANN C. 1979. "Protection of women workers and the courts: A legal history." *Feminist Studies* 5: 247–273.

HILL, DEBBIE. 1996. "3m women below 'decency threshold.'" *The Times of London* (September 29): 1(5).

HOBERMAN, JOHN. 1997. *Darwin's Athletes*. Boston: Houghton Mifflin.

HOCHSCHILD, JENNIFER L. 1995. *Facing Up to the American Dream: Race, Class and the Soul of the Nation*. Princeton, NJ: Princeton University Press.

HOFSTADER, RICHARD. 1955. *Social Darwinism in American Thought*. Boston: Beacon.

HOLMES, STEVEN A. 1996. "Income disparity between poorest and richest rises." *The New York Times* (June 20): 1–13A.

HOLMES, STEVEN A. 1997. "A rose-colored view of race." *The New York Times* (June 15): 4E.

HOOKS, BELL. 1984. *Feminist Theory from Margin to Center*. Boston: South End Press.

HOUT, MICHAEL; CLEM BROOKS; AND JEFF MANZA. 1993. "The persistence of classes in post-industrial society." *International Sociology* 8: 259–277.

HUBER, JOAN, AND WILLIAM H. FORM. 1973. *Income and Ideology*. New York: Free Press.

HUDDY, LEONIE, AND NAYDA TERKILDSEN. 1994. "The consequences of gender stereotypes for women candidates at different levels and types of office." *Political Research Quarterly* 46: 503–525.

HUDIS, PAULA M. 1977. "Commitment to work and wages: Earnings differences of black and white women." *Sociology of Work and Occupations* 4: 123–146.

HUNTER, TERA W. 1997. *To 'Joy my Freedom: Southern Black Women's Lives and Labor after the Civil War*. Cambridge, MA: Harvard University Press.

IRWIN, JOHN, AND JAMES AUSTIN. 1997. *It's About Time: America's Imprisonment Binge*. 2nd ed. Belmont, CA: Wadsworth.

JACKMAN, MARY R. 1979. "The subjective meaning of social class identification in the United States." *Public Opinion Quarterly* 43: 443–462.

JACKMAN, MARY R., AND ROBERT W. JACKMAN. 1983. *Class Awareness in the United States*. Berkeley: University of California Press.

JACKMAN, MARY R., AND MARY SCHEUER SENTER. 1982. "Different therefore unequal: Beliefs about trait differences between groups of unequal status." Pp. 123–134 in Donald J. Treiman and Robert V. Robinson (eds.), *Research in Stratification and Mobility*. Volume 2. Greenwich, CT: JAI Press.

JACKMAN, ROBERT W. 1979. *Politics and Social Equality: A Comparative Analysis*. New York: Wiley.

JACKMAN, ROBERT W. 1987. "Political institutions and voter turnout in industrial democracies." *American Political Science Review* 81: 405–423.

JACOBS, JERRY A. 1989. *Revolving Doors: Sex Segregation and Women's Careers*. Stanford, CA: Stanford University Press.

JACOBSEN, JOYCE P., AND LAURENCE M. LEVIN. 1995. "Effects of intermittent labor force attachment on women's earnings." *Monthly Labor Review* 118 (September): 14–19.

JAMES, DAVID R. 1988. "The transformation of the southern racial state: Class and race determinants of local-state structures." *American Sociological Review* 53: 191–208.

JAYNES, GERALD D., AND ROBIN M. WILLIAMS (eds.) 1989. *Common Destiny: Blacks and American Society*. Washington, DC: National Academy Press.

JEFFRIES-FOX, SUZZANNE, AND NANCY SIGNORIELLI. 1978. "Television and children's concepts of occupations." Paper presented at Telecommunications Policy Conference, Airlie House, VA.

JENCKS, CHRISTOPHER. 1994. *The Homeless*. Cambridge, MA: Harvard University Press.

JENCKS, CHRISTOPHER, AND PAUL E. PETERSON (eds.). 1991. *The Urban Underclass*. Washington, DC: The Brookings Institution.

JENSEN, JOAN M. 1980. "Cloth, butter and boarders: Women's household production for the market." *Review of Radical Political Economics* 12: 14–24.

JOHNSTON, WILLIAM, AND DOUGLAS BAER. 1993. "Class consciousness and national contexts." *Canadian Review of Sociology and Anthropology* 30: 271–295.

JONES, LEALAN AND LLOYD NEWMAN WITH DAVID ISAY. 1997. *Our America: Life and Death on the South Side of Chicago*. New York: Scribner.

JURAVICH, TOM, AND PETER R. SHERGOLD. 1988. "The impact of unions on the voting behavior of their members." *Industrial and Labor Relations Review* 41: 374–385.

KAHN, KIM F. 1992. "Does being male help? An investigation of the effects of candidate gender and campaign coverage on evaluations of U.S. Senate candidates." *Journal of Politics* 54: 497–517.

KAHN, KIM F., AND EDIE N. GOLDENBERG. 1991. "Women candidates in the news: An examination of gender differences in U.S. Senate campaign coverage." *Public Opinion Quarterly* 55: 180–199.

KALETTE, DENISE. 1991. "Swiss women strike for equal pay, benefits." *USA Today* (June 5): 6B.

KANTER, ROSABETH M. 1997. *Men and Women of the Corporation*. New York: Basic Books.

KATSILLIS, JOHN, AND RICHARD RUBINSON. 1990. "Cultural capital, student achievement, and educational reproduction: The case of Greece." *American Sociological Review* 55: 270–279.

KATZ, MICHAEL B. 1992. *The Undeserving Poor: From the War on Poverty to the War on Welfare*. New York: Pantheon.

KAUTSKY, JOHN H. 1996. "Contexts of conservatism, liberalism and socialism." *Society* 33 (March–April): 48–52.

KEEN, JUDY; JUDI HASSON; AND TOM SQUITIERI. 1997. "Dinner raised $488,000, and questions." *USA Today* (February 7): 4A.

KEPHART, WILLIAM E. 1994. *Extraordinary Groups*, 5th ed. New York: St. Martin's Press.

KERCKHOFF, ALAN C. 1976. "The status attainment process: Socialization or allocation?" *Social Forces* 55: 368–381.

KERCKHOFF, ALAN C. 1993. *Diverging Pathways: Social Structure and Career Deflections*. New York: Cambridge University Press.

KERCKHOFF, ALAN C. 1995. "Institutional arrangements and stratification processes in industrial societies." *Annual Review of Sociology* 21: 323–348.

KESSIN, KENNETH. 1971. "Social and psychological consequences of intergenerational occupational mobility." *American Journal of Sociology* 77: 1–18.

KESSLER-HARRIS, ALICE. 1982. *Out to Work*. New York: Oxford University Press.

KIESLER, SARA; LEE SPROULL; AND JACQUELYNNE S. ECCLES. 1983. "Second class citizens." *Psychology Today* 17: 40–48.

KILBORN, PETER T. 1990. "Automation: Pain replaces old drudgery." *The New York Times* (June 24): 1–22.

KILBORN, PETER T. 1995. "Up from welfare: It's harder and harder." *The New York Times* (April 16): 4E.

KIMBALL, MEREDITH M. 1989. "A new perspective on women's math achievement." *Psychological Bulletin* 105: 198–214.

KINGSTON, PAUL W., AND LIONEL S. LEWIS (eds.). 1990. *The High Status Track: Studies of Elite Schools and Stratification*. Albany, NY: State University of New York Press.

KINGSTON, PAUL W., AND JOHN C. SMART. 1990. "The economic pay-off of prestigious colleges." Pp. 147–174 in Paul W. Kingston and Lionel S. Lewis (eds.), *The High Status Track: Studies of Elite Schools and Stratification*. Albany, NY: State University of New York Press.

KIRK, MARGARET O. 1995. "When surviving just isn't enough." *The New York Times* (June 25): 11F.

KLEPPER, MICHAEL, AND ROBERT GUNTHER. 1996. *The Wealthy 100: From Benjamin Franklin to Bill Gates—A Ranking of the Richest Americans, Past and Present*. New York: Citadel Press.

KLUEGEL, JAMES R., AND ELIOT R. SMITH. 1986. *Beliefs about Inequality*. New York: Aldine de Gruyter.

KOHN, MELVIN L., AND CARMI SCHOOLER. 1983. *Work and Personality: An Inquiry into the Impact of Social Stratification*. Norwood, NJ: Ablex Publishing.

KOHN, MELVIN L., AND KAZIMIERZ M. SLOMCZYNSKAI. 1990. *Social Structure and Self Direction: A Comparative Analysis of the United States and Poland*. Cambridge, MA: Basil Blackwell.

KOLCHIN, PETER. 1988. *Unfree Labor: American Slavery and Russian Serfdom*. New York: Oxford University Press.

KORENMAN, SANDERS; JANE E. MILLER; AND JOHN E. SJAASTAD. 1995. "Long-term poverty and child development in the United States: Results from the NLSY." *Children and Youth Services Review* 17: 127–155.

KORETZ, GENE. 1995. "Prejudice: Still on the menu." *Business Week* (April 3): 42.

KRENDL, KATHY A.; MARY C. BROIHIER; AND CYNTHIA FLEETWOOD. 1989. "Children and computers: Do sex-related differences persist?" *Journal of Communication* 39: 85–93.

KUNEN, JAMES S. 1990. "Pop! Goes the Donald." *People* (July 29): 29–34.

LAMONT, MICHELE, AND ANNETTE LAREAU. 1988. "Cultural capital: Allusions, gaps and glissandos in recent theoretical developments." *Sociological Theory* 6: 153–168.

LAREAU, A. 1989. *Home Advantage: Social Class and Parental Intervention in Elementary Education*. New York: Falmer.

LAUMANN, EDWARD O. 1966. *Prestige and Association in an Urban Community*. Indianapolis, IN: Bobbs-Merrill.

LAVELLE, MARIANNE. 1997. "EPA goes to bat for Native Americans." *The National Law Journal* (April 8): 12A.

LEE, BARRETT A.; SUE HINZE JONES; AND DAVID W. LEWIS. 1990. "Public beliefs about the causes of homelessness." *Social Forces* 69: 253–265.

LEEPER, MARK S. 1991. "The impact of prejudice on female candidates: An experimental look at voter inference." *American Politics Quarterly* 19: 248–261.

LEGGETT, JOHN C. 1968. *Class, Race, and Labor*. New York: Oxford University Press.

LEMASTERS, E. E. 1975. *Blue-collar Aristocrats*. Madison, WI: University of Wisconsin Press.

LEONHARDT, DAVID. 1997. "Two-tier marketing." *Business Week* (March 17): 82–90.

LESLIE, CONNIE. 1991. "A rich legacy of preference." *Newsweek* (June 24): 59.

LESLIE, CONNIE, AND PAT WINGERT. 1990. "Not as easy as A, B or C." *Newsweek* (January 8): 56–58.

LEVELLE, MARIANNE. 1997. "A political elite joins lobby shop." *National Law Journal* (August 4): 1–26A.

LEVY, CLIFFORD. 1997. "Hispanic voters emerge as powerful force that democrats cannot take for granted." *The New York Times* (November 9): 39.

LEWCHUK, WAYNE A. 1993. "Men and monotony: Fraternalism as a managerial strategy at the Ford Motor Company." *Journal of Economic History* 53: 824–856.

LEWIS, MICHAEL. 1995. "The rich." *The New York Times Magazine* (December 19): 65–135.

LEWIS, OSCAR. 1966. *LaVida*. New York: Random House.

LICHTER, ROBERT S.; LINDA S. LICHTER; AND STANLEY ROTHMAN. 1991. *Watching America*. Englewood Cliffs, NJ: Prentice Hall.

LIGHT, IVAN. 1972. *Ethnic Enterprise in America*. Berkeley, CA: University of California Press.

LIGHT, LARRY, AND JULIE TILSER. 1994. "The big picture." *Business Week* (November 7): 6.

LIGHTFOOT, SARAH LAWRENCE. 1983. *The Good High School*. New York: Basic Books.

LII, JANE H. 1995. "Week in sweatshop reveals grim conspiracy of the poor." *The New York Times* (March 12): 1–40A.

LINDGREN, ETHEL J. 1938. "An example of culture contact without conflict: Reindeer Tungas and Cossacks of Northern Manchuria." *American Anthropologist* 40: 605–621.

LIPMAN-BLUMAN, JEAN. 1984. *Gender Roles and Power*. Englewood Cliffs, NJ: Prentice Hall.

LIPSET, SEYMOUR MARTIN. 1990. *Continental Divide: The Values and Institutions of the United States and Canada*. London: Routledge.

LIPSET, SEYMOUR MARTIN, AND WILLIAM SCHNEIDER. 1983. *The Confidence Gap: Business, Labor, and Government in the Public Mind*. New York: Free Press.

LOCKWOOD, DAVID. 1958. *The Blackcoated Worker*. London: Allen & Unwin.

LOEB, PENNY; WARREN COHEN; AND CONSTANCE JOHNSON. 1995. "The new redlining." *U.S. News & World Report* (April 17): 51–58.

LOEBER, JUDITH. 1994. *Paradoxes of Gender*. New Haven, CT: Yale University Press.

LOHR, STEVE. 1996. "Though upbeat on the economy, people still fear for their jobs." *The New York Times* (December 29): 1–22.

LOPREATO, JOSEPH, AND JANET S. CHAFETZ. 1970. "The political orientation of skidders: A middle range theory." *American Sociological Review* 35: 440–451.

MACKENZIE, GAVIN. 1973. *The Aristocracy of Labor*. New York: Cambridge University Press.

MACKINNON, CATHERINE A. 1993. *Only Words*. Cambridge, MA: Harvard University Press.

MACKINNON, NEIL J., AND TOM LANGFORD. 1994. "The meaning of occupational prestige scores." *The Sociological Quarterly* 35: 215–245.

MACLEOD, JAY. 1987. *Ain't No Making It*. Boulder, CO: Westview Press.

MARKLEIN, MARY BETH. 1997. "SAT scores up, but so too is grade inflation." *USA Today* (August 27): 1A–4D.

MARRIOTT, MICHAEL. 1997. "Black erotica challenges black tradition." *The New York Times* (June 1): 41–44.

MARSH, ROBERT M. 1971. "The explanation of occupational prestige hierarchies." *Social Forces* 50: 214–222.

MARX, KARL, AND FRIEDRICH ENGELS. 1959. *Marx and Engels: Basic Writings on Politics and Philosophy*. Lewis Feuer (ed.). Garden City, NY: Doubleday.

MARX, KARL, AND FRIEDRICH ENGELS. 1964. *Selected Writings*. T. B. Bottomore (ed.). New York: McGraw-Hill.

MASLAND, TOM; ROD NORDLAND; MELINDA LIU; AND JOSEPH CONTRERAS. 1992. "Slavery." *Newsweek* (May 4): 30–39.

MASSEY, DOUGLAS S.; GRETCHEN A. CONDRAN; AND NANCY A. DENTON. 1987. "The effect of residential segregation on black social and economic well-being." *Social Forces* 66: 29–56.

McCourt, Frank. 1996. *Angela's Ashes*. New York: Scribner.

McCurrer, Daniel P., and Amy B. Chasanov. 1995. "Trends in unemployment insurance benefits." *Monthly Labor Review* 118 (September): 30–39.

McDonald, William. 1997. "Movies find a way to close the class divide." *The New York Times* (April 6): 16–32H.

McKee, J. P., and A. C. Sherriffs. 1957. "The differential evaluation of males and females." *Journal of Personality* 25: 356–371.

McLanahan, S. S., and Gary D. Sandefur. 1994. *Uncertain Childhood, Uncertain Future*. Cambridge, MA: Harvard University Press.

Melich, Tanya. 1996. *The Republican War Against Women: An Insider's Report Behind the Lines*. New York: Bantam.

Milkman, Ruth. 1983. "Female factory labor and industrial structure: Control and conflict over 'women's work' in auto and electrical manufacturing." *Politics and Society* 12: 159–203.

Millan, Stan. 1997. "Enviro-bias is hot topic in facility siting." *The National Law Journal* (June 23): 8–13B.

Mills, C. Wright. 1951. *White Collar*. New York: Oxford University Press.

Mills, C. Wright. 1956. *The Power Elite*. New York: Oxford University Press.

Mincey, Ronald B.; Isabel Sawhill; and Douglas A. Wolf. 1990. "The underclass: Definition and measurement." *Science* (April 27): 450–453.

Mink, Gwendolyn. 1986. *Old Labor and New Immigrants in American Political Development*. Ithaca, NY: Cornell University Press.

Mintz, Beth. 1975. "The President's cabinet, 1897–1972: A continuation of the power structure debate." *Insurgent Sociologist* 5: 131–148.

Mitchell, Susan. 1996. *American Attitudes*. Ithaca, NY: New Strategist Publications.

Montefiore, Simon Sebag. 1996. "Black market." *The Times of London Sunday Magazine*. (November 17): 36–44.

More, Douglas M., and Robert W. Suchner. 1976. "Occupational status, prestige, and stereotypes." *Sociology of Work and Occupations* 3: 169-186.

Moss, Desda, and Gordon Dickson. 1994. "Homeless remembered." *USA Today* (December 23): 3A.

Muller v. Oregon, 1908. (118 U.S. 465).

Myerson, Allen R. 1996. "Executives are cradled while medical benefits are cut for rank and file." *The New York Times* (March 17): 1–13.

Myrdal, Gunnar. 1944. *An American Dilemma*. New York: McGraw-Hill.

Nagel, Joane. 1995. "Resource competition theories." *American Behavioral Scientist* 30: 442–458.

Nasar, Sylvia. 1992. "Women's progress stalled? Just not so." *The New York Times* (October 18): 1–10F.

National Center for Health Statistics. 1996. *Health, United States, 1995*. Hyattsville, MD: U.S. Public Health Service.

Neuborne, Ellen. 1990. "The young and wealthy take hands-on approach to philanthropy." *USA Today* (June 26): 6B.

Neuborne, Ellen. 1997. "Temporary workers getting short shrift." *USA Today* (April 11): 1–2B.

New York Times, The. 1988. "Philanthropy for the 21st century." *The New York Times* (July 12): 4F.

Newman, Katherine S. 1988. *Falling from Grace: The Experience of Downward Mobility in the American Middle Class*. New York: Free Press.

Nock, Steven L., and Peter H. Rossi. 1979. "Household types and social standing." *Social Forces* 57: 1325–1345.

Noel, Donald L. 1968. "How ethnic inequality begins." *Social Problems* 16: 157–172.

Norris, C.; N. Fielding; C. Kemp; and J. Fielding. 1992. "Black and blue: An analysis of the influence of race on being stopped by the police. *British Journal of Sociology* 43(2): 207–218.

Nottingham, Elizabeth K. 1954. *Religion and Society*. New York: Random House.

Nye, Joseph S.; Philip D. Zelikov; and David C. King, eds. 1996. *Why People Don't Trust Government*. Cambridge, MA: Harvard University Press.

OAKES, JEANNIE. 1985. *Keeping Track: How Schools Structure Inequality.* Santa Monica, CA: Rand Corporation.

O'FLAHERTY, BRENDAN. 1996. *Making Room: The Economics of Homelessness.* Cambridge, MA: Harvard University Press.

O'HARE, WILLIAM P. 1992. *America's Minorities: The Demographics of Diversity.* New York: Population Reference Bureau.

O'HARE, WILLIAM P. 1996. *A New Look at Poverty in America.* Washington, DC: Population Reference Bureau.

O'NEAL, GLENN. 1998. "Girls often dropped from computer equation." *USA Today* (March 10): 3D.

OLSTEN CORPORATION. 1996. "Downsizing results." *USA Today* (April 16): 1B.

OLZAK, SUSAN. 1996. *The Dynamics of Ethnic Competition and Conflict.* Stanford, CA: Stanford University Press.

ORDOVENSKY, PAT. 1989. "Minorities gain, but gaps remain." *USA Today* (September 12): 5D.

OSTRANDER, SUSAN. 1984. *Women of the Upper Class.* Philadelphia: Temple University Press.

OWEN, RICHARD. 1996. "Seventies dream of world with no hunger destroyed by conflict." *The Times of London* (November 14): 23.

PALMER, PHYLLIS. 1989. *Domesticity and Dirt: Housewives and Domestic Service in the United States, 1920–1945.* Philadelphia, PA: Temple University Press.

PAMMETT, JON H. 1987. "Class voting and class consciousness in Canada." *Canadian Review of Sociology and Anthropology* 24: 269–290.

PARSONS, TALCOTT. 1940. "An analytic approach to the theory of social stratification." *American Journal of Sociology* 45: 841–862.

PARSONS, TALCOTT. 1953. "A revised analytic approach to the theory of social stratification." Pp. 395–415 in Rinehard Bendix and Seymour Martin Lipset (eds.), *Class, Status and Party.* New York: Free Press.

PATERNOSTER, RAY. 1984. "Prosecutorial discretion in requesting the death penalty: A case of victim based racial discrimination." *Law and Society Review* 18: 437–478.

PEAR, ROBERT. 1996. "Thousands to rally in capital on children's behalf." *The New York Times* (June 1): 10.

PEASE, JOHN; WILLIAM H. FORM; AND JOAN HUBER RYTINA. 1970. "Ideological currents in American stratification." *The American Sociologist* 5: 127–137.

PENN, ROGER. 1975. "Occupational prestige hierarchies: A great empirical invariant." *Social Forces* 54: 352–364.

PETERSON, KAREN S., AND ANITA MANNING. 1996. "Trained women fit for heavy lifting jobs." *USA Today* (January 30): 7D.

PEYSER, MARC. 1997. "Question time: What will the 2000 census ask?" *Newsweek* (June 19): 14.

PHILLIPS, KEVIN. 1990. *The Politics of Rich and Poor.* New York: Random House.

PHYSICIAN TASK FORCE. 1985. *Hunger in America: The Growing Epidemic.* Middletown, CT: Wesleyan University Press.

PILIAVIN, IRVING, AND SCOTT BRIAR. 1964. "Police encounters with juveniles." *American Journal of Sociology* 70: 206–214.

PILIAVIN, IRVING; MICHAEL SOSIN; AND HERB WESTERFELT. 1987–88. "Tracking the homeless." *Focus* 10: 20–24.

PINES, DEBORAH. 1994. "Reebok gets the boot in its lawsuit against Kmart." *The National Law Journal* 16 (May 9): 27A.

POLIVKA, ANNE E., AND THOMAS NARDONE. 1989. "On the definition of contingent work." *Monthly Labor Review* 112: 9–16.

POPE, VICTORIA. 1997. "Trafficking in women." *U.S. News & World Report* (April 7): 38–44.

PORTER, J. R., AND R. E. WASHINGTON. 1993. "Minority identity and self-esteem." *Annual Review of Sociology* 19: 139–161.

POTOK, MARK. 1994. "Community, waste plant on common ground." *USA Today* (August 25): 8A.

POTOK, MARK. 1996. "Immigration's other side: Interdependence." *USA Today* (September 30): 19–20A.

PROSSER, WILLIAM R. 1991. "The underclass: Assessing what we know." *Focus* 13 (Summer): 1–18.

PROTHROW-STITH, DEBORAH. 1991. *Deadly Consequences*, New York: Harper.

PUENTE, MARIA. 1993. "Faces of nation's homeless take on a new look." *USA Today* (December 22): 3A.

PURITZ, PATRICIA. 1995. *A Call for Justice*. Chicago, IL: American Bar Association.

RACHIN, JILL. 1989. "The label that sticks." *U.S. News and World Report* (July 3): 51–52.

RAMSEY, PATRICIA. 1991. "Young children's awareness and understanding of social class differences." *Journal of Genetic Psychology* 152: 71–82.

RANSFORD, H. EDWARD. 1992. *Race and Class in American Society*, 2nd ed. Rochester, VT: Schenkman.

RANSFORD, H. EDWARD. 1994. *Race and Class in American Society: Black, Latino, Anglo*. Rochester, VT: Schenkman.

REIMAN, JEFFREY. 1996. *. . . and the Poor Get Prison: Economic Bias*. Boston, MA: Allyn & Bacon.

REINGOLD, JENNIFER. 1997. "Executive pay." *Business Week* (April 21): 58–66.

REMMINGTON, PATRICIA. 1981. *Policing*. Lanham, MD: University Press.

RESKIN, BARBARA, AND IRENE PADAVIC. 1994. *Women and Men at Work*. Thousand Oaks, CA: Pine Forge.

ROBERTS, SAM. 1994. "Black women graduates outpace male counterparts." *The New York Times* (October 31): 12A.

ROBINSON, ROBERT V. 1983. "Explaining perceptions of class and racial inequality in England and the United States." *British Journal of Sociology* 4: 344–366.

ROBINSON, ROBERT V., AND M. GARNIER. 1985. "Class reproduction among men and women in France: Reproduction theory on its home ground." *American Journal of Sociology* 91: 250–280.

ROBINSON, ROBERT V., AND JONATHAN KELLEY. 1979. "Class as conceived by Marx and Dahrendorf: Effects on income inequality, class consciousness, and class conflict in the United States and Great Britain." *American Sociological Review* 44: 38–58.

ROSE, ROBERT L. 1994. "Temporary jobs." *The Wall Street Journal* (October 25): 1A.

ROSEN, ELLEN ISREAL. 1987. *Bitter Choices: Blue-Collar Women In and Out of Work*. Chicago: University of Chicago Press.

ROSENBAUM, JAMES E. 1975. "The stratification of the socialization process." *American Sociological Review* 40: 48–54.

ROSENBERG, MORRIS. 1989. "Self-concept research: A historical overview." *Social Forces* 68: 34–44.

ROSENBERG, MORRIS, AND LEONARD I. PEARLIN. 1978. "Social class and self-esteem among children and adults." *American Journal of Sociology* 84: 53–77.

ROSENBERG, MORRIS; CARMI SCHOOLER; AND CARRIE SCHOENBACH. 1989. "Self-esteem and adolescent problems: Modeling reciprocal effects." *American Sociological Review* 54: 1004–1018.

ROSENWASSER, SHIRLEY MILLER, AND NORMA G. DEAN. 1989. "Gender role and political office." *Psychology of Women Quarterly* 13: 77–85.

ROSKIES, ETHEL, AND CHRISTIANE LOUIS-GUERIN. 1990. "Job insecurity in managers: Antecedents and consequences." *Journal of Organizational Behavior* 11: 345–359

ROSS, CHRISTINE; SHELDON DANZIGER; AND EUGENE SMOLENSKY. 1987. "The level and trend in poverty in the United States, 1939–1979." *Demography* 24: 587–600.

ROSS, ROBERT J. S., AND KENT C. TRACHTE. 1990. *Global Capitalism: The New Leviathan*. Albany, NY: State University of New York Press.

ROTHFEDER, JEFFREY, AND MICHELE GALEN. 1990. "Is your boss spying on you?" *Business Week* (January 15): 84–75.

RUBIN, LILIAN. 1976. *Worlds of Pain: Life in the Working Class Family*. New York: Basic Books.

RUNDEL, RHONDA. 1987. "New efforts to fight heart disease are aimed at blue-collar workers." *The Wall Street Journal* (March 16): 25.

RUSSELL, JAMES W. 1994. *After the Fifth Sun: Class and Race in North America*. Englewood Cliffs, NJ: Prentice Hall.

RYSCAVAGE, PAUL. 1994. "Gender-related shifts in the distribution of wages." *Monthly Labor Review* 117 (July): 3–15.

RYSCAVAGE, PAUL. 1995. "A surge in growing income inequality." *Monthly Labor Review* 118 (August): 21–28.

SALTZSTEIN, GRACE HALL. 1989. "Black mayors and police policies." *Journal of Politics* 51: 525–544.

SANDEFUR, GARY D.; RONALD R. RINDFUSS; AND BARNEY COHEN (eds.). 1996. *Changing Numbers, Changing Needs: American Indian Demography and Public Health*. Washington, DC: Committee on Population of the National Research Council.

SARGENT, ALLISON IJAMS. 1997. "The social register: Just a circle of friends." *The New York Times* (December 21): 1–2ST.

SCHEIN, VIRGINIA ELLEN. 1973. "The relationship between sex role stereotypes and requisite management characteristics." *Journal of Applied Psychology* 57: 95–100.

SCHNEIDER, MICHAEL. 1996. "Maryland drug squad searches more blacks than whites." *USA Today* (May 24): 12A.

SCHWARZ, JOHN E. 1997. *Illusions of Opportunity: The American Dream in Question*. New York: W. W. Norton.

SEGAL, ELIZABETH A., AND STEPHANIE BRUZY. 1995. "Gender and Congressional voting: A legislative analysis." *Affilia* 10: 8–22.

SEIDMAN, JOEL. 1942. *Needle Trades*. New York: Farrar and Rinehart.

SELTZER, RICHARD A.; JODY NEWMAN; AND MELISSA VOORHEES LEIGHTON. 1997. *Sex as a Political Variable*, Boulder, CO: Lynne Rienner.

SENNETT, RICHARD, AND JONATHAN COBB. 1973. *The Hidden Injuries of Class*. New York: Vintage.

SEWELL, WILLIAM H.; O. HALLER ARCHIBALD; AND G. W. OHLENDORF. 1970. "The educational and early occupational status attainment process: A replication and revision." *American Sociological Review* 35: 1014–1027.

SHAPIRO, LAURA. 1994. "How hungry is America?" *Newsweek* (March 14): 58–95.

SHAVIT, YOSSI, AND HANS PETER BLOSSFELD. 1993. *Persistent Inequality: Changing Educational Attainment in Thirteen Countries*. Boulder, CO: Westview.

SHIBUTANI, TAMOTSU, AND KIAN M. KWAN. 1965. *Ethnic Stratification: A Comparative Approach*. New York: Macmillan.

SHOSTAK, ARTHUR B. 1969. *Blue-Collar Life*. New York: Random House.

SIGELMAN, LEE, AND SUSAN WELCH. 1993. "The contact hypothesis revisited: Black–white interaction and positive racial attitudes." *Social Forces* 71: 781–795.

SILVESTRI, GEORGE T. 1995. "Occupational employment to 2005." *Monthly Labor Review* 118 (November): 60–84.

SIMMONS, ROBERTA G., AND MORRIS ROSENBERG. 1971. "Functions of children's perceptions of the stratification system." *American Sociological Review* 36: 235–249.

SIMPSON, IDA HARPER; DAVIS STARK; AND ROBERT A. JACKMAN. 1988. "Class identification processes of married, working men and women." *American Sociological Review* 53: 284–293.

SINGH, G. K.; K. D. KOCHANEK; AND M. F. MACDORMAN. 1996. "Advance report of final mortality statistics, 1994." *Monthly Vital Statistics Report* 45: 19–20.

SIO, ARNOLD A. 1965. "Interpretations of slavery: The slave status in the Americas." *Comparative Studies in Society and History* 7: 289–308.

SIVARD, RUTH LEGER. 1995. *Women . . . A World Survey*. Washington, DC: World Priorities.

SKAFTE, DIANNE. 1989. "The effect of perceived wealth and poverty on adolescents' character judgments." *Journal of Social Psychology* 129: 93–99.

SMEEDING, TIMOTHY M.; MICHAEL O'HIGGINS; AND LEE RAINWATER, eds. 1991. *Poverty, Income Inequality, and Income Distribution in Comparative Perspective*. Washington, DC: Urban Institute Press.

SMITH, CHRISTOPHER B. 1994. "Back to the future: The intergroup contact hypothesis revisited." *Sociological Inquiry* 64: 438–455.

SMITH, M. J.; P. CARAYON; K. J. SANDERS; S. Y. LIM; AND D. LEGRANDE. 1992. "Employee stress and health complaints in jobs with and without electric performance monitoring." *Applied Ergonomics* 23: 17–28.

SMITH, STEVEN K., AND CAROL J. DEFRANCES. 1996. *Indigent Defense*. Washington, DC: U.S. Government Printing Office.

SMITH, TOM. 1997. "Trends in confidence in government." *GSS News* 11 (August): 3.

SNIPP, C. MATTHEW. 1989. *American Indians: The First of This Land*. New York: Russell Sage.

SORENSON, ELAIN. 1989. "Measuring the effects of occupational sex and race composition on earnings." Pp. 49–69 in Robert T. Michael, Heidi I. Hartmann, and Brigid O'Farrell, (eds.), *Pay Equity: Empirical Inquiries*. New York: National Academy.

SPOHN, C., AND J. CEDERBLOM. 1991. "Race and disparities in sentencing: A test of the liberation hypothesis." *Justice Quarterly* 8: 305–327.

STANLEY, THOMAS, AND WILLIAM DANKO. 1996. *The Millionaire Next Door*. New York: Longstreet.

STEARNS, LINDA BREWSTER, AND JOHN R. LOGAN. 1986. "The racial structuring of the housing market and segregation in suburban areas." *Social Forces* 65: 28–42.

STERN, PHILIP M. 1992. *Still the Best Congress Money Can Buy*. Washington, DC: Regnery Gateway.

STEVENSON, HAROLD W. 1982. *School Experiences and Performances of Asian-Pacific American High School Students*. Washington, D.C.: U.S. Department of Education.

STEWART, SALLY ANN, AND WILLIAM DUNN. 1989. "Beverly Hills: A town apart." *USA Today* (January 27): 3A.

STOCKARD, J. AND W. WOOD. 1984. "The myth of female underachievement: A reexamination of sex differences in academic underachievement." *American Educational Research Journal* 21: 825-838.

STREITWEISER, MARY, AND JOHN GOODMAN. 1983. " A survey of recent research on race and residential location." *Population Research and Policy Review* 2: 253–283.

STROBEL, FREDERICK R. 1993. *Upward Dreams, Downward Mobility*. Lanham, MD: Rowman & Littlefield.

SUMNER, WILLIAM GRAHAM. 1914. *The Challenge of Facts and Other Essays*. New Haven, CT: Yale University Press.

SURO, ROBERTO. 1990. "Courts ordering financing changes in public schools." *The New York Times* (March 11): 1–28.

SWEENEY, GAEL. 1997. "The king of white trash culture." Pp. 249–266 in Matt Wray and Annalee Newitz (eds.). *White Trash: Race and Class in America*. New York: Routledge.

SWOBODA, FRANK. 1997. "Labor's dilemma on display at UPS." *The Washington Post* (August 20): 1–10A.

TANAKA, JENNIFER; DEBORAH BRANSCUM; AND PAULINA BORSOOK. 1996. "The wealth and avarice of the cyber-rich." *Newsweek* (December 30): 48–51.

TAYLOR, CHERYL. 1996. "Lordship prices are a'leaping." *The London Times* (November 30): 11.

TAYLOR, HUMPHREY. 1996. "The problem of homelessness." Harris Poll No. 34. New York: Louis Harris Associates.

TAYLOR, JOHN. 1989. *Circus of Ambition*. New York: Warner.

TAYLOR, ROBERT JOSEPH; LINDA M. CHATTERS; M. BELINDA TUCKER; AND EDITH LEWIS. 1990. "Developments in research on black families: A decade review." *Journal of Marriage and the Family* 52: 993–1014.

TERKEL, STUDS. 1972. *Working*. New York: Random House.

THOMAS, SUE. 1994. *How Women Legislate*. New York: Oxford University Press.

THOMAS, WILLIAM I. 1928. *The Child in America*. New York: Knopf.

TILGHER, ADRIANO. 1930. *Homo Faber: Work through the Ages*. New York: Harcourt, Brace and World.

TITTLE, CHARLES R., AND ROBERT F. MEIER. 1990. "Specifying the SES/delinquency relationship." *Criminology* 28: 292–319.

TOMASKOVIC-DEVEY, DONALD. 1993a. *Gender and Racial Inequality at Work*. Ithaca, NY: ILR Press.

TOMASKOVIC-DEVEY, DONALD. 1993b. "The gender and race composition of jobs and the male/female, white/black pay gap." *Social Forces* 72: 45–76.

TONER, ROBIN. 1989. "Americans favor aid for homeless." *The New York Times* (January 22): 1–21.

TONRY, M. 1994. "Racial disproportion in U.S. prisons." *British Journal of Criminology* 34: 97–115.

TOSCANO, GUY, AND JANICE WINDAU. 1994. "The changing character of fatal workplace injuries." *Monthly Labor Review* 117 (October): 17–27.

TREIMAN, DONALD J. 1977. *Occupational Prestige in Comparative Perspective*. New York: Academic Press.

TUCKER, CLYDE, AND BRIAN KOJETIN. 1996. "Testing racial and ethnic origin questions in the CPS supplement," *Monthly Labor Review* 119 (September): 3–7.

TUDOR, JEANETTE F. 1971. "The development of class awareness among children." *Social Forces* 49: 470–476.

TUMIN, MELVIN M. 1953. "Some principles of stratification: A critical analysis." *American Sociological Review* 18: 387–393.

TURNER, FREDERICK C. (ed.). 1992. *Social Mobility and Political Attitudes.* New Brunswick, NJ: Transaction.

TURNER, FREDERICK J. 1920. *The Frontier in American History.* New York: Henry Holt.

UNDP (UNITED NATIONS DEVELOPMENT PROGRAMME). 1995. *Human Development Report, 1995.* New York: Oxford University Press. 184–200.

U.S. BUREAU OF THE CENSUS. 1975. *Historical Statistics of the United States.* Washington, DC: U.S. Government Printing Office.

U.S. BUREAU OF THE CENSUS. 1979. *The Social and Economic Status of the Black Population in the United States, 1790–1978.* Washington, DC: U.S. Government Printing Office.

U.S. BUREAU OF THE CENSUS. 1987. Current Population Reports pp. 60–165, *Earnings of Married Couple Families, 1987.* Washington, DC: U.S. Government Printing Office.

U.S. BUREAU OF THE CENSUS. 1993. Current Population Reports pp. 60–187. *Child Support for Custodial Mothers and Fathers, 1991.* Washington, DC: U.S. Government Printing Office.

U.S. BUREAU OF THE CENSUS. 1995a. Current Population Reports pp. 60–189. *Money Income and Poverty Status of Families and Persons in the United States, 1994.* Washington, DC: U.S. Government Printing Office.

U.S. BUREAU OF THE CENSUS. 1995b. Current Population Reports pp. 70–47. *Asset Ownership of Households, 1993.* Washington, DC: U.S. Government Printing Office.

U.S. BUREAU OF THE CENSUS. 1996a. Current Population Reports pp. 60–189. *Income, Poverty, and Valuation of Non-cash Benefits, 1994.* Washington, DC: U.S. Government Printing Office.

U.S. BUREAU OF THE CENSUS. 1996b. Current Population Reports pp. 70–55. *The Dynamics of Economic Well-Being: Poverty 1992 to 1993.* Washington, DC: U.S. Government Printing Office.

U.S. BUREAU OF THE CENSUS. 1996c. *November 1994 Voting and Registration.* "Voting and Registration of Employed Persons by Race, Hispanic Origin, Sex, and Major Occupational Group." http://www.census.gov/population/socdemo/voting/work/tab11.txt

U.S. BUREAU OF THE CENSUS. 1996d. Current Population Reports pp. 60–193, *Money Income in the United States, 1995.* Washington, DC: U.S. Government Printing Office.

U.S. Bureau of the Census. 1996e. Current Population Reports pp. 20–487, *School Enrollment—Social and Economic Characteristics of Students: 1994.* Washington, DC: U.S. Government Printing Office.

U.S. BUREAU OF LABOR STATISTICS. 1995c. *Occupational Injuries and Illness.* Bulletin 2455. U.S. Government Printing Office.

U.S. COMMISSION ON CIVIL RIGHTS. 1987. *New Evidence on School Desegregation.* Washington, DC: U.S. Government Printing Office.

U.S. CONGRESS. 1986. Joint Economic Committee. *The Concentration of Wealth in the United States.* Washington, DC: U.S. Government Printing Office.

U.S. DEPARTMENT OF JUSTICE. 1988. *Criminal Victimization in the United States, 1986.* Washington, DC: U.S. Government Printing Office.

U.S. DEPARTMENT OF LABOR. 1985. *Handbook of Labor Statistics.* Washington, DC: Government Printing Office.

U.S. GENERAL ACCOUNTING OFFICE, 1988. *Sweatshops in the U.S.* Washington, DC: U.S. Government Printing Office.

U.S. GENERAL ACCOUNTING OFFICE. 1991. *Workers at Risk.* Washington, DC: U.S. Government Printing Office.

U.S. GENERAL ACCOUNTING OFFICE. 1994. *Child-care Subsidies Increase Likelihood That Low-income Mothers Will Work.* Washington, DC: U.S. Government Printing Office.

U.S. HOUSE OF REPRESENTATIVES. 1990. Select Committee on Hunger. *Food Security in the United States.* Washington, DC: U.S. Government Printing Office.

U.S. IMMIGRATION AND NATURALIZATION SERVICE. 1997. *Statistical Yearbook, 1997.* Washington, DC: U.S. Government Printing Office.

USEEM, MICHAEL. 1983. *The Inner Circle: Large Corporations and the Rise of Business Activity in the U.S. and U.K.* New York: Oxford University Press.

USEEM, MICHAEL, AND JEROME KARABEL. 1986. "Pathways to top corporate management." *American Sociological Review* 51: 184–200.

VALDES, DENNIS N. 1991. *Al Norte: Agricultural Workers in the Lakes Region.* Austin: University of Texas Press.

VANNEMAN, REEVE, AND LYNN WEBER CANNON. 1987. *The American Perception of Class.* Philadelphia, PA: Temple University Press.

VANNEMAN, REEVE, AND FRED C. PAMPEL. 1977. "The American perception of class and status." *American Sociological Review* 42: 422–437.

VEBLEN, THORSTEIN. 1899. *The Theory of the Leisure Class.* New York: Macmillan.

VERBA, SIDNEY; NORMAN H. NIE; AND JAE-ON KIM. 1978. *Participation and Political Equality: A Seven-Nation Comparison.* New York: Cambridge University Press.

WALKER, SAMUEL; CASSIA SPOHN; AND MIRIAM DeLONE. 1996. *The Color of Justice,* Belmont, CA: Wadsworth.

WARING, STEPHEN P. 1991. *Taylorism Transformed: Scientific Management since 1945.* Chapel Hill, NC: University of North Carolina Press.

WARNER, W. LLOYD, AND PAUL LUNT. 1941. *The Social Life of a Modern Community.* New Haven: Yale University Press.

WAYNE, LESLIE. 1997. "A special deal for lobbyists: A getaway with lawmakers." *The New York Times* (January 26): 1–16.

WEBER, MAX. 1946. *From Max Weber: Essays in Sociology.* H. Gerth and C. W. Mills (trans.). New York: Oxford University Press.

WEBER, MAX. 1947. *Theory of Social and Economic Organization.* (A. M. Henderson and Talcott Parsons, eds.) New York: Oxford University Press.

WEBER, MAX. 1958. *The Protestant Ethic and the Spirit of Capitalism.* New York: Scribner.

WEINBERG, DANIEL H. 1996. *A Brief Look at Postwar U.S. Income Inequality.* Current Population Reports pp. 60–191. Washington, DC: U.S. Government Printing Office.

WENNEKER, MARK B.; JOEL S. WEISSMAN; AND ARNOLD M. EPSTEIN. 1990. "The association of payer with utilization of cardiac procedures in Massachusetts." *Journal of the American Medical Association* 264: 1255–1263.

WENTZEL, KATHRYN R. 1988. "Gender differences in math and English achievement: A longitudinal study." *Sex Roles* 18: 691–699.

WEST, CANDACE, AND SARAH FENSTERMAKER. 1995a. "Doing difference." *Gender & Society* 9: 8–37.

WEST, CANDACE, AND SARAH FENSTERMAKER. 1995b. "Reply: (Re)doing difference." *Gender & Society* 9: 506–513.

WESTERN, MARK, AND ERIK OLIN WRIGHT. 1994. "The permeability of class boundaries to intergenerational mobility among men in the United States, Canada, Norway and Sweden." *American Sociological Review* 59: 606–630.

WHITMAN, DAVID. 1989. "Shattering myths about the homeless." *U.S. News & World Report* (March 20): 26–28.

WHYTE, MARTIN K. 1990. *Dating, Mating and Marriage.* New York: Aldine.

WILL, GEORGE. 1993. "A measure of morality." *The Washington Post* (December 16): 25A.

WILLIAMS, J. ALLEN, JR., AND SUZANNE T. ORTEGA. 1990. "Dimensions of ethnic assimilation: An empirical appraisal of Gordon's typology." *Social Science Quarterly* 71: 697–710.

WILLIAMS, JOHN E., AND DEBORAH L. BEST. 1990. *Measuring Sex Stereotypes: A Multination Study.* Newbury Park, CA: Sage.

WILLING, RICHARD. 1997. "Courting the young and the rich." *USA Today* (March 17): 3A.

WILSON, WILLIAM JULIUS. 1987. *The Truly Disadvantaged.* Chicago: University of Chicago Press.

WILSON, WILLIAM JULIUS. 1996. *When Work Disappears: The World of the New Urban Poor.* New York: Knopf.

WINFIELD, IDEE; RICHARD T. CAMPBELL; ALAN C. KERCKHOFF; DIANE D. EVERETT; AND JERRY M. TROTT. 1989. "Career processes in Great Britain and the United States." *Social Forces* 68: 284–308.

WIRTH, LOUIS. 1945. "The problem of minority groups." Pp. 347–372 in Ralph Linton (ed.), *The Science of Man in the World Crisis*. New York: Columbia University Press.

WONG, MORRISON G. 1983. "Chinese sweatshops in the United States: A look at the garment industry." *Sociology of Work* 2:357–379.

WRAY, MATT, AND ANNALEE NEWITZ (eds.) 1997. *White Trash: Race and Class in America*. New York: Routledge.

WRIGHT, ERIK OLIN. 1985. *Classes*. London: New Left Books.

WRIGHT, ERIK OLIN. 1989. *The Debate on Classes*. London: Verso.

WRIGHT, ERIK OLIN. 1997. *Class Counts*. Cambridge, England: Cambridge University Press.

WRIGHT, ERIK OLIN, AND BILL MARTIN. 1987. "The transformation of the American class structure, 1960–1980." *American Journal of Sociology* 93: 1–29.

YBARRA, MICHAEL. 1996. "Don't ask, don't beg, don't sit." *The New York Times* (May 19): 5E.

ZEDLEWSKI, SHEILA; SANDRA CLARK; ERIC MEIER; AND KEITH WATSON. 1996. *Potential Effects of Congressional Welfare Reform Legislation on Family Incomes*. Washington, DC: Urban Institute Press.

ZINGRAFF, RHONDA, AND MICHAEL D. SCHULMAN. 1984. "Social bases of class consciousness." *Social Forces* 63: 98–116.

ZIPP, JOHN F., AND ERIC PLUTZER. 1985. "Gender differences in voting for female candidates: Evidence from the 1982 election." *Public Opinion Quarterly* 49: 179–197.

ZIPP, JOHN F., AND ERIC PLUTZER. 1996. "Wives and husbands: Social class, gender, and class identification in the United States." *Sociology* 30: 235–252.

Name Index

Widdison, Harold A., 110, 112
Will, George, 147
Williams, Darrell L., 141
Williams, J. Allen, Jr., 65
Williams, John E., 73, 79
Williams, Linda, 177
Williams, Robin M., 140
Willing, Richard, 126
Wilson, William Julius, 47, 48, 194, 209
Windau, Janice, 153
Winfield, Idee, 205
Wingert, Pat, 198
Wirth, Louis, 7
Wolch, Jennifer R., 98
Wolf, D. M., 159
Wolf, Douglas A., 48
Wong, Morrison G., 63

Wray, Matt, 105, 122
Wright, Erik Olin, 17, 21, 24, 25, 33, 52, 82, 193

X

Xin, Shaomin, 3, 108

Y

Ybarra, Michael, 99
Yuan Shuan, 197

Z

Zedlewski, Sheila, 97
Zelditch, Morris, Jr., 120
Zelikov, Philip D., 143
Zimmerman, Wendy, 78, 204
Zingraff, Rhonda, 180
Zipp, John F., 139, 184

Subject Index

A
Achieved prestige, 111–112
African Americans, 8
  class consciousness and, 177
  criminal justice system and, 147–50
  discrimination in hiring and, 204
  earnings gap and, 83–88
  educational attainment of, 203
  educational segregation and, 117
  health care system and, 152, 153
  homeless, 98
  income by class and gender, 16
  infant mortality rates for, 152
  institutionalization of inequality and, 61, 62, 72
  intermarriage and, 118
  net worth of, 89
  political participation of, 134, 136–37, 140–42
  population size of, 9
  poverty and, 91, 93, 96, 98, 193
  residential segregation and, 114–17
  self-identification among, 9–10
  slavery and, 9, 37–38, 62–63, 66
  social mobility of, 192–93, 203, 206
  stereotyping of, 66–67
  unemployment and, 206
Agricultural society, division of labor in, 70

American Conference of Governmental Industrial
  Hygienists (ACGIH), 130
American dilemma, 78–79, 207–8
American Dream, 55–61, 79
Anglo-conformity, 65
Annual income, 82–88
Ascribed prestige, 109–11
Asian Americans, 8
  academic test scores of, 199
  earnings gap and, 83
  educational segregation and, 117
  immigrants, 39
  independent businesses and, 208
  infant mortality rates for, 152
  population size of, 9, 10
  residential segregation and, 116
Assimilation theory, 65
Authority, 4

B
Beliefs, 13
Black Americans (*see* African Americans)
Blue-collar work (*see also* Working class)
  occupational safety and health and, 153–54
  social mobility and, 192–93
  social status and, 106, 111